NUTSHELL SERIES

Debtor-Creditor Law, 2nd Ed., 1980, 324 pages, by David G. Epstein, Professor of Law, University of Texas.

Employment Discrimination—Federal Law of, 2nd Ed., 1981, 402 pages, by Mack A. Player, Professor of Law, University of Georgia.

Energy Law, 1981, 338 pages, by Joseph P. Tomain, Professor of Law, Drake University.

Environmental Law, 1983, approximately 332 pages by Roger W. Findley, Professor of Law, University of Illinois and Daniel A. Farber, Professor of Law, University of Minnesota.

Estate Planning—Introduction to, 3rd Ed., 1983, 370 pages, by Robert J. Lynn, Professor of Law, Ohio State University.

Evidence, Federal Rules of, 1981, 428 pages, by Michael H. Graham, Professor of Law, University of Illinois.

Evidence, State and Federal Rules, 2nd Ed., 1981, 514 pages, by Paul F. Rothstein, Professor of Law, Georgetown University.

Family Law, 1977, 400 pages, by Harry D. Krause, Professor of Law, University of Illinois.

Federal Estate and Gift Taxation, 3rd Ed., 1983, 509 pages, by John K. McNulty, Professor of Law, University of California, Berkeley.

Federal Income Taxation of Individuals, 3rd Ed., 1983, approximately 425 pages, by John K. McNulty, Professor of Law, University of California, Berkeley.

Federal Income Taxation of Corporations and Stockholders, 2nd Ed., 1981, 362 pages, by Jonathan Sobeloff, Late Professor of Law, Georgetown University and Peter P. Weidenbruch, Jr., Professor of Law, Georgetown University.

Federal Jurisdiction, 2nd Ed., 1981, 258 pages, by David P. Currie, Professor of Law, University of Chicago.

Future Interests, 1981, 361 pages, by Lawrence W. Waggoner, Professor of Law, University of Michigan.

Government Contracts, 1979, 423 pages, by W. Noel Keyes, Professor of Law, Pepperdine University.

Historical Introduction to Anglo-American Law, 2nd Ed., 1973, 280 pages, by Frederick G. Kempin, Jr., Professor of Business Law, Wharton School of Finance and Commerce, University of Pennsylvania.

Injunctions, 1974, 264 pages, by John F. Dobbyn, Professor of Law, Villanova University.

Insurance Law, 1981, 281 pages, by John F. Dobbyn, Professor of Law, Villanova University.

Intellectual Property—Patents, Trademarks and Copyright, 1983, approximately 410 pages, by Arthur R. Miller, Professor of Law, Harvard University, and Michael H. Davis, Professor of Law, University of Tennessee.

International Business Transactions, 1981, 393 pages, by Donald T. Wilson, Professor of Law, Loyola University, Los Angeles.

Introduction to the Study and Practice of Law, 1983, approximately 400 pages, by Kenney F. Hegland, Professor of Law, University of Arizona.

Judicial Process, 1980, 292 pages, by William L. Reynolds, Professor of Law, University of Maryland.

Jurisdiction, 4th Ed., 1980, 232 pages, by Albert A. Ehrenzweig, Late Professor of Law, University of California, Berkeley, David W. Louisell, Late Professor of Law, University of California, Berkeley and Geoffrey C. Hazard, Jr., Professor of Law, Yale Law School.

Juvenile Courts, 2nd Ed., 1977, 275 pages, by Sanford J. Fox, Professor of Law, Boston College.

Labor Arbitration Law and Practice, 1979, 358 pages, by Dennis R. Nolan, Professor of Law, University of South Carolina.

Labor Law, 1979, 403 pages, by Douglas L. Leslie, Professor of Law, University of Virginia.

Land Use, 1978, 316 pages, by Robert R. Wright, Professor of Law, University of Arkansas, Little Rock and Susan Webber, Professor of Law, University of Arkansas, Little Rock.

Landlord and Tenant Law, 1979, 319 pages, by David S. Hill, Professor of Law, University of Colorado.

Law Study and Law Examinations—Introduction to, 1971, 389 pages, by Stanley V. Kinyon, Late Professor of Law, University of Minnesota.

Legal Interviewing and Counseling, 1976, 353 pages, by Thomas L. Shaffer, Professor of Law, Washington and Lee University.

Legal Research, 3rd Ed., 1978, 415 pages, by Morris L. Cohen, Professor of Law and Law Librarian, Yale University.

Legal Writing, 1982, 294 pages, by Dr. Lynn B. Squires, University of Washington School of Law and Marjorie Dick Rombauer, Professor of Law, University of Washington.

Legislative Law and Process, 1975, 279 pages, by Jack Davies, Professor of Law, William Mitchell College of Law.

Local Government Law, 2nd Ed., 1983, approximately 345 pages, by David J. McCarthy, Jr., Professor of Law, Georgetown University.

Mass Communications Law, 2nd Ed., 1983, 473 pages, by Harvey L. Zuckman, Professor of Law, Catholic University and Martin J. Gaynes, Lecturer in Law, Temple University.

Medical Malpractice—The Law of, 1977, 340 pages, by Joseph H. King, Professor of Law, University of Tennessee.

Military Law, 1980, 378 pages, by Charles A. Shanor, Professor of Law, Emory University and Timothy P. Terrell, Professor of Law, Emory University.

Oil and Gas, 1983, approximately 365 pages, by John S. Lowe, Professor of Law, University of Tulsa.

Personal Property, 1983, approximately 318 pages, by Barlow Burke, Jr., Professor of Law, American University.

Post-Conviction Remedies, 1978, 360 pages, by Robert Popper, Professor of Law, University of Missouri, Kansas City.

Presidential Power, 1977, 328 pages, by Arthur Selwyn Miller, Professor of Law Emeritus, George Washington University.

Procedure Before Trial, 1972, 258 pages, by Delmar Karlen, Professor of Law, College of William and Mary.

Products Liability, 2nd Ed., 1981, 341 pages, by Dix W. Noel, Late Professor of Law, University of Tennessee and Jerry J. Phillips, Professor of Law, University of Tennessee.

Professional Responsibility, 1980, 399 pages, by Robert H. Aronson, Professor of Law, University of Washington, and Donald T. Weckstein, Professor of Law, University of San Diego.

Real Estate Finance, 1979, 292 pages, by Jon W. Bruce, Professor of Law, Vanderbilt University.

Real Property, 2nd Ed., 1981, 448 pages, by Roger H. Bernhardt, Professor of Law, Golden Gate University.

Regulated Industries, 1982, 394 pages, by Ernest Gellhorn, Dean and Professor of Law, Case Western Reserve University, and Richard J. Pierce, Professor of Law, Tulane University.

Remedies, 1977, 364 pages, by John F. O'Connell, Professor of Law, Western State University College of Law, Fullerton.

Res Judicata, 1976, 310 pages, by Robert C. Casad, Professor of Law, University of Kansas.

Sales, 2nd Ed., 1981, 370 pages, by John M. Stockton, Professor of Business Law, Wharton School of Finance and Commerce, University of Pennsylvania.

Secured Transactions, 2nd Ed., 1981, 391 pages, by Henry J. Bailey, Professor of Law Emeritus, Willamette University.

Securities Regulation, 2nd Ed., 1982, 322 pages, by David L. Ratner, Dean and Professor of Law, University of San Francisco.

Sex Discrimination, 1982, 399 pages, by Claire Sherman Thomas, Lecturer, University of Washington, Women's Studies Department.

Titles—The Calculus of Interests, 1968, 277 pages, by Oval A. Phipps, Late Professor of Law, St. Louis University.

Torts—Injuries to Persons and Property, 1977, 434 pages, by Edward J. Kionka, Professor of Law, Southern Illinois University.

Torts—Injuries to Family, Social and Trade Relations, 1979, 358 pages, by Wex S. Malone, Professor of Law Emeritus, Louisiana State University.

Trial Advocacy, 1979, 402 pages, by Paul B. Bergman, Adjunct Professor of Law, University of California, Los Angeles.

Trial and Practice Skills, 1978, 346 pages, by Kenney F. Hegland, Professor of Law, University of Arizona.

Trial, The First—Where Do I Sit? What Do I Say?, 1982, 396 pages, by Steven H. Goldberg, Professor of Law, University of Minnesota.

Unfair Trade Practices, 1982, 444 pages, by Charles R. McManis, Professor of Law, Washington University, St. Louis.

Uniform Commercial Code, 1975, 507 pages, by Bradford Stone, Professor of Law, Detroit College of Law.

Uniform Probate Code, 1978, 425 pages, by Lawrence H. Averill, Jr., Dean and Professor of Law, University of Arkansas, Little Rock.

Welfare Law—Structure and Entitlement, 1979, 455 pages, by Arthur B. LaFrance, Dean and Professor of

Law, Lewis and Clark College, Northwestern School of Law.

Wills and Trusts, 1979, 392 pages, by Robert L. Mennell, Professor of Law, Hamline University.

Hornbook Series

and

Basic Legal Texts

of

WEST PUBLISHING COMPANY

P.O. Box 3526

St. Paul, Minnesota 55165

May, 1983

Administrative Law, Davis' Text on, 3rd Ed., 1972, 617 pages, by Kenneth Culp Davis, Professor of Law, University of San Diego.

Agency, Seavey's Hornbook on, 1964, 329 pages, by Warren A. Seavey, Late Professor of Law, Harvard University.

Agency and Partnership, Reuschlein & Gregory's Hornbook on the Law of, 1979 with 1981 Pocket Part, 625 pages, by Harold Gill Reuschlein, Professor of Law, St. Mary's University and William A. Gregory, Professor of Law, Southern Illinois University.

Antitrust, Sullivan's Hornbook on the Law of, 1977, 886 pages, by Lawrence A. Sullivan, Professor of Law, University of California, Berkeley.

Common Law Pleading, Koffler and Reppy's Hornbook on, 1969, 663 pages, by Joseph H. Koffler, Professor of Law, New York Law School and Alison Reppy, Late Dean and Professor of Law, New York Law School.

Common Law Pleading, Shipman's Hornbook on, 3rd Ed., 1923, 644 pages, by Henry W. Ballentine, Late Professor of Law, University of California, Berkeley.

Conflict of Laws, Scoles and Hay's Hornbook on, Student Ed., 1982, 1085 pages, by Eugene F. Scoles, Professor

IX

of Law, University of Illinois and Peter Hay, Dean and Professor of Law, University of Illinois.

Constitutional Law, Nowak, Rotunda and Young's Hornbook on, 2nd Ed., Student Ed., 1983, approximately 1100 pages, by John E. Nowak, Professor of Law, University of Illinois, Ronald D. Rotunda, Professor of Law, University of Illinois, and J. Nelson Young, Professor of Law, University of North Carolina.

Contracts, Calamari and Perillo's Hornbook on, 2nd Ed., 1977, 878 pages, by John D. Calamari, Professor of Law, Fordham University and Joseph M. Perillo, Professor of Law, Fordham University.

Contracts, Corbin's One Volume Student Ed., 1952, 1224 pages, by Arthur L. Corbin, Late Professor of Law, Yale University.

Contracts, Simpson's Hornbook on, 2nd Ed., 1965, 510 pages, by Laurence P. Simpson, Late Professor of Law, New York University.

Corporate Taxation, Kahn's Handbook on, 3rd Ed., Student Ed., Soft cover, 1981 with 1982 Supplement, 614 pages, by Douglas A. Kahn, Professor of Law, University of Michigan.

Corporations, Henn's Hornbook on, 3rd Ed., Student Ed., 1983, approximately 1167 pages, by Harry G. Henn, Professor of Law, Cornell University.

Criminal Law, LaFave and Scott's Hornbook on, 1972, 763 pages, by Wayne R. LaFave, Professor of Law, University of Illinois, and Austin Scott, Jr., Late Professor of Law, University of Colorado.

Damages, McCormick's Hornbook on, 1935, 811 pages, by Charles T. McCormick, Late Dean and Professor of Law, University of Texas.

Domestic Relations, Clark's Hornbook on, 1968, 754 pages, by Homer H. Clark, Jr., Professor of Law, University of Colorado.

Environmental Law, Rodgers' Hornbook on, 1977, 956 pages, by William H. Rodgers, Jr., Professor of Law, University of Washington.

Estate and Gift Taxes, Lowndes, Kramer and McCord's Hornbook on, 3rd Ed., 1974, 1099 pages, by Charles L. B. Lowndes, Late Professor of Law, Duke University, Robert Kramer, Professor of Law Emeritus, George Washington University, and John H. McCord, Professor of Law, University of Illinois.

Evidence, Lilly's Introduction to, 1978, 486 pages, by Graham C. Lilly, Professor of Law, University of Virginia.

Evidence, McCormick's Hornbook on, 2nd Ed., 1972 with 1978 Pocket Part, 938 pages, General Editor, Edward W. Cleary, Professor of Law Emeritus, Arizona State University.

Federal Courts, Wright's Hornbook on, 4th Ed., Student Ed., 1983, 870 pages, by Charles Alan Wright, Professor of Law, University of Texas.

Federal Income Taxation of Individuals, Posin's Hornbook on, Student Ed., 1983, approximately 421 pages, by Daniel Q. Posin, Jr., Professor of Law, Hofstra University.

Future Interest, Simes' Hornbook on, 2nd Ed., 1966, 355 pages, by Lewis M. Simes, Late Professor of Law, University of Michigan.

Income Taxation, Chommie's Hornbook on, 2nd Ed., 1973, 1051 pages, by John C. Chommie, Late Professor of Law, University of Miami.

Insurance, Keeton's Basic Text on, 1971, 712 pages, by Robert E. Keeton, Professor of Law Emeritus, Harvard University.

Labor Law, Gorman's Basic Text on, 1976, 914 pages, by Robert A. Gorman, Professor of Law, University of Pennsylvania.

Law Problems, Ballentine's, 5th Ed., 1975, 767 pages, General Editor, William E. Burby, Late Professor of Law, University of Southern California.

HORNBOOKS & BASIC TEXTS

Legal Writing Style, Weihofen's, 2nd Ed., 1980, 332 pages, by Henry Weihofen, Professor of Law Emeritus, University of New Mexico.

Local Government Law, Reynolds' Hornbook on, 1982, 860 pages, by Osborne M. Reynolds, Professor of Law, University of Oklahoma.

New York Practice, Siegel's Hornbook on, 1978, with 1981–82 Pocket Part, 1011 pages, by David D. Siegel, Professor of Law, Albany Law School of Union University.

Oil and Gas, Hemingway's Hornbook on, 2nd Ed., Student Ed., 1983, approximately 507 pages, by Richard W. Hemingway, Professor of Law, University of Oklahoma.

Poor, Law of the, LaFrance, Schroeder, Bennett and Boyd's Hornbook on, 1973, 558 pages, by Arthur B. La-France, Dean and Professor of Law, Lewis and Clark College, Northwestern School of Law, Milton R. Schroeder, Professor of Law, Arizona State University, Robert W. Bennett, Professor of Law, Northwestern University and William E. Boyd, Professor of Law, University of Arizona.

Property, Boyer's Survey of, 3rd Ed., 1981, 766 pages, by Ralph E. Boyer, Professor of Law, University of Miami.

Real Estate Finance Law, Osborne, Nelson and Whitman's Hornbook on, (successor to Hornbook on Mortgages), 1979, 885 pages, by George E. Osborne, Late Professor of Law, Stanford University, Grant S. Nelson, Professor of Law, University of Missouri, Columbia and Dale A. Whitman, Dean and Professor of Law, University of Missouri, Columbia.

Real Property, Burby's Hornbook on, 3rd Ed., 1965, 490 pages, by William E. Burby, Late Professor of Law, University of Southern California.

Real Property, Moynihan's Introduction to, 1962, 254 pages, by Cornelius J. Moynihan, Professor of Law, Suffolk University.

Remedies, Dobb's Hornbook on, 1973, 1067 pages, by Dan B. Dobbs, Professor of Law, University of Arizona.

Sales, Nordstrom's Hornbook on, 1970, 600 pages, by Robert J. Nordstrom, former Professor of Law, Ohio State University.

Secured Transactions under the U.C.C., Henson's Hornbook on, 2nd Ed., 1979, with 1979 Pocket Part, 504 pages, by Ray D. Henson, Professor of Law, University of California, Hastings College of the Law.

Torts, Prosser's Hornbook on, 4th Ed., 1971, 1208 pages, by William L. Prosser, Late Dean and Professor of Law, University of California, Berkeley.

Trial Advocacy, Jeans' Handbook on, Student Ed., Soft cover, 1975, by James W. Jeans, Professor of Law, University of Missouri, Kansas City.

Trusts, Bogert's Hornbook on, 5th Ed., 1973, 726 pages, by George G. Bogert, Late Professor of Law, University of Chicago and George T. Bogert, Attorney, Chicago, Illinois.

Urban Planning and Land Development Control, Hagman's Hornbook on, 1971, 706 pages, by Donald G. Hagman, Late Professor of Law, University of California, Los Angeles.

Uniform Commercial Code, White and Summers' Hornbook on, 2nd Ed., 1980, 1250 pages, by James J. White, Professor of Law, University of Michigan and Robert S. Summers, Professor of Law, Cornell University.

Wills, Atkinson's Hornbook on, 2nd Ed., 1953, 975 pages, by Thomas E. Atkinson, Late Professor of Law, New York University.

Advisory Board

LOCAL
GOVERNMENT LAW
IN A NUTSHELL

DAVID J. McCARTHY, Jr.

Professor of Law

Georgetown University Law Center

SECOND EDITION

ST. PAUL, MINN.

WEST PUBLISHING CO.

1983

COPYRIGHT © 1975 By WEST PUBLISHING CO.
COPYRIGHT © 1983 By WEST PUBLISHING CO.

50 West Kellogg Boulevard
P.O. Box 3526
St. Paul, Minnesota 55165

Printed in the United States of America

Library of Congress Cataloging in Publication Data

McCarthy, David J.
  Local government law in a nutshell.
  (Nutshell series)
  Includes index.
  1. Local government—Law and legislation—United
States. I. Title. II. Series.
KF5300.Z9M3   1983   342.73'09   83–12535
                          347.3029

ISBN 0–314–75415–6

McCarthy Local Govt. Law 2nd Ed. NS

TO MY WIFE

*

XVII

PREFACE

This text is intended to aid students who seek to learn Local Government Law. It is hoped that it will also be of assistance to practicing attorneys who seek an overview of all or part of the subject matter. The relationships between local governments, their citizens, their states and the federal government are so pervasive that choices of emphasis must of necessity be made in a text of this size. Because Local Government Law tends to overlap some other law school courses, the choice herein was to address at least as many areas as could accurately convey the scope of these relationships and to treat in greater detail areas which are not likely to be pursued in such detail in the core courses common to all law school curricula.

The vast scope of the subject inevitably means that individual authors and editors will approach it with differing views of the most interesting and instructive theme and focus. Witness the various casebooks presently available. The choice of this text has been the central theme of delegated power and the limitations imposed upon its exercise. Such limitations may derive from restrictions imposed by the people upon all exercises of power in the state, restrictions imposed in furtherance both of the cession of powers to the federal government and of the protection of individual rights, restrictions accompanying the delegations of local powers, and the restrictions resulting from political realities and the limitations upon the local ability to raise and spend revenues. The text attempts to interweave concepts of practical reality in presenting this most practical of subjects.

Occasionally, throughout the text, comments and queries will be addressed in attempts to provoke reader reaction (agreement or disagreement) to the status or trend of particular legal principles and of local government policies. Frequently, illustrations will be used to assist in understanding the text. Many of the illustrations are drawn from actual cases.

While many cases, books and casebooks were consulted in the preparation of the text, with much gratitude particular note should be made of the major assistance of the following: Antieau, Local Government Law (Matthew Bender, 1966); Fordham, Local Government Law (The Foundation Press, Inc., 1949), Revised Edition (The Foundation Press, Inc., 1975); Mandelker, Managing Our Urban Environment (Bobbs-Merrill 1963), Second Edition (Bobbs-Merrill, 1971); Michelman & Sandalow, Materials on Government in Urban Areas (West Publishing Company, 1970); Reynolds, Handbook of Local Government Law (West Publishing Company, 1982); Sato & Van Alstyne, State and Local Government Law (Little, Brown, 1970), Second Edition (Little, Brown, 1977), and supplement; and Valente, Local Government Law: Cases and Materials (West Publishing Company, 1975), Second

Edition (West Publishing Company, 1980), and supplement.

Permit me also to express my gratitude to some of the people whose assistance and efforts have contributed to this book: to my respected former colleague, Professor Chester J. Antieau, whose contributions to my knowledge and this text began when he taught me Local Government Law, and have continued to the suggestion and offering of materials assisting all aspects of the research; to my research assistants, Laura Farrand, Steven Sarfatti, Neal Tonken, Robert Varney and L Mark Winston and, for this second edition, Christopher Whitney, whose efforts during the periods of initial and final research and writing have been major factors without which the book would not have been completed; and to the Law Center faculty-support service personnel for their indispensable assistance.

DAVID J. McCARTHY, JR.

Washington, D.C.
March, 1983

*

OUTLINE

	Page
Preface -------------------------------------	XIX

CHAPTER I—LOCAL GOVERNING POWER: GENERAL ASPECTS, LIMITATIONS, RESOLUTION OF POWER CONFLICTS AND CHALLENGES

A. Introduction ------------------------- 1
Sec.
  1. Basic Questions and Terms ------- 1
  2. Focus and Approach ------------- 6
  3. Local Governing Entities --------- 7
  4. An Illustration ------------------ 10
  5. Comment ---------------------- 13

B. Sources of Local Governing Powers ---- 14
  1. Dillon's Rule --------------------- 14
  2. Express Grants of Authority ------- 15
  3. Interpretation and Implication ----- 18
  4. Comment ---------------------- 23

C. Limitations on State Power Over Municipal Corporations ------------- 24
  1. "Plenary" Power ----------------- 24
  2. State Constitutional Provisions, Generally -------------------------- 26
  3. Provisions Limiting Expenditures --- 27
  4. Provisions Insuring Local Accountability -------------------------- 28

Page

C. **Limitations on State Power Over Munici-pal Corporations**—Continued
    5. Provisions Protecting Local Autonomy   30

D. **Resolution of Competing Power Con-siderations** --------------------   38
    1. Two Views of Predominance ---------   38
    2. Competing Federal Power Considera-tions -------------------------   40
    3. Competing State Power Considerations   45
    4. Competing Local Power Considerations   47
    5. Federal and State Constitutional Pre-dominance ----------------------   48

CHAPTER II—FORMATION OF THE LO-CAL GOVERNMENT, ALTERATION, BOUNDARY CHANGES; SOME PROBLEMS OF ORGANIZATION AND OPERATION: OFFICERS, EM-PLOYEES, ALLOCATION AND DEL-EGATION OF FUNCTIONS, ELEC-TIONS

A. **Some Aspects of Organization and Alter-ation Choices** ------------------   51
    1. Introduction: Choices for Unin-corporated Areas ---------------   51
    2. Introduction: Choices for Incorporated Areas -------------------------   53

B. **Considerations Common to Statutory In-corporation or Alteration Pro-cedures** -----------------------   55
    1. Specific Provisions ----------------   55
    2. Mandatory and Directory -----------   58

Page

C. **Formation of the Local Governing Unit** __ 59
  1. Incorporation of the Local General Government _____ 59
  2. Formation of Special Districts _____ 62
  3. Comment on the Special District and Other Forms of Decentralization ___ 63

D. **Alteration, Boundary Changes** _____ 64
  1. Extraterritorial Exercise of Power ___ 64
  2. Annexation _____ 66
  3. Dissolution, Division and Detachment 72
  4. Political Realities and Constitutional Implications _____ 74
  5. Cross-Boundary Cooperation: Consolidation and Federation _____ 82

E. **Some Problems of Organization and Operation: Officers, Employees, Allocation and Delegation of Functions, Elections and Referenda** ___ 86
  1. Introduction _____ 86
  2. Employee Profile _____ 87
  3. Officers _____ 89
  4. Devices to Protect Against Conflicts of Duty and Interest _____ 90
  5. Residency Requirements _____ 95
  6. Challenged Employment Practices ___ 97
  7. Public Employee Unions _____ 103
  8. Restrictions on the Exercise of Executive, Administrative, Legislative and Judicial Functions _____ 107
  9. Delegation of Implementation Authority _____ 113

E. Some Problems of Organization and Operation: Officers, Employees, Allocation and Delegation of Functions, Elections and Referenda
—Continued **Page**

   10. Elections and the Fourteenth Amendment 119

CHAPTER III—REGULATION OF CONDUCT AND THE USE OF LAND

A. **The Police Power** 126

   1. Relation to Zoning Power 126

   2. Challenges to Police-Power Exercise .. 127

   3. Appropriate Objects for Police-Power Exercise 131

   4. Relation of Means to Object 135

   5. Specific Constitutional Limitations .. 138

   6. Regulation and Prohibition 144

   7. Licenses, Permits, Fees 146

   8. Nuisances 148

   9. Investigation, Enforcement and Penalties 149

   10. Discriminatory Enforcement 153

   11. Estoppel 154

B. **Regulation of Land Use** 155

   1. Functional Components in the Land Regulatory Process 155

   2. The Role of Planning 160

   3. "Plans" and "Maps" 161

B. Regulation of Land Use—Continued

Page

4. Techniques of Plan Implementation: Official Maps, Master Plans, Subdivision Control, and Other Devices 163
5. Zoning _____ 170
6. Rezoning _____ 173
7. Zoning Devices: Euclidean, Floating, Conditional, Contract, and Cluster, Planned Unit Development _____ 174
8. Flexibility Devices: Exemptions, Accessory Uses, Special Exceptions, Variances, Non-conforming Uses, and Cumulative Zoning _____ 180
9. Enforcement _____ 189
10. Accompanying Land Use Regulations 189
11. Challenges to Land-Use Restrictions _ 194
12. "Exclusionary Zoning" _____ 199

CHAPTER IV—ACQUISITION, LIMITATIONS ON USE, AND DISPOSITION OF GOODS, SERVICES AND PROPERTY

A. Acquisition by Contract _____ 208
    1. Introduction _____ 208
    2. Authority to Contract _____ 212
    3. Conflict of Interest _____ 213

A. **Acquisition by Contract**—Continued   **Page**
    4. Other Contracts Against Public Policy   215
    5. Bidding Requirements 219
    6. Limitations to Assure Citizen Vigilance 226
    7. Agency 226
    8. A Note on Some Common Municipal
       Contract Clauses 227
    9. Relief and Restitution 228

B. **Other Methods of Property Acquisition:**
    Gift, Dedication, Adverse Pos-
    sesion, Prescription and User 231
    1. Public Purpose and Methods of Ac-
       quisition 231
    2. Illustration 232
    3. Estate Obtained: The Fee (Directly or
       by Implication); Aquisition with
       Conditions 233
    4. Estate Obtained: Easement 235
    5. Effect of Estate Obtained and Method
       of Acquisition Upon Municipal Flex-
       ibility 236

C. **Acquisition Under Eminent Domain** 238
    1. Authority 238
    2. Some Interests Subject to Eminent Do-
       main 239
    3. Necessity and Public Use or Purpose
       Requirements 243
    4. Excess Condemnation 246
    5. Quick Condemnation 247

C. Acquisition Under Eminent Domain—
Continued

Page

6. Some Aspects of Just Compensation: Fair Market Value, Methods of Appraisal, Apportionment, Highest-and-Best-Use Factors, and Substitution _____ 248
7. Consequential and Severance Damages, Offsetting Benefits _____ 254
8. Comment on Extent of Just Compensation _____ 257

D. Some Limitations on Municipal Use of Acquired Property _____ 258
1. Nuisances _____ 258
2. Inconsistent Private Uses _____ 258
3. Constitutional Limitations _____ 259
4. Holding City to Present Use _____ 260
5. Change of Use of Property Held in Fee 262

E. Disposition and Loss of Municipal Property _____ 263
1. Abandonment _____ 263
2. Lease _____ 264
3. Franchises _____ 265
4. Vacation of Streets _____ 267
5. Gift, Pledge, Mortgage _____ 268
6. Sale _____ 269
7. Adverse Possession, Estoppel to Claim Title _____ 270
8. Reversion _____ 271
9. Eminent Domain, Compulsory Transfer _____ 271

CHAPTER V—MUNICIPAL
REVENUES

Page

A. Important Sources of Revenue Which Generally Are Not Major Contributors to the Municipality's Total Revenues ------------------ 274

1. Licensing ------------------------ 274
2. Local Income Taxes --------------- 280
3. Sales, Use and Gross Receipts Taxes -- 282
4. Other "Minor" Revenue Sources ----- 287
5. Special Assessments -------------- 288

B. Important Sources of Revenue Which Constitute Major Contributions to the Revenue Picture --------------- 302

1. Intergovernmental Transfer of Revenues ---------------------------- 303
2. Property Taxes (Real and Personal) -- 305
3. Borrowing ----------------------- 315
4. Warrants ------------------------ 316
5. Bonds -------------------------- 318
6. Debt Limitations ----------------- 324
7. Illustration: Industrial Revenue Bonds 329
8. Practical Considerations: Borrowing Restraints -------------------- 333
9. Practical Considerations: Federal Taxation ------------------------- 336

C. Some Additional Considerations Relevant to Municipal Expenditures ------ 338

1. Constitutional Restrictions on Expenditure Objectives --------------- 338
2. Expenditure Method Restrictions ---- 339

C. **Some Additional Considerations Relevant to Municipal Expenditures—** Cont'd

Page

   3. Officer Liability for Unlawful Expenditures ------------------------- 341

CHAPTER VI—CONSIDERATIONS PERTINENT TO CITIZEN LITIGATION WITH LOCAL GOVERNMENTS

A. **Citizen Tort Claims Against the Local Government** -------------------- 343

   1. Customary Theories ---------------- 343
   2. Ultra Vires ----------------------- 345
   3. Statutes of Limitations ------------ 345
   4. Notice Requirements -------------- 345
   5. Municipal Immunity -------------- 348
   6. Some Notes Concerning Damages, Execution, Contribution and Indemnity 359

B. **Standing** ----------------------------- 362

   1. The Requirement's Rationale -------- 362
   2. "Adverse" Effect of Government Action; Illustrative Questions ------- 363
   3. Taxpayer Suits -------------------- 365
   4. Note on Federal Cases ------------- 369

Index ------------------------------------ 375

*

XXXI

LOCAL
GOVERNMENT LAW
IN A NUTSHELL

SECOND EDITION

*

CHAPTER I

LOCAL GOVERNING POWER: GENERAL ASPECTS, LIMITATIONS, RESOLUTION OF POWER CONFLICTS AND CHALLENGES

A. INTRODUCTION

§ 1. Basic Questions and Terms. Broadly considered, the study of Local Government Law is the study of local governing powers exercised by entities subsidiary and largely subordinate to the state. When government at any level plans to act, a basic question is whether the proposed activity is an appropriate one for government. "Should government get into the business of owning and operating airports?"

Since all government is restricted within limits constitutionally structured by the people, the next question may be whether the governmental entity can act as planned. "Can government get into the business of owning and operating an airport?"

When the prospective actor is a government of delegated authority, the question of its ability to act would perhaps be phrased, "Does *this* city possess the authority to own and operate this airport?"

[1]

a.   While legislative and judicial attempts to answer these questions may frequently be characterized as unsatisfactory, resolution of the questions is at the heart of local governance. The decision to what extent the local government either ought to or can initiate activity which might be the subject of private action or governmental involvement at another level is, in the first instance, committed to the local legislative body. The courts often defer to this decision, especially as to the appropriateness of activity. When a judicial decision of appropriateness is made, it may be expressed in a determination whether the activity serves a public purpose, or serves to protect the public health, safety, morality or general welfare. "The expenditure of funds for the purchase and operation of the airport will expedite public travel, will ensure the safety of air traffic operation, will increase local business access to economical commercial routes, will create more jobs, will protect residential areas, and thus will serve a public purpose."

b.   Judicial determination of the local government's ability to act will be the result of reference to the sources of its power. As we shall see, these sources may be constitutional and statutory grants and limitations subject to judicial interpretation. If the questioned power exercise is neither expressly approved nor specifically prohibited, inference of its approval by implication will be tested by the reasonableness of the desired inference and its obvious or attenuated relationship to expressly authorized activities. "The court concludes that the power to own and operate a municipal airport may not reasonably be inferred from the statutory authorizations to regulate traffic and to provide parks and recreational facilities."

It can readily be seen that if the relationship between the asserted implied power and the powers expressly granted is not too attenuated, the determination whether the implication is a reasonable inference may involve a decision, albeit frequently unspoken, that the activity is or is not appropriate.

c. This questioning of the value of action initiated by the local government may also underlie judicial determination of the level of government which should be permitted to act. The question may arise in deciding whether the local government is authorized to act. It may arise because both the state and the local government have enacted legislation on the precise point. It may arise because both have legislated in the area, although not in a conflicting manner. It may arise because the state has attempted to interpose its authority either legislatively or through administrative boards over a matter which allegedly is within the constitutionally protected area of local government.

[*3*]

To illustrate, let us assume that the state legislature has enacted a public disclosure law designed to provide voters with information to make judgments concerning the allegiances and possible conflicts of interest of electoral candidates and public officials throughout the state. Let us further assume that the local government's legislature subsequently has enacted a local public disclosure law designed to meet the same objectives regarding candidates and officials in the local jurisdiction, but with stricter disclosure requirements. The latter law is challenged in court.

The court may decide that the local government had no authority at all to enact the law. As noted above, if such authority is argued to be by interpretation of express language or implication, evaluation of the appropriateness of the local action may underlie the decision.

The court may decide that without regard to the state's action, the matter of public officials and elections is one committed by the state constitution, or by statute, to the state's purview. Even if, by state law, the local government is permitted to initiate action, without further authorization, on matters of local concern (home rule, as we shall see), the court may conclude that this matter has consequences beyond the boundaries of the locality, and is more appropriately committed to statewide action. Perhaps, then, the ques-

[4]

tion of local initiative will turn on judicial decision as to its appropriateness in light of its external consequences.

The court has additional choices. It may deem the local action authorized and merely supplemental to or in augmentation of the state legislation. Conversely, it may determine that the local law "prohibits what state law permits" in an area partaking of statewide concern and strike it down on that ground. Whatever the court's decision, the classification of the activity as "local" or "general" may turn on the appropriateness of governmental action at the level in question.

d. Governing activity, of course, is not limited to regulations designed to *protect* the public interest and to *preserve* the public health, safety, morality and general welfare. Much government action is designed to *promote* such objectives. This is particularly true at the local level where the desire for services may constitute a primary motivation for the local entity's organization. In promoting such activities, the municipality will have concluded that, for a variety of reasons, governmental action is preferable to that of the private sector and is to that extent appropriate. As we shall see, the people of many states have in constitutional amendments declared that such activities should be protected against state legislative or administrative incursion. Where such incursion is alleged to have occurred, judicial decision concerning the appropriate governmental level may call for designation of the questioned local power exercise as either "governmental" (and thus, perhaps, within state legislative purview) or "proprietary." The latter activities may also be called "municipal" or "corporate."

e.   Thus, an exercise of local governing power will be upheld if it serves a "public purpose," if its implied existence is "reasonable," if the matter in question is of "local" rather than "statewide" concern, or if the activity is "municipal," or "corporate," or "proprietary" rather than "governmental." The seeming simplicity of the classification process is, of course, deceptive. As in other areas of the law, once the "label" has been affixed, predictable results corresponding to that label will follow. The much more difficult and unpredictable determination whether to affix a particular label will bring into operation precedent, political theory, and persuasion.

§ 2.   **Focus and Approach.**   Our study must accordingly begin with the sources of local governing power, the limitations upon state interference with that power, the resolution of competing governmental claims to power priority, and illustrations of challenges seeking to assert protection of citizens' rights from power exercise. Thereafter, we shall engage in a more discrete analysis of the following particular manifestations of local governing power:

[*6*]

a. The formation of the local entity, alteration, boundary changes, internal operating problems, delegations of responsibility, elections and referenda;

b. The police and zoning powers, i.e., regulation of citizen conduct, business activity and land use, without compensation, to protect the public health, safety, morality and general welfare;

c. The acquisition, use and disposition of goods, services and property; and

d. The acquisition and expenditure of revenues derived from taxation, assessments, borrowing and investments.

Our study will close with a brief view of citizen suits against the local government, seeking damages for injury, or seeking to block or compel government activity.

§ 3. Local Governing Entities. We have spoken of local governing power seemingly divorced from the entity exercising it. To a large extent, our study will follow that approach. Nevertheless, from the fact that more than 80,000 governmental units are in operation, all but fifty of which exercise, broadly or narrowly, local governing power, it is evident that promotion or challenge of a particular activity must occasionally involve recognition of the nature of the entity engaging in it. Illustratively, a school district may not be able to levy taxes. A city's population may not be of sufficient size to include it within a class to which home rule has been granted, or to which the power to act extraterritorially has been accorded. A county may not be able to withstand annexation by an adjoining city. Many of these considerations are relevant to the existence of authority to act or to the manner in which action must be taken.

a. The entity most frequently referred to herein will be the basic unit of local general government, the unit possessing the authority to exercise the widest range of governing power while being not only subordinate to the state but also subject to local citizen political accountability. For ease of reference, the terms "city," "municipality" or "municipal corporation" will be used interchangeably. However, in some states, notably in the south, counties and occasional independent cities meet this definition of the basic unit of broad local general government. In other states, the county may not exist, or may be the local agent of designated state powers. Similarly, "towns" may be basic local governing units or the state's limited local agents. Those counties, townships or towns which act as a state's local agent and which are involuntarily created are sometimes called quasi-municipal corporations.

The range of powers exercised by local general governments will differ in many states according

[*8*]

to classification (township, borough, cities of the first, second, third or fourth class, villages).

b. In addition to local general governments, special purpose, limited, governmental structures, customarily called special districts, abound. They have been created in attempts to bypass normal governmental borrowing limitations, to "insulate" certain activities from traditional political influence, to allocate functions to entities reflecting particular expertise, to provide services in otherwise unincorporated areas, or to bring certain functions within closer local citizen control. Such special districts may serve only a single purpose (fire protection, mosquito abatement, e.g.), or may serve multiple purposes (provision of water and removal of sewage, lighting and sanitation, parks and planning, e.g.). They may be accountable to the electorate (some school districts, e.g.) and may have the power to tax to support their activity (commonly ad valorem taxes). They may fall within, share or extend across other municipal boundaries, may be dependent for revenues upon or controlled by other municipal entities, or may be independent thereof, and may be temporary or permanent in nature.

There are thousands of such entities throughout the country, with school districts the most prevalent. In metropolitan areas, a multitude of "local governments" may exercise local governing powers in connection with overlapping geographical areas, populations, and functions.

Sometimes indistinguishable from the special districts are ad hoc entities commonly referred to as public or special authorities which often operate bond-funded facilities, have no defined geographic or population extent, and are under comparably closer control of their creator-governments. Both special districts and public authorities should be distinguished from those "districts" created to provide a local benefit paid for through special assessments imposed upon property owners specially benefiting from the improvement.

Whether special districts serve the need for expertise or compound the "red tape" incident to government activity, whether they serve the purposes for which they were designed or create fiefdoms impervious to citizen need, whether they expedite government activity or enable unwise expenditure, whether they reflect valid judgments of the wisdom of local control or serve to insulate society from compelling social problems are questions which illustrate the controversial nature of the special district form.

§ 4. An Illustration. A further illustration may help to put the foregoing in perspective. Assume that the government of the city of Allgood wishes to build a domed stadium in order to attract major sports teams and sporting events.

City officials think that local business will be aided by such a venture and that the sports attractions will provide desirable recreation for the citizens and will spur the development of athletic programs for adults and children. In addition, the possible attraction of "major league" teams may increase a sense of citizen identification with the city which will have spillover effects in housing, renewal and commerce.

Critics raise in opposition the sizeable debts which may result, the "horror stories" of other cities' failures, and the need for expenditure of effort and funds in areas of higher priority.

As we have seen, the matter will begin with the question of the city's authority to engage in the project. Is there express statutory authority for the city to build a domed stadium? Is this city within the class to which such authority has been granted? If there is express authority, several battles remain to be fought through the judicial and electoral processes to enforce the respective public-involvement or private-sector views.

If there is not express authority, the public-private-priority struggle will be engaged on the question whether authority can be inferred from existing constitutional or statutory grants. For example, can approval be inferred from customary parks and recreation authority? Putting the same basic priority question in another form, "Will the necessary expenditure of funds be for a

[*11*]

public purpose, or will the use of the property be a public use?"

Assume that stadium opponents seek the aid of the state in opposition. Does the city's contemplated action conflict with specific statutory provisions or does it enter a field specifically reserved to the state? Does the decision to build and operate a stadium involve such consequences external to the city (economic disruption in other areas of the state, e.g.) that it should be denied status as a purely local matter even if the city's authority is asserted from a position of home rule? If the authority question is answered favorably from the city's point of view, should a state constitutional clause barring state delegation to administrators of authority over "municipal" ("corporate," "proprietary") affairs prevent supervision or assumption of the matter by the State Board of Economic Improvement? Is this the sort of local benefit that the people, through their constitution, wished to leave to the discretion and judgment of the citizens who formed the city?

Implementation of the plan will bring additional questions concerning the exercise of specific powers. If the land upon which the stadium is to be constructed is outside the city, may the city annex the land? May it be acquired through eminent domain? If the city is authorized to build, may the power to condemn land outside its

boundaries be inferred? Does the city have the
necessary power to rezone the land for its prospective use? How will the necessary revenues
be raised? Will the city's taxing power support
promises to bondholders? Will the city's financial position necessitate creation of a special authority to build and operate the stadium? Will
there be special districts responsible for sanitation and lighting? If there are injuries in connection with the venture, is the activity one which
should be protected from citizen recovery? If citizens wish to challenge, who has standing to do
so? May the facilities, when completed, be leased
to organizations which discriminate on the basis
of race or creed?

§ 5. **Comment.** a. The history of local government offers plentiful assurance that the domed
stadium project will be challenged through the
electoral, legislative and judicial processes in
every conceivable way, only a few of which are
illustrated above. Clearly the validity of the
city's assumption of benefit will play a vital,
though frequently unspoken, role in the outcome.
Nevertheless, what some hope would be a decision expeditiously implemented may instead be a
tortuous exercise in political interplay and public
accountability. Such complexity offers to the local citizenry, through referendum provisions, bidding and conflict-of-interest requirements, and
debt limitations, some protection against unwise

[*13*]

commitments. Such complexity also serves to provide inordinate delay, harassing challenge, sizeable cost increases and manifest inefficiency.

b. The relative merit of the multiplicity of protections and the prices of inefficiency is but one of the dilemmas facing the student who wishes to assess the value of local government. Others include such questions as what level of government possesses the fiscal power best to support certain governmental activities. What governmental decisions are more appropriately decided at relatively local levels? Despite citizens' historic compulsion for local government and the apparent revitalization of local government by federal policy and U.S. Supreme Court decisions, one might ask, then, for what purposes and benefits is politically accountable government below the state level of continuing viability.

These questions, while clearly beyond the scope of this text, will assuredly, though silently, accompany our study of the success and implementation of local governing power.

B. SOURCES OF LOCAL GOVERNING POWERS

§ 1. **Dillon's Rule.** Whether the city of Allgood can build and operate the stadium, whether the other municipalities can own and operate an airport or can enact a public disclosure law, whether

[*14*]

any municipal corporation can act, depends in the first instance upon its authority so to act.

More often than not, discussions of local governing authority begin with Dillon's Rule: Municipal corporations have and can exercise only those powers expressly granted, those necessarily or fairly implied therefrom, and those that are essential and indispensable. This often repeated formulation, of course, indicates the process of determining whether the power exists, not the answer itself. Originally applied strictly, its present application is more likely to be accompanied by degrees of liberality. While it may be mentioned in some home-rule determinations, it is not a helpful process of power analysis in such cases.

§ 2. **Express Grants of Authority.** The search begins with powers expressly granted. Is the city empowered by its charter to act in this matter? The term "charter" referred at one time to the crown charters granted newly organizing municipalities in the colonies. Today it may refer to the charter proffered by legislation and chosen by the city, or the charter drafted and approved by the citizens in a home-rule jurisdiction. Occasionally, it is used to refer to the compendium of express powers accorded to a particular city by state constitutional provisions, organizational statutes and a plethora of specific power grants scattered throughout other state statutes. Since, as we have noted earlier, some municipalities may

[*15*]

initiate activity within a reservoir of power designated by the title "home rule," it is important to determine under which of the customary forms of core power delegation the municipality was organized. It is also important, of course, because the methods of amendment will obviously differ.

a. The municipality may derive its basic authority by direct delegation from the people through one or more state constitutional provisions. The provisions may be simple or detailed in nature, and may create autonomy over local matters or municipal affairs (most prevalent) or over almost all matters not denied to the municipality by its charter or by general law. This is termed "constitutional home rule" and will be discussed in more detail later in this chapter. Such a constitutional delegation is often supplemented by additional power grants in a multitude of state statutes. While debatably the power thus reposed may be exercised in the absence of an actual charter, charters are universally drafted and approved by the voters of the municipality. Customarily, such charters express the powers of the corporation and allocate the functions therein. It should be noted that California and perhaps other jurisdictions consider the home-rule charter provisions to be not expressions of power but limitations on the reservoir of governing authority constitutionally delegated. This view analogizes the

[*16*]

charter to a state constitution which serves the same purpose.

b.   The municipality may derive its basic authority under state legislation granting home rule to it and members of its class usually with such state enactment authorized by constitutional provision.   This "legislative home rule" is conceptually less secure than its constitutional counterpart, although for a variety of reasons including judicial interpretations, some of such local governments may in fact be the more powerful. Charter enactment and amendment may proceed as in constitutional home-rule jurisdictions, and additional powers may derive from additional state statutes.   It should be noted that in both types of home-rule jurisdictions, home-rule status may be granted only to some classes of cities, or to cities and counties, or to counties and independent cities.   Special-district claims of home-rule authority will be unavailing.

c.   Non-home-rule municipalities may receive express authority by particular state legislation applicable specifically to them.   This method is not frequent today because, as we shall see, state constitutions commonly ban "special," "one city" legislation.   More commonly, non-home-rule municipalities qualify in accordance with the class they fit (usually on the basis of population) for a "charter" consisting of a state legislative grant of powers to respective classes of municipalities.

[*17*]

This state legislation sometimes takes the form of alternative "charters" or governmental forms from which the municipality of a particular class elects the one under which it will operate (commonly, by voter preference). Again, the powers thus derived are frequently and substantially augmented by authority sprinkled throughout the state legislative enactments.

§ 3. Interpretation and Implication. Even if our illustration cities seeking stadium, airport or public disclosure authority possess home-rule status, unless there is expressed in accompanying state statutes or in the special or general state statutory "charters" specific stadium, airport or public disclosure authority, our search must turn to the area of implication and interpretation.

Needless to say, the role of the judiciary in this area is substantial. A restrictive court can strictly limit municipal operation and flexibility by deciding: that charter or statutory expressions should not be interpreted to include the power in question; that the permission to act is an improper delegation of legislative authority by the legislature; that it is not a local matter or municipal affair; that it is not necessarily or fairly to be implied from express authority; or that it is not an indispensable attribute of local government.

a. Legislative documents and charters contain language which is, of course, subject to varying interpretations. Indeed, the political process

[*18*]

leading to their drafting, enactment or approval often results in intentional ambiguities designed to achieve support of those who would have to oppose more explicit language. Consequently, the determination whether a power is expressed may eventually involve judicial interpretation of the "legislatively or constitutionally intended" meaning of terms. The reader should not confuse the sources of federal legislative history with the all too common paucity of such materials at the state and local levels. The flexibility of local power exercise is in the hands of the courts.

b. The problem of delegation of legislative power is a complex one frequently (and fortunately) overlooked by the courts. It is clear that a state legislature may delegate administration or implementation of state legislation to local governments under fairly general standards. It is by no means equally clear whether a particular delegation qualifies for this description. "All cities of population greater than 500,000 . . . may own and operate municipal airports provided that no such airport shall be within five miles of a built-up residential area, and provided that no such airport shall employ tower personnel who are not licensed by the Federal Aviation Agency. . . . " Is such a provision a delegation of legislative or administrative authority?

It is also clear that the delegation problem is avoided when the original delegation is made di-

rectly by the people to the local governments in
the state constitution. Similarly, the constitutional provisions authorizing home-rule delegation
would seem to approve the delegation of legislative authority by the state.

Strict adherence to the doctrine of non-delega-
tion would strangle local government. Thus, a
practical though conceptually unreconcilable exception permits the state legislature to delegate
to local units legislative power incidental, appropriate or related to municipal affairs or local self-
government, with little cavil over what is a local
or municipal matter. Where called upon to do so
the majority of American courts would not include within the exception a delegation to the local entity of the authority to determine its form
or powers. Local-option legislation which permits local units to accept or reject the application
of state enactments in their city (liquor-by-the-
drink approval, e.g.) and local opportunity to
choose among statutory alternatives of forms of
government can and do survive most challenges
of improper legislative delegation.

Finally, constitutional provisions may by their
terms prohibit delegation of legislative power to
certain kinds of local units (counties, e.g.). And
courts will occasionally disapprove delegations
which appear to violate provisions of the constitution conferring power to act in the matter upon
the state legislature. Illustratively a constitu-

[*20*]

tional provision declaring that "the Legislature shall have the power to prescribe the manner of conducting . . . elections, the qualifications of candidates for public office . . . " might be held to bar a delegation to our city of the power to enact a public disclosure law.

The cognate problem of state legislatures delegating to special state-created commissions the power over certain municipal functions and the vestiges of the doctrine of inherent right of local self-government, though somewhat relevant here, will be discussed in our examination of limitations of state power over municipal affairs.

c. Judicial decision whether a matter is local (within home rule) or general in nature is theoretically possible whether or not the state has acted and will be discussed infra. As a practical matter, the question will often arise in determining whether existing state legislation preempts, conflicts with or usurps local prerogatives, and will be discussed in that connection.

d. Whenever the search for express authorization has been concluded unsuccessfully, there remains the broad area of implied powers. Can the airport, stadium or public disclosure authority be fairly or necessarily implied from existing express grants? It is this question which underlies much of the power-source litigation. And here, of course, precedent and persuasion play a great role. Here a court can effectively extinguish municipal flexibility. Courts can decide that the authority to regulate parking does not imply authority to prohibit it. Courts can decide that the authority to regulate parking does not imply authority to create a rebuttable presumption that an "illegally parked" vehicle was parked there by its owner. Using such traditional principles of construction as "ejusdem generis," courts can decide that authority to act to protect the public welfare does not imply authority to impose land use restrictions on purely aesthetic grounds.

On the other hand courts can decide that the power to regulate implies the power to set conditions under which existence of the subject of regulation will be permitted. Courts can decide that effective regulation implies the power to create presumptions which expedite enforcement. Courts can decide that aesthetic considerations form a proper basis for protection of land values, healthy and safe living conditions, and tourist-aided economic values.

The city of Allgood, for example, might successfully make the following argument: express authority to create parks and promote citizen recreation implies power to build and operate the stadium. Moreover, when land for the expressly authorized recreational projects is not available within the city, the state legislature may have implied the authority to obtain the land outside the

[*22*]

city, even by the expressly granted power of eminent domain.

e. Because powers which are essential or indispensable are easily implied from any rationally designed grant of express authority, there has been little need to identify a separate category of powers thus classified. Presumably, providing a meeting place for the city council might be such a power. Removal of "impeachable" officers may be another. Our cities would have no success under this classification regarding the airport and stadium. A more plausible argument, that for the public disclosure law, would no doubt fail as well.

§ 4. **Comment.** Whether as a general rule courts have been unduly restrictive in reviewing power exercises by local government units, home rule or no, is a matter of some dispute. Some proponents of flexible and powerful local government argue the affirmative. Their position is bolstered by the apparent necessity of constitutional amendments in two heavily populated states calling for liberal judicial power-interpretation. Others conclude with some support in the cases that, particularly in home-rule jurisdictions, courts have been receptive to municipal undertakings. It is one thing to ask the court to approve municipal flexibility and imaginative government in the absence of extraterritorial consequences or state expressions in the area. It is quite another

[*23*]

to ask approval despite extraterritorial consequences, or in the face of state activity in the
matter, or in the face of due concern by the judge
for the separate prerogatives of the state legislative branch.   It has been in part the failure of advocacy to assess and attempt to overcome the reluctance engendered by these considerations
which has resulted in the "illiberal" decisions.   It
is arguable that alleged municipal "powerlessness" is more the result of this failure of advocacy and the failure of courage in city hall than of
judicial restrictiveness.

C.   LIMITATIONS ON STATE POWER
OVER MUNICIPAL CORPORATIONS

§ 1.   **"Plenary" Power.**   It is frequently said
that the state possesses plenary power over its
municipal corporations and may create, dissolve
and realign them, may deny them power and may
direct them to accomplish governmental objectives.   As a description of the position of a municipality vis-a-vis its state when the municipality
seeks a protected status under the Federal Constitution, where no individual person's rights are
at issue, the "plenary power" description approaches accuracy.   Cities have been uniformly
unsuccessful in attempts to protect themselves
from state power exercise by invoking the indi-
vidual- or contract-rights protections of the Federal Constitution.   But when the state action af-

fects not only the rights of city citizens as members of the city but also their rights given protected status under the federal and state constitutions (voting rights, creditors' rights, e.g.), the description, though strongly urged, is inapplicable. In addition, there have been occasions, even to the point of suit by the city against its state, when municipalities have successfully withstood normally superior state power because they have been acting under federally conferred power deemed within the ambit of the Federal Constitution's Supremacy Clause.

To be sure, where the municipality is exercising those powers classified as governmental, i.e., where it may be said to be exercising governing powers which the state might exercise if the city did not exist as a "local agent," state power is superior to that of the city. The state may require the city to act or may prevent city action. Additionally while the state may be barred, as we shall see, from meddling in "municipal" affairs, appropriate exercise of such state governmental power as the police power may be upheld even if it interferes with what are alleged to be the local unit's local affairs. Finally, the state may require its local unit to recognize claims against it which are morally but not legally binding. (Municipal appropriation of funds to pay morally binding claims has been upheld.) The state legislative requirement may be either the waiver of technical defenses (state created) or a directive to pay the claim.

§ 2. State Constitutional Provisions, Generally. a. The above circumstances and the totality of state-local relations are circumscribed by the state constitutions which contain numerous provisions, some very detailed, affecting state-local relations. Most fall into one of three categories: (i) those which attempt to prevent unwarranted expenditures; (ii) those which enshrine certain activities for which there should be local political accountability; and (iii) those which serve to create and protect local autonomy.

b. These amendments have been responses to historical abuses of the late Nineteenth and early Twentieth Centuries. (i) States and cities (with apparent state blessing) engaged in unwarranted and injudicious expenditures involving not only the potential of graft, but also the serious risks of poor investment. Notorious among these were the investments in railroads. (ii) As the populations moved to urban density and the impact of cities on state affairs became more pronounced, state legislatures began more and more to meddle in the local units' affairs, often with capricious results. Responsive to constituent and special interest pressures, legislatures would involve themselves with the most menial of local activities. State legislatures became, in effect, "legislatures of appeals," responding to override local

[*26*]

initiative at the behest of those disappointed with the response at the local level. (iii) Also during this time, some courts gave short life to a principle which although now unspoken, has never died: the inherent right to local self-government. Cases are no longer decided on the ground that there is a basic, common-law-if-you-will, unbreachable right to local self-government which at some point serves as a barrier to incremental state meddling. But state constitutional provisions survive as memorials to the doctrine's former vitality. And, as some recent state-constitutional reformation results and attempts to introduce state land use control attest, the doctrine lives on as a practical reality of political psychology.

c. The present impact of these remedies for earlier state and local excesses should not be underestimated. While judicial interpretation may have in some cases eroded their remedial intent (debt limitations avoided by special authorities, e.g.) and the demands of modern society may have occasionally burst through their apparent inflexibility (urban renewal and private investment, e.g.), they are nonetheless viable limitations which serve occasionally as protections and occasionally as obstacles to municipal or state innovation.

§ 3. Provisions Limiting Expenditures. Illustrative of the constitutional provisions guarding against unwarranted and injudicious expenditures are those which prohibit states from lending their credit to private enterprises or to local units; those which prohibit the state from authorizing its local governments to lend their credit to private enterprises; those which impose ceilings on local government debt; those which prohibit the state and its local government units from paying extra compensation to public officers or employees, increasing public officer compensation during term of office, or paying compensation to public contractors above the contract price; and those which prohibit the payment of unauthorized or illegal claims.

Would these strictures impede the following plan? The state legislature has voted to authorize the city of Allgood (1) to purchase the land and construct the domed stadium; (2) to pay a generous bonus to the general contractor and subcontractors if the stadium is built on time; (3) to borrow the necessary funds through a bond issue; (4) to enter into an agreement with the nationally known firm Pro Sports, Inc., whereby the latter will lease the stadium from the city for a number of years, operate it for profit, and pay rental to the city; (5) to use the rental payments to retire the bonds which are to be limited to the rental revenues.

§ 4. Provisions Insuring Local Accountability. Provisions which are intended to insure that certain functions retain local political accountability include: those prohibiting the state legislature from imposing taxes for local units' corporate purposes, and from delegating to special commissions the power to perform, supervise or interfere with municipal or corporate functions; and those requiring local selection of local officers, and local approval of changes in county seats, county consolidations, street railway franchises, and a host of particular subjects.

It is important to note that the general protection is given to corporate or municipal affairs and purposes, i.e., those benefit-promoting services and functions which serve the exclusive interests of the citizen-members of the corporation, and which may have constituted one of the primary motivations for organizing the local unit. Those clauses which refer to or are construed as limited to such local matters do not bar state activity in connection with the local unit's governmental activities, i.e., the core functions of government in general, basic powers therefore of the state, and responsibilities locally implemented in an "agency" capacity. It has previously been indicated that there are substantial numbers of local activities whose placement in one category or the other is highly debatable. For example, should a municipal water and sewage system be "governmental" or "corporate?"

§ 5. Provisions Protecting Local Autonomy.
Two kinds of constitutional provisions serve to
protect local autonomy: those which seek to ban
"local," "one-city" legislation, and those which
delegate or authorize delegation of home rule.

a.   Prohibitions of "local," "one-city" legislation take many forms. They may require state
legislative enactments to be general and of uniform applicability. They may prohibit the passage of local or special laws. They may require
that no special law be enacted in any case where
a general act can be made applicable. They may
in summary or particular detail enumerate the
subject matters upon which no special laws may
be enacted. Neither the scope of subject matter
nor the pattern are uniform among the states and
combinations of the above may be found. While
their purpose may be to protect municipalities or
particular local matters in a municipality from
"selected target" attack by the state legislature,
this may not always be the practical result. Indeed, it would be misleading to convey a picture
of the city fighting to prevent state intrusion.
Frequently, the "target city" is seeking to obtain
the very authorization from the state legislature.

(i) Absent any other constitutional impediment,
the state legislature may, of course, enact legislation of general applicability to which the "target
city" and others may be required to conform. In
addition, unless classification itself is constitu-
[*30*]

tionally prohibited or limited, the state may enact laws which are of general and uniform applicability to a particular class of local units. Such units are frequently classified by population, but may be grouped according to geographic considerations, the presence of facilities (colleges, hospitals, e.g.), financial resources, or the like. Courts often defer to legislative classification but may occasionally disapprove a "grouping" which merely masks a special law. There is no rule of thumb which divides a law of "general" and "uniform" applicability within a class from its converse, the special law. A classification which contains but one municipality and which appears closed to a projected future membership increase is obviously suspect, but in an appropriate case (the only seaport, e.g.) it may withstand challenge.

(ii) The provisions which require general laws where practicable afford the additional difficulty of identifying the ultimate arbiter of practicability. In some jurisdictions, the legislature's determination is final. In others, the legislative determination may only be set aside if it is arbitrary, unreasonable, or a clear abuse of discretion. In yet others, the decision is purely for the courts.

(iii) Our illustration city has sought from the state legislature authority to own and operate the desired airport. The city of Allgood hopes for authorization from its state legislature to build the

domed stadium. In the present legislative sessions, the state legislatures respectively enact
and the governors sign the following:

"All cities with populations greater than
500,000 . . . in which annual commercial
gross revenues from intrastate and interstate
commerce exceed $100 million . . . are au-
thorized to construct, own and operate municipal
general business aviation airports. . . ."

"Whereas the city of Allgood is the capital of
this state and is the only city whose population
exceeds 1,000,000 persons, and is the center of
the only major metropolitan area in the state, the
city of Allgood may take all steps necessary to
construct and operate a domed stadium.
. . . . "

Would either of the above withstand challenge
based upon state constitutional provisions prohibiting special laws relating to local government
units and requiring that laws be of general and
uniform applicability? Would your answer be
different if the provision in Allgood's state allowed a special law where a general one would be
impracticable? Would your answer differ if the
airport city were the only one in its state now
meeting or in the foreseeable future likely to
meet the statutory criteria?

b. To the extent that home rule creates local
autonomy, it serves as a significant limitation up-

on the power of state legislatures. We have seen that home-rule status may devolve upon particular local units directly from constitutional clauses or may be accorded by state legislation constitutionally authorized. We have seen that charters will be drafted, and amended by the local electorate. The significance of home rule to local units is not without its detractors and is difficult to measure. It clearly has been a sizeable source of local governing power, though whether the same power would not have been granted by the legislature in non-home-rule contexts is open to some question.

(i) Implementation of the home-rule concept involves several problems, none of which has thus far been satisfactorily resolved. The constitutional delegations are generic, summary and subject to substantial judicial interpretation. The delegations include such terminology as:

". . . may make and enforce all laws and regulations in respect to municipal affairs . . . ;"

". . . to exercise all powers of local self-government and to adopt and enforce within their limits such police, sanitary and other similar regulations, as are not in conflict with general law;"

"The legislative assembly shall provide by law for the establishment of home rule in the cities and villages. It may authorize such cities and villages to exercise all or a portion of any power or function which the legislative assembly has power to devolve upon a nonhome rule city or village, not denied to such city or village by its own home rule charter and which is not denied to all home rule cities and villages by statute." (Note that some constitutional authorizations for legislative home-rule grants speak in mandatory terms. The practical effect of this is still unclear.)

Statutory delegations enumerate in much more specific terms but conclude with similar catch-all phrases. As a result, there is no clear indication of what powers are within local autonomy. On the other hand, the inflexibility of specific indication may argue in favor of lack of specificity.

What local units should have home rule? Should they be allowed to opt for it (some states)? Should it be limited to major governmental units? The home-rule jurisdictions are not consistent in their answers and there is some suspicion that there has been insufficient coordination of the powers provided and the capacities of the units granted the powers.

In part to react to the intensified stratification of local home rule in areas of wide ranging regional problems, several states have authorized home rule for counties. While several urbanized counties have availed themselves of home rule, it cannot yet be said that county responses have been uniformly participatory.

[*34*]

As we indicated previously, a major area of dispute surrounds the classification of governmental functions as "municipal" or "local" and the identification of the functions within the class. Many argue that governmental functions cannot be thus compartmentalized. The complexity of the problems facing government today lends credence to this. More and more courts are sensitive to the external implications of so-called local action. For example, consider the effect on other local units of an exclusionary zoning ordinance.

We mentioned earlier the failure of courage at city hall. There is some reason to believe that the "municipal affairs" or "local self-government" limitations upon local autonomy serve to dampen municipal enthusiasm for venturing into uncharted waters. City hall must consider not only the disruption of eventual disapproval of its venture, and attendant political consequences, but also the costs of aborted implementation and protracted litigation.

(ii) Given the broad areas for judicial resolution, it is no wonder that commentators have differed in their assessment of judicial receptivity to home-rule power exercise. In judging the competence of municipal legislation courts, after all, can reject a municipal exercise as not involving a local matter and not otherwise authorized, occasionally because there is no precedent for local government action of this type, or because the court deems the action one beyond the bounds of appropriate governance. For example, our illustration city's attempted public disclosure law may have no precursors in other similar localities or may be too intrusive upon privacy rights when balanced against the importance of many of the pertinent local offices.

The courts may decide that the locally initiated action involves not only the trappings of a local affair but also external consequences which are of such magnitude as to make it more appropriate for governmental purview at a higher level. Our airport and stadium could present such difficulties.

The courts may find that other provisions of the state constitution seem to confer authority over a matter (such as income taxes) upon the state legislature. They will read even the constitutional home-rule delegation in conjunction with the other provisions and reject the local power exercise.

Finally, the courts may strike down the local ordinance because, in resolving a conflict of legislation, state legislative patterns have indicated preemption of the field or because the court concludes that the ordinance and state statutes are in direct conflict. The decision will more than likely involve a combination of the above, of course.

[*36*]

Conversely, if a conflicting state law is deemed to cover a local matter in jurisdictions granted local autonomy, the state enactment may be deemed preempted by the local enactment. And results in cases involving internal local matters such as civil service, police-power matters such as land use, and local acquisition of goods and services demonstrate that local exercise in the absense of state competition may be deemed appropriate.

(iii) The inevitable uncertainty attending the local-statewide dichotomy has taxed the ingenuity of courts attempting to resolve conflicts between inconsistent legislation of the state and its home-rule city. For example, one court has attempted to restrict municipal dominance to the structure and procedures of local agencies and uphold state dominance in substantive social, economic or regulatory objectives unless the law is shown to be irreconcilable with the locality's freedom to choose its own political form. This restrictive attempt to clarify, imposed in what had been a liberal home-rule jurisdiction, has been couched with so many qualifications that it may simply have substituted one set of uncertainties for another. Also illustrative of attempts to resolve the difficulty of defining the area of local autonomy are the suggested (with few adoptions to date) constitutional clauses reposing full governmental authority upon local governments and leaving to the

[*37*]

local citizenry (in the charters) and the state legislatures (by general law) the task of limitation. Such proposed authority conferrals would exclude the power to create civil relationships, although they might include authority allowing a traffic ordinance to be deemed the negligence standard of care, and would further exclude the power to specify felonies. The exclusions conform to established consensus concerning outer limits of local power. Do the suggestions seem to assume that all levels of government possess full competence to govern? Is their premise that it will be easier to prevent the enactment of state limitations than to obtain state power authorizations a valid one?

D. RESOLUTION OF COMPETING POWER CONSIDERATIONS

§ 1. **Two Views of Predominance.** Earlier in the text we discussed appropriateness as a consideration in governmental activity and in the level of government which engaged in that activity. Our discussion of home rule also indicated that various interests would be balanced in resolving the validity of local power exercise. Since government exercise is the exercise of power, one can view the matter from a perspective of predominance, not only as a method of resolving competing and inconsistent power exercises but also as a question of the perception of power.

[*38*]

Many allocations of power are accomplished by
state and federal constitutions; much, however,
is left to the courts. Whether the government in
question be federal, state or local, with respect to
a particular subject matter, one can ask whether
it can act at all. Is it acting within the sphere of
its own constitutional or judicially determined
competence? If it is, can another level of government also act on the same subject matter? If
both act, when do both actions stand? If the actions are inconsistent, the allocation of power and
the balancing of interests will lead to the predominance of one. Even if the actions are not inconsistent, the allocation of power and the balancing
of interests may so weigh in favor of one level of
government that it is permitted to preempt action
by any other level.

Here we are concerned about local power and
the local government's sphere of competent activity, especially in light of state and federal competence and predominance. Of course, in addition
to the local matters which the federal (liquor,
twenty-first amendment to the U.S. Constitution,
e.g.) and state (local officers, e.g.) governments
may be constitutionally required to avoid, there
are numerous situations in which there is deference to local governing even though the matters
are fully capable of general power exercise.
Nevertheless, courts are repeatedly called upon
to reconcile competing claims of predominance.

[*39*]

Illustratively, the airport, public-disclosure and domed-stadium ordinances of our cities not only have to be competent actions of those cities standing alone, but also may face, respectively, federal air-traffic noise controls less stringent than those desired by the city, a state public-disclosure statute, and zoning and traffic regulations of the surrounding county inimical to extraterritorial location and operation of the stadium.

§ 2. **Competing Federal Power Considerations.** a. Consider the federal role from both the perceptional and the allocation-of-power perspectives. Clearly federal law can predominate but not because the federal government is "higher" in any hierarchical sense of federal-state-local government. Both the federal and local governments are entities of delegated authority, possessing those powers ceded or delegated by the states. So, while a state may, in the exercise of eminent domain power, condemn a locality's governmental land for a public purpose without required compensation to the local government, a similar federal condemnation would require compensation.

b. In an allocational sense, the federal government cannot act competently to exercise powers not ceded by or, as in the twenty-first, eleventh and tenth amendment contexts, reserved to the states. Even in the federal exercise of such ceded authority as the commerce, tax and spending powers, a balancing of important interests may lead to a competency question. While the federal Congress may have an affirmative grant of legislative authority, there are limits upon the power of Congress to override state sovereignty. It may not exercise federal power in such a way as to impair the states' integrity or their ability to function effectively in a federal system through regulation of the states as states by directly displacing or impairing, in non-emergency contexts, essential state policies concerning the conduct of matters unquestionably the attributes of state sovereignty, integral governmental functions or the ability to deliver traditional, citizen-required, governmental services.

The outcome of the balancing of these federal systemic interests and the scope of the limitation are by no means clear in this continually evolving area. Thus, for example, the federally required minimum wage and maximum work-hour provisions may not be applied directly to public employees of the states and their political subdivisions performing integral functions (but such may not include mass transit workers). But federal age discrimination, equal-pay and Title VII-reporting requirements may be so applied because the activities sought to be remedied are not attributes of state sovereignty, because valid state objectives may be achieved in other ways, and perhaps because the remedies are authorized

[*41*]

to implement the U.S. Constitution's fourteenth amendment, an amendment directly addressed to the balancing of state and national power in the federal system.

Similarly, Congress' establishment of a regime of competition as the fundamental principle governing commerce in the nation must not prohibit the sovereign from imposing as an act of government certain anticompetitive restraints. But where local governments are alleged to have exercised their powers to achieve anticompetitive objectives violative of the national policy, there must be a clearer indication of state policy and authorization than either the customary generic local power authorization or the allocation of home rule. In the absence of specifically express or inferable state authorization, supervision (where private parties are involved) and policy, the local power exercises will not be deemed exempt from federal antitrust laws. It is unclear, however, whether in all instances the remedies available against the participating private violators will be appropriate to the non-exempt municipal actions if they are proved to be violations.

Again, judicially implied, state immunity from direct federal taxation exists and may play a role in federal reluctance to tax the interest on municipal bonds. It does not extend, inter alia, to an annual registration tax on all civil aircraft, including state owned aircraft used exclusively for po-

[42]

lice functions, a non-discriminatory, user-fee, revenue measure ensuring that each member of a special benefited class pays a reasonable approximation of its fair share of the cost of a national program to the federal government. Note that while the state's interest is a governmental function, also at issue is the cost of a federal program which the state is using to perform the function.

Finally, while the federal government may, in the balancing of interests, be able to set regulatory standards which local governments, like private citizens, must observe, and while federal involvement in, and inducement of, a host of local endeavors, even accompanied by the carrot and stick of federal funds gained or lost, may constitute a weighty, indeed a distorting presence, it may not be able to mandate the exercise of state or local regulatory powers to achieve the federal objective.

c.   Whether the foregoing be perceived as a question of federal competency, or the resolution of power conflict, predominance depends upon the balancing of federal power and state sovereignty in the federal system. Where that issue is not involved, it is possible that federal and state or local actions can coexist because such complementary actions are contemplated by the respective levels of government. Thus, Congress' nuclear-power role has been held to have left sufficient authority in states to determine on eco-

nomic grounds that there may be a slowing of or
a moratorium on reactor construction because a
lack of adequate interim storage capacity for
spent fuel and national policy for permanent storage will make such reactor an uneconomic operation.   Similarly, locally imposed emplaning
charges of up to one dollar per commercial airline
passenger to defray the costs of airport construction are not taxation in violation of the federal
Commerce-Clause prerogatives, not a burden on
or discrimination against interstate commerce,
and do not conflict with federal policies further-
ing uniform, national air-transportation regulation. (Nor do they impinge upon the passengers'
constitutionally protected right to travel.)

Where there is a conflict between the respective exercises of power, predominance has to be
determined and, as we have seen, will not necessarily favor the federal interest.   Absent the
state-sovereignty issue, federal exercise of a ceded power will be supreme. Perhaps the most
graphic example is that of a city exercising what
amounts to federally licensed power predominat-
ing over its state under the federal constitution's
Supremacy Clause. The city, federally licensed
to build a dam on "navigable waters," could and
did withstand contrary direction imposed by the
state legislature and by state citizen initiative.

d. As our earlier analysis indicated, in addition to competency, complementary assertions

[44]

and conflict resolution, there remains the possibility that the federal government, competent and not prohibited to act, might so act as to occupy the field and preempt state or local action on that subject matter. In such circumstances, federal law in a matter within federal competence will supercede even the historic state-source local police power if such predominance was the "clear and manifest purpose of Congress." The courts will reach this conclusion if the scheme of federal regulation is so pervasive as to imply that Congress left no room for state supplementation, if the field in question is one in which the federal interest is so dominant that preclusion of state laws may be assumed, if the object sought by the federal law and the character of the obligations imposed by it reveal the pervasive or dominant purpose, or if the state-local enactment's policy would produce a result inconsistent with the federal statute's objective. Our illustration city's attempt to impose severe air traffic noise restrictions would fail this test.

§ 3. Competing State Power Considerations.

a. Similarly imprecise standards govern determination of state-local dominance. Ordinances enacted by a municipality in the exercise of power conferred upon it either expressly or by implication will generally be upheld if they are not inconsistent with state law. But ordinances which conflict with statutes enacted within the competence of the state legislature will thereby be rendered invalid. Such a conflict exists when both the ordinance and the statute contain express or implied terms which are irreconcilable.

This conclusion is sometimes expressed by stating that the ordinance permits (forbids) what the statute forbids (permits). When a contrary conclusion is reached, it is said that the ordinance is merely additional and complementary to or in aid and furtherance of the statute. For example, the local public disclosure ordinance, more stringent than that of the state, could be deemed to conflict, or could be said to be in furtherance of state law because the city could well have determined that greater information was necessary in elections where the candidates might be less well known and in a structure where officials might function less in the public spotlight. Could a person have observed the requirement of both laws?

b.   While the local ordinance may not conflict, it may nonetheless be preempted because the state has "occupied the field." The subject matter may have been so completely covered by general law as to indicate that it has become exclusively a matter of state concern. Or the subject matter may have been partially covered by general law couched in terms indicating that a "paramount state concern will not tolerate further or additional local action." Again, the subject matter may have been partially covered by state law

[*46*]

and the subject is of such a nature that "the adverse effect of a local ordinance on the transient citizens of the state outweighs the possible benefit to the municipality." Compare the state's occupation of the field of licensing drivers with motor vehicle registration where in some states additional local vehicle registration may be required.

c. It must be emphasized that, like the federal government, the state must be acting in an area within its competence. If the subject matter is committed by law to local autonomy (a local matter), it is the state action which will be rendered inoperative in the particular locality. Not only is there much dispute concerning conflict and occupation of the field, there are also questions whether an ordinance which merely duplicates the state law may stand, whether an ordinance may stand until a state statute is enacted on a matter not deemed local or municipal, and whether in the converse situation the state law is operative until a local law is enacted. The jurisdictions answer these questions inconsistently.

§ 4. **Competing Local Power Considerations.**
Conflicting power exercises among political subdivisions within a state produce judicial resolutions which have been markedly inconsistent. The conflict in question may be resolvable through state statutory formulae or by intergovernmental-agreement mechanisms. The courts

may be able to interpret the respective actions and ordinances in such a way as to "harmonize" them. Traditional deferral of the later action to the earlier may be invoked (annexations, e.g.). The courts may choose the entity having the more favored status (home-rule city vs. non-home-rule county, e.g.), or the "higher function," (governmental over proprietary, e.g.). The state authorization of action by one may be interpreted to intend preclusion of reaction or resistance by the other. Thus, the conflict between Allgood's stadium and the neighboring county's zoning can be resolved in Allgood's favor (home-rule city or state authorized preclusion) or in favor of the county (zoning-governmental over stadium-proprietary).

§ 5.   Federal and State Constitutional Predominance.

a. Consider predominance from another perspective. We have examined competing exercises of power among various levels of government. When authority, conflict and preemption issues have been resolved, however, there remains the dominant position given to constitutionally protected rights of persons—aliens, citizens, taxpayers—who may feel the impact, or be the subject of the intended impact of the exercise of traditional government powers.

Federal and state constitutional protections against unwarranted, uncontrolled or improper imposition of local governing power over the rights of citizens will, of course, predominate over authorized local power exercises which violate them. Such provisions include the federal Contracts Clause, the Federal Bill of Rights, the fourteenth and fifteenth amendments to the Federal Constitution, and the state constitutional provisions banning lending of credit, insisting upon a public purpose, prohibiting municipal indebtedness above specified limits, requiring a thorough and efficient public education, and setting forth state bills of rights.

For example, where the state exercised its "plenary power" to dissolve an existing city and to create another municipal corporation composed of substantially the same community, bondholder-creditors' constitutional rights to contract adherence unimpaired by this action required that the new corporation, capable of doing so, be responsible for full performance.

Otherwise unquestionable state discretion to allow its localities to choose whether particular state laws shall apply could not insulate from individuals' successful equal-protection challenge a county choice to close its public schools in the face of judicial desegregation orders.

b. We have alluded to the presence of equal-protection and right-to-travel issues in earlier examples. Consideration of constitutionally protected alien, citizen and taxpayer rights, naturally, accompanies the state's or local government's exercise of powers to determine form, structure and personnel policies, and of the police, land use, acquisition, expenditure and revenue powers. There has been an exponential increase in the number of cases inviting judicial protection of civil rights under fourteenth-amendment jurisprudence in boundary decisions, personnel requirements, elections and referenda, land-use regulation, uses of municipal property, provision of municipal services, taxation, and fiscal support for such local services as education. Although its earlier cases were not as clear, and other courts differed, the U.S. Supreme Court has insisted upon proof of racially discriminatory intent or purpose in order to show a violation of the equal protection clause and to trigger strict scrutiny. Disproportionate impact, while not irrelevant, is not the "sole touchstone" of invidious racial discrimination.

c.   It should be noted that the predominance of individual rights often results from statutory implementation of constitutionally protected status in such areas as civil rights and voting rights. The number of challenges to local government power exercises is substantial and the burden on the challenger is not as strict as in fourteenth-amendment cases.

CHAPTER II

FORMATION OF THE LOCAL GOVERNMENT, ALTERATION, BOUNDARY CHANGES; SOME PROBLEMS OF ORGANIZATION AND OPERATION: OFFICERS, EMPLOYEES, ALLOCATION AND DELEGATION OF FUNCTIONS, ELECTIONS

A. SOME ASPECTS OF ORGANIZATION AND ALTERATION CHOICES

§ 1. Introduction: Choices for Unincorporated Areas. a. The objectives which motivate choices concerning municipal organization and alteration run the gamut from aggressive and defensive political considerations to the economics of efficient service management and distribution. For example, the residents of an unincorporated area may choose to remain unincorporated to avoid the tax supported costs of an additional level of government. (The term "choose" is used to denote a selection despite the fact that the area meets the criteria for incorporation in that state.) The choice of status quo would probably mean that service needs are few or are met sufficiently by the county and that there is no likelihood or fear of annexation by existing municipalities.

[*51*]

The choice to remain unincorporated where incorporation is possible also may denote a strong county, weak existing cities structure, or may indicate a judgment that unmet service needs and risk of annexation are offset by unwillingness to underwrite the costs of local government status.

b.   If service needs are paramount, the people in the area may choose to avail themselves of the state's procedures for creating a special district. As we noted in Chapter I, this entity may be sufficiently powerful to impose and collect ad valorem taxes, and superintend multiple functions, and may often be governed by elected officials.   Such an entity would nonetheless differ from an incorporated city because, in the case of a special district, the priority of needs to be served was chosen in its creation.   Therefore, it would not possess the city's flexibility to promote the public good or regulate in areas additional to its original purposes.   While this governmental form can provide identifiable, needed services with the least complex governmental structure, thus allowing our hypothetical unincorporated area to remain close to its original status, it will not likely serve to protect against the possibility of annexation.

c.   If the motives for change include a desire to allow the political process to determine service priorities or to avoid adverse economic, social or political consequences of annexation by existing cities, the choice will be incorporation as the broad based, politically accountable governing unit, to the extent existing state classification and related powers legislation allow. "Defensive incorporation" offers the opportunity to withstand expansion by other cities if begun first, and if the newly acquired corporate status is by law shielded from incursion. One drawback of such a protective device is that it may serve to thwart growth as a desirable urban-problem-solving tool of the other cities. Such "defense" might be unnecessary if the state's law posited the affirmative vote of those to be annexed as prerequisite to successful annexation.

§ 2. Introduction: Choices for Incorporated Areas. a. Let us assume that our hypothetical area is an incorporated "city." Its government and citizens may desire to maximize economies of scale in providing services, or may seek to enlarge its tax base (although it will customarily need more than this as justification). It may seek to avail itself of extraterritorial facilities or geographic advantages, or may wish to solve on a broader base a multiplicity of urban problems. A number of choices are available. The city may use existing, or seek state legislative authorization of, extraterritorial powers in its planning, regulatory or utility functions. It may enter into an area-wide council of governments whereby its goals may be reached through mutual planning

[*53*]

and discussion and concomitant governmental actions by the allied independent localities. It may, if authorized, enter into contractual agreements with other municipal entities for provision of services. It may join in the formation of a metropolitan district, a special district extending across municipal boundaries empowered to perform one or more desired functions (water and sewage removal, e.g.). It may invoke the procedures necessary to annex the adjoining areas. It may enter into one of a variety of governmental "mergers," city-county, federation, or city-city consolidation, to accomplish its goals. All of these choices present in varying degrees the problem of state authorization and the obstacles of geopolitical reality and citizen resistance which may make them difficult or impossible to accomplish.

b. Citizens of an area within an incorporated city may seek to gain a greater voice in municipal affairs or may desire to "secede" from the city. In the former situation, the city may respond by forms of decentralization ranging from local advisory boards to partial functional control within an area by the residents of that area. The "secession" objective, an extremely difficult one, may result in return to unincorporated status or disconnection with city A in order to be annexed to city B.

c. It should be recalled that the state itself may accomplish any of the above status alterations by legislative direction if not prohibited from doing so by home rule, prohibition of special legislation, or other constitutional limitations.

B. CONSIDERATIONS COMMON TO STATUTORY INCORPORATION OR ALTERATION PROCEDURES

The political realities of the choices introduced above are self-evident. All aspects of "structure" deal with schools, services, regulation, taxes, entrenched pre-existing governmental structures and officeholders, and social relations— each politically volatile. During the course of our more specific ensuing discussion, the reader may wish to evaluate the legislatively or judicially required procedures of organization or alteration in terms of their effectiveness in accommodating political realities and in defusing or channeling the virtually inevitable explosion of opposition.

§ 1. **Specific Provisions.** a. There are several aspects common to almost all statutory schemes authorizing organization or alteration with attendant issues requiring the attention of proponents and providing grist for opponents. For our purposes, it suffices to indicate the patterns and the issues for which local law provides the answers.

Many processes begin with petitions. Must the process begin by petition or is legislative action by the sponsoring local government sufficient? If petitions are necessary, or are at least permitted, how many signatures are required? Who may sign, all residents of the area in question or only those owning property? Must the petition not only contain the signatures of a specified percentage of the population but also reflect a specified percentage of real property ownership? When must the petition be filed? How long before the result sought must it be filed? Is there a time period within which signatures can be withdrawn? If the petition fails, when may another attempt be made?

b.   The petitions and the government's initiating or responsive resolutions will customarily be accompanied by required descriptions of boundaries, maps, demographic data and the like. The requirements may insist upon accurate specificity and may even in some jurisdictions call for annexation "environmental impact statements."

c.   At several points during the process, it will be necessary to give notice to affected persons of the proposed action. What must the notice contain? What degree of specificity and completeness is required? How is the notice to be conveyed to the affected persons? Dissemination of the notice will customarily involve publication in a newspaper of general circulation at specified intervals. Sometimes, dissemination may be accomplished by mail or by posting signs near the

[*56*]

affected area. Do not be misled by the requirement that notice of the pending action be dissemi-
nated. *Effective* notification will almost uniformly require vigilance on the part of the affected
persons. They will be deemed to have "seen"
signs or "read" the public notices in the general-
circulation newspaper which successfully bids for
the contract to publish column upon column of
such notices. This constructive notice will be effective so long as the method of notification com-
plies with the jurisdiction's requirements.

d. The proposed action may have to be approved by a county or state board or commission
whether or not it is eventually to be submitted to
the electorate. The approving entity may be a
legislative or administrative body. Some processes may instead require judicial imprimatur. The
intervention of these governmental organs may
only be necessary in response to a specified number of remonstrances, i.e., protest provisions
which may raise the questions alluded to in the
above discussion of petitions.

e. The final result or the matter to be submitted to the electorate will entail the drafting of a
document (charter, e.g.) and the framing of the
question to be voted upon. Either or both may
be set forth in the statutes, and must then conform to the required formulations.

f. The customary referendum presents numerous questions concerning the jurisdictions

whose electorates must be allowed to participate, the limitations if any (caveat constitutional implications) upon who may vote, the manner of determining whether the question has been approved or disapproved, and sometimes such specifics as the location of polling places.

g.   A host of practical intergovernmental regulatory and economic consequences are reflected in many of the statutory patterns. Where they are not, difficult problems arise. For example, who is to bear the costs of the process? Who retains or obtains title to preexisting government property? How are assets and liabilities to be transferred or shared? What is the tenure of officeholders and employees of preexisting governments? What are the powers of the new entity? What laws govern the new entity? Are power exercises of preexisting government units of continuing validity and applicability? Formulae may be included for necessary intergovernmental agreements.

h.   The state legislation will contain provisions for publication of the results of the process which may frequently envision certification by governmental officials such as the county board or the secretary of state.

§ 2. **Mandatory and Directory.** a. Of overriding concern, as with all state legislative direction, is the intent of the state legislature, as construed by the courts, to require compliance with the letter of some or all of the statutory procedures. Where such intent is found, or judicially declared, failure to comply literally with the statutory steps, thus deemed "mandatory," is fatal to the process. Substantial compliance with other statutory steps, deemed "directory," will be satisfactory.

C. FORMATION OF THE LOCAL GOVERNING UNIT

§ 1. **Incorporation of the Local General Government.** We have seen the sources of municipal power and the methods of municipal organization. Statutory patterns such as those outlined above, involving petition, notice, drafting, election and certification procedures, will be followed by citizens seeking to incorporate under constitutional or legislative home-rule power grants or general state legislative authorizations with local unit classifications. Once again, grant of a charter by special act of the legislature is a rarely permitted occurrence.

a. In addition to strict or substantial compliance with statutory incorporation procedures, certain prerequisites must be met. Constitutional or statutory terms such as "city," "community" or "village," even in those jurisdictions where specific minimum requirements are not set forth in the statutes, have been given meaning by the courts so that everywhere, the area to be incorporated must contain a minimum population and density (often expressed per acre). The territory must be contiguous, must have definitely ascertainable boundaries, must constitute a community (a concept at once geographic, sociological, economic and political), and must contain only property which is adaptable for municipal uses and which will, at least in the foreseeable future, benefit from existence within the municipality. These prerequisites are not as strictly applied as to require an identifiable "downtown," although some mutual-benefit attraction must be present. They are not limited to land already platted but some future benefit other than tax revenues to the city must be predictable. In short, while the state legislature may delegate some legislative authority to the politically accountable, multi-powered local unit, the courts will find the state's power to create such local delegate limited to potentially benefited, preexisting communities.

b. Challenges may be raised to a local unit's legitimate existence, either by the state in the customary quo warranto proceeding, or by persons who hope to avoid a particular power exercise. Where incorporation proceedings were fatally defective and void, such collateral attack by individuals is permitted. But for reasons of stability of the social order, courts do not welcome collateral attacks on the local unit's validity. Frequently, the outcome will be a declaration of

[*60*]

the unit's existence as a "de facto municipal corporation." Such status obtains where there is legislative authority for the chosen form of municipal corporation, and where there has been not only a good faith undertaking to organize thereunder, resulting in apparent compliance with the legislation but also subsequent exercise of corporate powers. Concern for the stability of the social order and practical realities have also motivated frequent curative state legislation validating prior faulty municipal incorporations. Such enactments are uniformly upheld. It should be noted that direct and collateral attacks upon annexations, may be more liberally viewed than those upon incorporation.

c. Charter amendment and revision may be accomplished by constitutional amendment. It may also be done by state general legislation, state special acts or action by the local citizens depending upon the original source of the municipality's power.

d. The form of the incorporated unit, like the decision to incorporate, will be chosen to accomplish objectives such as political responsiveness and accountability (e.g., large city council with small constituencies); administrative competence and an appropriate independence from political pressures (e.g., weak executive, appointed manager, and council with "non-partisan" election); check-and-balance distribution of executive and

[*61*]

legislative power or desirability of charismatic leadership (e.g., strong executive and council); or simplicity of governmental operations (e.g., commissioners board, often misleadingly labelled "court," with an appointed administrator or the mixture of legislative and executive functions). Experience indicates that many local units have selected forms which are not now fully responsive to their size, complexity or sociological composition.

§ 2. Formation of Special Districts. The formation of special authorities and districts is everywhere governed by statutes which may permit creation by the local electorate or by one or more existing local governments. Many are of course directly created by state statutes. Boundary ascertainment and referenda may be required in a manner similar to our above legislative patterns.

a. As we have seen, such entities may be remote from political control or may themselves be subject to the electorate. Divorce from political control is, however, never complete because the district's governors may be appointed by elected governments, local or state. And many structures allow for "interlocking" governance whereby locally elected officials serve on the district's board or commission.

b. We shall see in our subsequent discussion of finances that such a special district differs from a municipal administrative department in that it may permit the incurring of debt not aggregated with that of the "sponsoring" city for the purpose of determining the city's position vis-a-vis the constitutional debt limitations.

§ 3.   Comment on the Special District and Other Forms of Decentralization.   a.   The availability to existing municipalities of special-district forms for accomplishing municipal objectives has been suggested as one method of decentralizing local government.   Other proposals range from those which accord substantial governance authority to small geopolitical areas within the city to those which contemplate the location of "branch city halls" throughout the community. The drive for decentralization has been spawned by the felt needs to revitalize waning citizen involvement and to provide better or more appropriate services to areas of the city previously underserved for economic or social reasons.

b.   While the objectives have much merit and the felt needs are real, and while the simpler proposals (mini-city-halls; advisory neighborhood councils, e.g.) have beneficial impact on citizen morale and improvement of services, the decentralized-control-with-power programs, whether under federal community action program requirements or state or local arrangements such as those dealing with schools, have not been notable for their success.   There may, of course, be exceptions.   If there were nonpolitical or nonvolatile matters which could be within decentralized partial control, the concept of decentralization could well be a fruitful one. In reality, however, the matters over which decentralized control is sought are emotionally provocative and have a high political profile, because they are matters as to which the geopolitical areas within the city feel growing political impotence. For this reason, the structures of power-decentralization predictably succumb to the crippling chaos and political crossfire which critically undermine their effectiveness. Moreover, the careful mixture of sub-local control and traditional city power necessary to avoid challenge as an improper delegation of authority to private citizens feeds suspicion that only cosmetic change has been applied to political impotence.

c. Finally, since a primary objective is to provide an antidote to the frustration of apparent political powerlessness, the politically sterile, indirectly accountable, special-district or authority form is manifestly unsuited to its solution.

D.   ALTERATION, BOUNDARY CHANGES

§ 1.   **Extraterritorial Exercise of Power.** a. Our Chapter I illustrations concerning the domed stadium and the airport alluded to the possible ability of a city to exercise extraterritorial power without expanding its boundaries. Such a possibility raises the question whether such extraterritorial power must be express or can be implied. The answer will differ, depending upon the power in question and upon whether the express power giving rise to the inference of implied power is itself extraterritorial in application. If the power under scrutiny is "proprietary," extraterritoriality may be less difficult an implication. For example, city utility storage and sources and the provision of utility services by cities with a surplus to fringe users outside city boundaries have been upheld.

b.   Much more commonly, however, state statutes authorize the exercise of municipal powers, including parks and recreation, airports, utilities, roads, planning, eminent domain and subdivision control and other police powers, in limited areas immediately outside city lines. When an extraterritorial power is thus authorized, powers necessary to its fulfillment will sometimes be deemed included. Were our illustration city statutorily empowered to construct its airport outside its boundaries, would use of the power of eminent domain to obtain the necessary land be upheld?

c.   Courts most rigorously scrutinize attempted extraterritorial exercise of "coercive" powers to protect health, safety, morality and the general welfare, looking for express authorization. Where authority to exercise extraterritorial

power is not found, the exercise will be ultra
vires and reliance upon it by those outside the
city will be unavailing. Where authority is
found—and it is found in some form in at least
two thirds of the states—the legislative motivation may be the probability of eventual annexation, the control of matters which may be
indirectly detrimental to governmental responsibilities within the city, recognition of the
embryonic "metropolitanism," or provision of services to unincorporated areas. The frequent
challenge to "governing without the consent or
votes of the governed" has rare success in the
face of state authorization, although a different
result might be reached where a city has so extended the full panoply of its powers as to have
"annexed" the area outside its borders in all but
name.

§ 2. **Annexation.** The statutory methods permitting expansion of municipal boundaries reflect
no consistent pattern throughout the United
States. The several methods may at one time
have been responsive to the demographic facts of
life in the particular states. The segmented incorporation patterns of the country's metropolitan areas, most graphic in the megalopolis along
the northeast Atlantic seaboard, and the jurisdictions' acceptance with some judicial support of
the relative inviolability of local government
boundaries have resulted in the dilution of annex-

ation as a tool for urban-problem solutions. The methods which may have originally been responsive now offer frequently archaic procedures which serve to compound the inflexibilities of annexation. Hence there is impetus for the exploration of federation and other forms of metropolitanism. Nevertheless, annexation remains for many areas a mechanism to satisfy growth needs or to fulfill expansionist tendencies.

Annexation may be accomplished by special act of the state legislature in the few jurisdictions allowing it. Absent permitted special legislation, the procedures of annexation, governed by statute everywhere, may at the risk of oversimplification be classified as (a) those which are within the home rule power of the annexing city; (b) those which are initiated by or require the consent of the territory to be annexed; (c) those which require the approval of governmental legislative or administrative boards; (d) those which require substantive approval of the courts; and (e) those which are submitted to arbitration. It should be noted that some classes of cities within a particular state may be authorized to annex in one manner, while other classes may be permitted to do so by another method. Additionally, the annexation methods in several states may combine elements from the above groupings.

a.   A few cities have been deemed to possess unilateral power to annex as an attribute of home rule sovereignty. In the past, the inevitable expanionist tendencies were not troublesome in less dense demographic circumstances. However, Texas, the notable example of annexation by city resolution, found it necessary to circumscribe this unilateral power by statutes authorizing extraterritorial jurisdiction over a limited unincorporated area, restricting annexations generally to land within this extraterritorial jurisdiction, limiting area of annexation in any one calendar year, requiring pre-annexation hearings open to all interested persons, and providing rather liberal judicial disannexation standards for areas not appropriately benefited by the annexation. Nevertheless, problems in one Texas city, including degenerating services and federal Voting-Rights-Act challenges to dilution of minority voting strength, suggest that such circumscription may not sufficiently control tax-base-motivated, repeated annexations. In North Carolina, unilateral annexation authority is accompanied both by rather specific statutory standards with municipal adherence measured by the courts upon residents' appeal, and by required municipal exposition of the services to be provided to the annexed area with mandamus available to assure judicial enforcement of this service commitment.

b.   Annexation methods involving the consent of the territory to be annexed take several forms. First, the territory may be allowed to petition for annexation with response by the city's government perhaps subject to referendum. Second, the annexing municipality may be able to accomplish annexation only upon an affirmative vote in the territory to be annexed or affirmative votes in both the city and the territory. Conceivably, annexation might be authorized when the combined total vote of the city and territory approve.

It should be noted that the requirement of concurrent majorities for approval is very common throughout the states. Most commonly, the territory to be annexed is not an incorporated political subdivision. Where it is, the procedure is normally termed "consolidation" and is governed by a different statutory scheme. Some statutes give additional protection to the territory to be annexed. For example, there may be an option for a community municipal corporation which would have, for a specified, limited time, in such matters as land use controls, effective decentralized power over the extension of the annexing city's governance into the area.

c. Some statutory annexation procedures require substantive approval of boards or commissions, either legislative entities, such as a board of county commissioners, or administrative boards at state or regional levels. The objectives are, of course, not the same. Where a county commissioner's unit is specified, the state is both invoking the regional considerations which may

[*69*]

have a positive or negative bearing, and, in order to preserve stronger or at least viable counties, inviting a "bias" against local expansionism which would alter the power balances. The role of the administrative board is to combine expertise and regional or statewide considerations in the evaluation of the annexation. Such a goal strikes a responsive chord among commentators who believe that the competitive or expansionist instincts of cities and the benefits of annexations to citizens are best handled at the state level with expertise independent of, or somewhat remote from, the local pressures.

d. While virtually all methods of attempted annexation can face some review in the courts, there are some which envision full substantive judicial review. Because incorporation and power existence are legislative matters committed to the state legislatures and not delegable by them, substantive judicial oversight has presented the inevitable question of improper delegation. While the challenge has not been entirely unsuccessful, especially in jurisdictions where its imminence has kept the courts from carving out a larger role, the "judicial annexation" jurisdictions' courts have overcome it by reference to legislatively posited standards, however sweeping. Thus, Virginia courts in judging whether the proposed annexation is "necessary" and "expedient" require from the annexing government a substantial

[70]

showing of benefits to the city and the territory to be annexed, service comparisons, economic data and the like (the "annexation environmental impact" showing mentioned supra). The courts may approve, reject or modify the proposal, setting terms and conditions for approval. The city in turn, if it does not wish to meet the terms, may abandon the proposal.

In variations of this idea, other states' procedures permit bypassing such judicial oversight unless a specified number of remonstrances or a citizen-initiated challenge is filed. The courts then undertake to apply standards some of which are somewhat more detailed in a thorough judicial review of the annexation. Note that in substantive judicial reviews, the burden of establishing the reasonableness of the annexation may be upon the annexing entity.

e. Perhaps a method provided in some states, notably New Mexico, deserves emulation. In a frank recognition of the fact that annexation is a political decision and that the terms and conditions would be least objectionable if they could be evaluated by persons elected from the interested areas, this procedure calls for submission of the approval question to an arbitration panel consisting of seven members, three elected by the city, three elected by the territory to be annexed, and one neutral selected by the six.

[71]

§ 3. **Dissolution, Division and Detachment.**
Conceivably, municipal powers, once obtained for
a particular area, may now lie dormant because
conditions have radically changed. More likely,
as noted earlier, economic considerations,
changed geopolitical conditions, or failure to realize annexation benefits may bring about a desire
to "secede" from a municipal unit and return to
unincorporated status or join another municipality. Each of these objectives may be achievable
by the local area pursuant to statutory procedures often accompanied by a substantial role for
the judiciary. Of course, each of these objectives
may also be achieved by the state legislatures if
no state constitutional limitation intervenes.
State power, even without such limitation, must
further observe the protections of individual
rights in the federal and state constitutions. For
example, state-legislated detachment of sections
of a city which resulted in the local disen-
franchisement of almost all of the city's black
voters were held to be a violation of the fifteenth
amendment to the U.S. Constitution.

a. Dormancy of the municipality's total powers alone will generally not accomplish dissolution although there are a few statutes so providing. The municipal corporation may only
terminate with the permission of the state legislature either by officially surrendering its corporate status or by state legislated dissolution, or

by voter petition, election, judicial or state decree and certification.

b. Division of a municipality whereby its territory is divided between it and another may be accomplished by appropriate state legislative enactment or by adherence to state legislative procedures for disannexation followed by annexation. For example, where changing conditions would seem to indicate that a particular area was in fact becoming part of a community other than the one in whose boundaries it was located, some jurisdictions allow disannexation from the latter and annexation to the former with the consent of the governing municipal bodies. The courts will scrutinize the withholding of consent by the "loser," allowing it to be voluntary and more than ministerial but rejecting arbitrary or unreasonable recalcitrance.

c. Again, outright detachment, severance, ouster or disannexation of an area from the municipality may be accomplished by state legislative enactments or under procedures envisioning judicial or administrative agency determination that the area in question is not now receiving and will not in the foreseeable future receive municipal benefits, so that municipal retention is unreasonable, motivated solely for revenue purposes. Disannexation, we have seen, is sometimes provided as in Texas where expected municipal benefits have not materialized within a specified time period.

Statutes frequently provide for adjustment of assets and liabilities when such municipal contractions occur. In addition, courts will occasionally make adjustments. In the absence of such, the original municipality retains all of its original powers and real property within its revised boundaries, and all of its personal property. It also remains solely liable even for its preexisting debts.

§ 4. **Political Realities and Constitutional Implications.** It bears repeating that the political realities and constitutional implications of boundary alteration are a significant and constant source of difficulty and challenge. For example, let us assume that our illustration cities' airport and domed-stadium desires envision annexations of their respective locations some miles outside the cities. Neither city intends to annex sizeable portions of the intervening areas which are largely populated by economically poor minorities living in service-poor conditions. Assume that the annexations must either be initiated by or receive the consent of the areas to be annexed. Our cities' plans would be vulnerable because the territories are arguably not contiguous. They might be thwarted by defensive incorporation of the areas in question. The price of consent may be in-

[74]

ordinate. The plans may face serious constitutional challenge.

a. It is uniformly a requirement of both original incorporation and annexation that the territory in question be contiguous. Problems arise when the desired area is only contiguous if certain geographical factors are ignored or if the requirement is satisfied by a connecting link of minimum dimensions. Courts have sometimes resolved the former problem in favor of annexation, thus approving the joining of areas on two sides of a railroad, or a river. Such favorable reaction is by no means certain, however.

The judicial reaction to "corridor annexation" is much less favorable, though far from consistent. Accordingly, attempted annexations which would result in a city of "barbell" dimensions would be a risky undertaking. When rationally applied, the contiguity requirement serves not only to support the desire that municipalities be the corporate reflection of real communities, but also to prevent expansionist tendencies motivated by the acquisition of desirable areas and the avoidance of those more needing municipal services.

b. Because, as we have seen, annexation is generally not permitted where the territory to be annexed has separate incorporated status, perhaps the most effective line of resistance is separate incorporation. And because the proceeding first begun takes priority, the community on de-

fense will race to begin incorporation steps before annexation steps have begun. While it is
possible that the area will not qualify for incorporation, statutory standards and judicial requirements are likely to be so minimal as not to constitute a major barrier. Accordingly, a state
legislature which seeks to foster effective local
government realignment must set more stringent
standards for incorporation. Since it is rarely difficult to determine which proceeding first began,
litigation will more likely constitute an attack by
the later on the degree of adherence by the prior
to statutory provisions which the later will urge
as mandatory. These seemingly hypertechnical
disputes and procedural haggling, of course,
mask the underlying causes of resistance: unwillingness to be subjected to predictably increased
taxation; maintenance of original escape from urban problems; fear of racial, ethnic or economic
integration; undesirability of the annexing city's
school policies on such matters as sex education,
textbooks or corporal punishment; protection
against unwanted land use controls; limitation of
improperly motivated urban expansionism; and
retention of the historic or traditional character
of the territory to be annexed.

It is worth noting here, although we shall see
more later, that in the face of urban strangulation resulting from multiplicity of corporations,
many of them defensively organized for the

above-enumerated reasons, courts have recently been more willing to scrutinize the external consequences of corporate power exercises particularly in the control of land use.

Such urban strangulation has motivated commentators to urge governmental restructuring more in line with geopolitical reality and power realignment more reflective of supporting revenue sources. Some have urged abolishment of local government—an impossible objective, although in more "virgin" territory, Hawaii and Alaska have with much success attempted to avoid many of the pitfalls of corporate multiplicity.

c. The price attached to a territory's affirmative participation, where necessary, may be so great as to outweigh the benefits of annexation from the annexing city's point of view. We have seen that state legislation may authorize temporary mini-municipal corporations with near veto power in matters such as land use in order to protect annexed areas. We have also seen that annexing municipalities may be required to observe pre-annexation service commitments or to extend to annexed areas within a specified time services commensurate with those throughout the original city.

Even more costly may be the "voluntary" quid pro quo for consent, involving tax considerations, additional services, waiver of construction financial requirements, undertaking of promotional activities and the like. Such "hard bargains" are sometimes necessary where the area to be annexed is largely controlled by a developer or subdivider, not within the extraterritorial control of the annexing city, and resistant to annexation.

d. Annexations, local-government and special-district boundaries have come under increasing challenge on federal constitutional grounds. Although such challenges enjoyed some initial judicial receptivity, the courts have eventually rejected:

An attempt to derive from a U.S. Supreme Court ruling to the effect that redrawing of municipal lines to exclude blacks who previously were voting citizens of the city was unconstitutional, a conclusion that an annexation which avoided adjoining areas of heavy black and poor population was thereby defective;

An attempt to dissolve an annexation or to remedy by restructured municipal election districts a dilution of the black vote allegedly intentionally accomplished by the annexation; and

Attempts to impose multidistrict remedies to single district de jure school segregation in circumstances where the other districts were not found to have failed to operate unitary school districts within their systems, where the districts' boundary lines were not found to have been es-

[78]

tablished to foster segregation, and where the state, arguably responsible for its political subdivisions, was not found to have acted in the city to affect school composition outside the city, or the converse.

While the matter of constitutional rights and existing boundaries of municipalities and special districts does not always lead to predictable results, the U.S. Supreme Court's and lower federal courts' decisions do signal certain tendencies. Opinions have reaffirmed the importance of local government, the significance of the traditional allocation of certain matters to local control, and the "sacrosanctity" of traditional local boundaries, city, county or school district. Intent and impact are required for a constitutional violation. A proposed remedy which affects local-government boundaries and units is to be limited to the scope of the problem, although the courts will not readily assume multi-entity impact of the proposed remedy. The courts refuse to impose a remedy extending across boundaries or to decree restructured operation of local units if the additional governmental entities are not implicated in the constitutional violation or, while linked in past actions, have not been integral to those presently under attack.

Where the courts have found that constitutional rights have been intentionally harmed by multidistrict or multi-unit actions, the multiplicity of lo-

[*79*]

cal entities has not precluded multiple-entity remedy. For example, consideration of a metropolitan as well as a city-only school desegregation remedy was deemed appropriate where there was a cooperative segregation effort on the part of the city and suburban school districts and where racially discriminatory exclusion of the city from state legislation reorganizing the state's school districts prevented the State Board from considering consolidation of the city and other districts to alter racial proportions. And attempts to carve out a new school district from an existing district which was in the process of dismantling a dual school system were declared unconstitutional because, whatever the motive, the effect was to hinder the process of school desegregation.

It should be noted that it is purposeful discrimination which federal courts require. For example, the absence of such proof motivated the U.S. Supreme Court to remand the assertion that the establishment of city-county metropolitan government without concomitant school-district realignment, inter alia, required interdistrict remedies transferring black students to suburban systems, and insisting that the housing authority expand throughout the metropolitan area its city-only activities which reinforced black-white housing patterns. Statutory protections, where applicable, may not require such stringent proof. The federal Voting Rights Act requires, in covered jurisdictions, specified court or executive approval of changes which, whatever the intent, affect the voting rights of minorities. Such actions include not only alterations in the electoral process, but boundary changes as well and must have neither discriminatory intent nor discriminatory impact.

e. We have earlier seen that procedures for construction of or provision of local benefit often include creation of an "improvement district" for this purpose. Such an entity presents its own possibility of boundary challenge. Improvement districts are limited to those properties which obtain special benefit from their operation. As we shall see in Chapter V, this benefit may be translated into the property's appreciation in market value and the financial support of the district's operations may result from assessments reflective of this appreciation, rather than from ongoing taxes. While there is little a person can do beyond opposition through the legislated incorporation procedures and election to avoid inclusion in a municipal corporation, when that corporation is a "benefit" district of the type above described, there is the additional infrequent opportunity to demonstrate that no benefit thus contemplated will accrue to the property in question. In this manner, for example, a person whose property constituted an island rising 175 feet above surrounding marshy land demonstrated that the property could not directly or indirectly be benefited by inclusion in a drainage improvement district. The U.S. Supreme Court decided that inclusion of this property solely for the purpose of deriving taxes for the benefit of other lands would be violative of the due process requirements of the fourteenth amendment to the U.S. Constitution.

§ 5. Cross-Boundary Cooperation; Consolidation and Federation.

As has been mentioned, a number of other alternatives are available to citizens and local governments desiring to adapt to meet changing economic, geopolitical and social conditions. These involve intergovernmental cooperation, intergovernmental agreements and sharing of power in a variety of ways.

a.   In all states there is likely to be authority for contractual arrangements among designated municipalities for the accomplishment of certain objectives. There are a great number of such intergovernmental arrangements throughout the country covering information exchange, sharing of facilities, mutual aid, provision by one of services for the other, and the like, which make possible maximum utilization of expensive or unique facilities, economies of scale, services which a particular locality is too small to provide for itself, and mutually beneficial development of specialized resources by local municipality-members of the joint enterprise.

b.   Regional councils of government officials are a recent and potentially significant development fostered in part by federal grant planning requirements.   These groups (COGs) consist of the chief elected officials of the region's local governments (sometimes of interstate regions), who with the assistance of staff concern themselves with many and varied areawide problems. While the COGs cannot compel local government action, COG-developed plans, policies and solutions will often be followed by concomitant governmental actions of the independent municipality-members.

c.   One or more functions or services for which an area's municipalities may be individually responsible could perhaps be more economically or effectively managed on an areawide basis. Hence, such municipalities will take advantage of state legislative authorization to create a special metropolitan district for this purpose.   Frequently, the district will be governed by a board consisting of some of the elected officials of the municipalities or their appointees.

d.   Imaginative consideration of the concepts of interlocal agreements and metropolitan service districts naturally has led to study of the possibilities of metropolitan government in a broader sense.   There has long been available the ability of one local government to merge with another, thereby creating a new entity.   Not all states have satisfactory consolidation procedures, but in many, the authorization for, and details and results of, city-city consolidation are very specifically set forth.

Ventures in broad metropolitanism have taken one of what might, at the risk of some oversimplification, be classified as two forms: federation or city-county consolidation.

Some major metropolitan areas have been involved. While in many cases it may still be somewhat early to make a fair assessment, substantial success seems to have outweighed political upheaval and such other problems as constitutional challenges, increased service expectations and cost savings which did not meet projections.

(i) Federation consists of the creation of a multipurpose metropolitan district assigned many particularly designated functions previously the responsibility of the federated localities, and charged with many regional policy and planning functions with power to compel local unit compliance. The metropolitan district will have sufficient power to be seen to be a functioning central government (and indeed is so promoted). Yet the local units will retain some independence and their identity.

It can readily be seen that this metropolitan remedy is politically difficult (e.g., for the reasons supporting defensive incorporation) and probably requires a metropolitan condition in which the suburban communities must see the center city or cities as important to their continued growth or existence. Such precondition may be affected by decisions to transfer commerce and industry to the suburbs or to remain in or return to the city.

(ii) City-county relationships have followed diverse routes where the city was entirely within the county. Several cities were allowed to achieve independent status leaving the balance of the county to continue its separate existence. In some instances, the major city through a form of consolidation with the county undertook to perform some of the county governmental functions, although other intra-county localities remained in existence. In some jurisdictions such consolidations occurred long ago. Nevertheless, it is this method of creating a general metropolitan government by centralizing major functions while permitting retention of local identity which has been recently undertaken in some large metropolitan areas. This method utilizes what may not be available to a proposed federation, viz., a traditional governmental unit to which there has long been citizen "allegiance," or at least some sense of belonging, as a shell for the creation of the metropolitan central government. But it is faced with the same political and practical realities. Thus, for example, the new "unigovernment" may have to create two service districts, a gener-

[*85*]

al one embracing the entire county area, and an urban service district consisting of the total area of the principal city.

The consolidation may have been pressed to improve the city's deteriorating tax base (indeed, in one case under pressure by the major employer) with resulting disagreements among area voters. Challenges to the procedure for voter approval and to the failure to reorganize services which affect minorities may also accompany the venture.

E. SOME PROBLEMS OF ORGANIZATION AND OPERATION: OFFICERS, EMPLOYEES, ALLOCATION AND DELEGATION OF FUNCTIONS, ELECTIONS AND REFERENDA

§ 1. **Introduction.** Incident to the organization and basic to the operation of local government units are the internal structure, the relationship of subordinate functionaries, the allocations of power within the unit, the ability to enact and implement legislation, and the involvement of the citizens in ongoing regulation, in effectuating political accountability or in overseeing government activity. A complete examination of the myriad details of employment relationships, typical offices, the legislation enactment process and council meetings, methods of daily operation and the specific jurisdictional election and referendum differences is beyond the scope of this text. Nevertheless, certain significant matters deserve attention. For example, we shall briefly explore policies designed to assure proper motivation and integrity in government, and attempts to protect government employees and applicants from discriminatory treatment.

Earlier in this chapter, the various alternative forms of local government executive-legislative structure were mentioned. While there are apparent mixtures of classic governing roles, we shall see that there are policies designed to preserve the identity of the legislative, executive and administrative or judicial processes even where all are exercised by the same entity.

Frequently, for political-protection or citizen-involvement reasons, private citizen roles in the governing process will raise suspicion that power has moved from publicly accountable officials to unaccountable private citizens who may act arbitrarily. Yet, as we shall see, some "citizen delegations" of power are approved by the courts.

Finally, at many points in the governing process from officer election to ordinance referendum the necessity of, scope of and limitations upon the elective process must be paramount considerations in the exercise of local governing power.

§ 2. **Employee Profile.** a. In several cities most employees are in classified service. In

others, a substantial number of the employees
are protected against the adversities of changing
government administrations. In yet others, few
employees are in classified service. Of course,
municipal creation of a civil service requires state
authorization where not an attribute of home
rule. Frequently, government employees may be
classified on a statewide basis and state legislative or administrative efforts in conflict with local
policies involving local employees produce the inevitable preemption questions, particularly in
home-rule states.

    b. A municipality which has created a govern-
ment employee cadre protected from the political
vicissitudes may consist of the following: elected
officials who are not in the classified service; a
number of appointed officials whose positions are
excepted from the classification system because
their duties involve professional relationships,
confidential relationships with elected officials, or
functions which are viewed as necessarily or de-
sirably politically accountable; civil service appointees who are chosen because of qualifications
suitable for a particular position but who are not
on a career competitive ladder with expectations
of promotion; and employees in the career service, selected for examination-indicated potential
and competing for merit system promotions and
greater responsibilities.

c. The civil-service and career-service components of the merit system will likely be accompanied by appropriate and reasonable classification of positions and specificity of job descriptions, pay standardization for parallel positions and classes of positions, methods of selection and promotion including examination of pertinent skills and certification of results, provision for armed service veterans' preference in selection, selections in order from lists of eligible candidates, limitations on avoidance of the merit system by municipal contracts for services with outside concerns, provisions governing discharge and reduction in force, and retirement provisions (sometimes including pension fund, investment protections and policies).

§ 3. **Officers.** a. When the employment position is a public office, excepted from the merit system, the duration of the officer's entitlement to hold office is generally fixed by constitution, statute or charter. It may be for a specific length of time or at the pleasure of a higher officer. The incumbent may continue to hold office validly until a successor qualifies. An officer, elected or appointed, may be removed for cause through procedures set forth in existing legislation. There is authority supporting a common law power of local governments to remove for cause, an example of the essential powers.

b. Typically, the attributes which distinguish an office from an employment position are powers conferred by law, a fixed or specified tenure, and the authority to exercise sovereign governmental functions. For example, one acting as legal officer of the city, representing it in court actions, and drafting or approving legal instruments to which the city may be a party, has been held to be invested with elements of the sovereign power of the city government. This distinction becomes necessary when cities attempt to create positions additional to those authorized by statute or charter in a manner neither expressed nor implied in their sources of power. The distinction may also be significant in interpreting the intent of dual officeholding prohibitions.

§ 4. Devices to Protect Against Conflicts of Duty and Interest. a. A number of constitutional, statutory, charter or ordinance provisions are designed to ensure that a public official (many extend to government employees as well) serves in the pertinent office solely motivated to perform its functions for the public good. These provisions seek to avoid the complications inherent in dual officeholding and the conflict of the public interest with the officeholder's personal financial interests or allegiances to a relative, patron, political party or foreign power. Such provisions may invite citizen vigilance by including public disclosure of personal finances, public

[*90*]

meeting requirements of public bodies (extending, for example, even to state university faculty meetings), and some popular access to legislative and administrative proceedings and records. All such protections have been the basis for much litigation in which personal rights of the individual contest against the public interest. Thus, the freedom of association and privilege against self-incrimination provisions of the first and fifth amendments to the U.S. Constitution have limited overreaching governmental attempts to "guarantee the loyalty" of government employees.

b. Constitutional, statutory, charter, or ordinance provisions or the common law itself may support a prohibition against dual officeholding. The common law doctrine is limited to "offices," although legislation may be more inclusive. The prohibition is intended to avoid the incompatibility which results from a conflict or inconsistency in the functions of offices held by one person where in the planned government structure one office is subordinate or subject to the supervision or control of another, or where the duties conflict, motivating the incumbent to choose one obligation over the other. Illustratively, a state legislator was not prevented by the common law doctrine from holding simultaneously a local position as township attorney even though the township was entitled to lobby to seek or prevent state legislation because neither the decision to lobby nor the duty to carry it out were necessary responsibilities of the attorney's office. The limitation of the common law prohibition to *incompatible* offices, not simply to plural officeholding, has prompted more inclusive state constitutional or legislative prohibitions against the latter, and regulation of how the holder of one office seeks another. As in so many other areas, the question of equal protection of the laws can arise, for example, in classifying which officers must resign to seek another office and which may retain their present office until their quest for another is successful.

c.   The incompatibility of an office subordinate to another need not always result in vacation of one of the incumbencies (usually the first). Frequently when the superior office becomes vacant, the subordinate officer assumes its duties in a de facto, acting capacity under the applicable law. This does not violate the rule. Moreover, in jurisdictions where the common law rule is recognized, there exist numerous statutory authorizations of such situations as city councillors serving as special-district board members. Where legislative approval exists, the common law rule is inapplicable.

d.   The efforts to guard against conflicts of interest giving rise to potential improper motivation have support at common law and are manifested by numerous provisions invalidating

[*92*]

municipal action and penalizing officers and employees who act in such circumstances.

e. The subtleties of conflicts of interest are such that many critics deem the traditional protections insufficient at best. National, state and local governments have faced a formidable crisis of credibility and trust with the electorate. As a result, governments at all levels through legislative action and the people of several states through popular initiative are enacting laws requiring disclosure of campaign contributions and expenditures, limiting contributions and expenditures and requiring disclosure by public officials and candidates of personal financial information in sufficient detail to permit citizen vigilance and to prevent improper influence by the threat of public disclosure and penalties for failure to disclose including disqualification for office.

Despite the laudable purpose of such laws and the overwhelming evidence of the necessity for additional protection, they have frequently been found to be too intrusive. On a policy level, critics are not unmindful of the fact that many persons serve government at all levels at some sacrifice who would for valid reasons prefer to keep elements of their financial circumstances private. Would the loss of these people to government service be too high a price to pay for the unproved benefits of public disclosure?

[*93*]

In many instances, the courts have found other "prices" too high. Personal-finance disclosure requirements have been invalidated as constituting an overbroad intrusion upon the right of privacy and thereby an unconstitutional restriction upon the right to seek or hold public employment or office. Required disclosure of campaign contributions and expenditures has been reviewed and found wanting under the U.S. Constitution's first amendment where minor parties, their supporters and those doing business with them may suffer official and private harassment as a result of such disclosures. While the state's interest has supported strictly defined limitations on group contributions, limits on individual contributions and the use of personal funds have run afoul of the first amendment. Strict scrutiny under the Equal Protection Clause and due process requirements of specificity in penal clauses (especially in light of the first-amendment implications) have resulted in invalidation of offending provisions. Laws which are held to impose additional eligibility requirements to those set forth in state constitutions for constitutionally enshrined offices are thereby invalidated. Of course, localities attempting to improve upon state law are running into the preemption problems discussed earlier.

f. Our illustration city's attempted public disclosure law will therefore require not only appropriate authorization, but also careful drafting to avoid the substantial constitutional problems. Its authors must carefully assess the objectives to be achieved. The depth of citizen feeling throughout the country cannot be underestimated. Accordingly, some legislatures and legislative drafters have reduced their expectations and attempted to devise laws which more closely meet constitutional objectives, laws which reflect the first amendment interests, which are aimed only at substantial potentiality of conflict, which are more generic in the categories of personal details to be disclosed, and which are designed to relate more specifically to appropriately regulatable conduct and information. Needless to say, the final chapter has not been written in this area of the difficult balance of constitutional and societal interests.

§ 5. Residency Requirements. Some offices and positions in government are circumscribed by many other provisions which, like the foregoing, are designed to insure proper motivation and the appearance thereof, the absence of favoritism, full attention to duty and the use of government positions for their intended purposes. Illustrative are restrictions on nepotism, on outside work and on political activity. Yet other provisions, residency requirements, are designed to improve local knowledgeability and responsiveness. There are three discrete residency requirements which serve three distinct goals. The first two

may be characterized as prior-residency requirements; the third, as a requirement of continuing
residency.

a.   The first requirement, applicable to all voters in a jurisdiction, demands a period of residency as a prerequisite to registration and voting.   It
is designed to ensure voter knowledgeability.   Although such residency periods were at one time
substantial, they have been sharply limited
(though not completely outlawed) by the courts.
One of the limitations' effects has been the en-
franchisement of college students in the jurisdiction of their college residence.

b.   The second requires that persons who seek
to be candidates for public office reside in the appropriate jurisdiction for a specified time prior to
the election.   It is designed to ensure that potential public officers are locally knowledgeable.   Judicial receptivity to lengthy requirements has
been mixed.

c.   The third requires that, in order to hold a
public position, the person in question either be a
resident, or take up residence within the particular jurisdiction by a specified time after election
to public office or entry upon employment.

Their premise is that more responsible and responsive government will result when government officials and employees are themselves
members of the community being governed.

[*96*]

Continuing residency requirements have been held not to implicate an asserted constitutional right to travel, and where reasonable, i.e., where there is a reasonable link between the residency and the position for which it is required, successfully withstand challenge under the federal constitution. They are more likely to be the subject of political rather than legal dispute. Nevertheless, such requirements may occasionally be invalidated under state constitutional or (if local) statutory provisions.

In urban communities, citizens are pressing for more stringent official and employee residency requirements with particular attention to teachers, welfare personnel and police. Ironically, wealthier communities have had to relax their requirements where the local cost of living was felt to be a hindrance to effective employee recruitment and retention.

§ 6. Challenged Employment Practices. a. The ever-expanding scope of challenges to government employment practices includes assertions of federal constitutional and statutory protections against discrimination and unequal treatment in the obtaining and retention of positions, and assertions of federal first-amendment rights in connection with restrictions on political practices in non-partisan electoral circumstances (often upheld) and dismissals from government employment.

[*97*]

b. Traditional municipal hiring, job assignment and retention, and promotion policies have come under considerable attack. Such challenges have included position availability, entrance examinations, educational requirements, height and weight minimums, examination achievement levels as a condition of continued employment, physical skill, strength and endurance tests, job assignments and non-rotation policies harmful to promotion possibilities, merit promotion examinations, racial assignment of employee facilities, pay classifications, and maternity leave policies. The effect of such standards, policies and requirements was alleged and in many cases demonstrated to be discriminatory on the basis of race, ethnic background, alienage, age and sex in violation of the constitutional demands of equal protection or of federal statutory provisions prohibiting such discrimination.

Courts have engaged in strict scrutiny and demanded compelling justification in adjudicating the constitutional equal-protection claims. The results may be unpredictable because the U.S. Supreme Court has held that the discrimination must be purposeful. Intent must be proved. Unpredictability may also result from the inevitably difficult balancing of interests in such constitutional cases. For example, aliens may not be excluded from every government position; they may be barred from "sensitive" posts such as state policeman or teacher. When a position largely affects economic considerations, discrimination based on alienage must be compellingly justified. If the position involves largely political objectives, a rational relationship to the public interest suffices.

In cases involving statutory prohibitions, disparate impact of the challenged employment practice is sufficient for a prima facie case for one whose opportunity for nondiscriminatory treatment is protected by the statute, even if the employer's employee-profile results do not appear disparate and no proof of intent is made. The government-employer has the burden of explaining that the challenged practice was supported by nondiscriminatory reasons, but not of persuading the court that the reasons were justified. Note again that the application to local governments of federal statutes prohibiting employment discrimination is not barred by interpretations of state sovereignty under the tenth amendment.

As in school desegregation cases, the most difficult and politically volatile aspect of the cases has been the remedy, for the courts required not only future good conduct but back pay and remedial efforts to make amends for past discrimination. Thus, a civil service commission might be ordered to make a new, non-discriminatory examination available to all applicants; to place successful Black and Spanish-surnamed examinees

[*99*]

who had failed past examinations in a priority pool, if otherwise qualified; to create a second pool of eligibles from among those not identifiable as discriminated against; to certify to requisitioning police departments eligibles from the two pools on a formula of one from the priority pool to every one to three from the second pool. Or, a city might be ordered to hire as many black teachers for the forthcoming school year as is necessary to attain the racial ratio that existed before discriminatory in-service testing and minimum achievement requirements were instituted.

The courts are being called upon to answer such questions as: whether the government employer has a duty to hire minority or female applicants whenever their qualifications are equal to white male applicants (absent a remedial order, no); whether a local government may constitutionally impose a quota system for the hiring of minorities in an effort to respond to a history of past local hiring discrimination (unclear); and whether in responding to economic-exigency employment dismissals by governments engaged in directed remedial efforts, traditional "last-in-first-out" seniority rules may be followed when the impact is disproportionately upon minorities (unresolved).

c.   The matter of dismissals has other constitutional perspectives involving the federal first-amendment and due-process requirements.

[*100*]

Among the many first-amendment concerns incident to local-government employment are those
related to patronage and those asserted in challenging dismissals or failures to rehire. While
the dimensions of the full practical impact have
not yet been realized, the federal first-amendment rights have been held to predominate over
traditional patronage considerations where retention of the government position in question requires allegiance to a particular political party (although coercion to join another party need not be
proved), unless such political affiliation be shown
to be an appropriate requirement for the effective
performance of the policy making or confidentiali-
ty-preserving duties of the specific position. It
should be noted that while case-by-case determinations are more firmly establishing this principle, the decisions are not signaling a trend to
overturn traditional restrictions on candidacy for
local office or customary limitations on partisan
political activity by classified civil servants.

When a local-government employee (teacher,
e.g.) challenges dismissal or failure to reemploy
as an improper decision implicating first-amendment rights, the challenger faces a considerable
burden of proof. It must be shown that the employee's actions were constitutionally protected
and were a substantial or motivating factor in the
dismissal or refusal to reemploy. If the government employer can then show by a preponder-

ance of the evidence that the same decision would have been reached even in the absence of the protected conduct, the employee's claim will fail. Compare dismissal for speaking publicly on a matter of legitimate public concern (invalid), with dismissal after internal-office speaking on matters of limited public concern, substantially including employee grievances not protected by the first amendment for private employees (valid).

Due-process implications in dismissals from public employment have expanded well beyond the vestigial theory that no one has a right to government employment. Explanations for discharge must be given and opportunity to respond must be afforded in the appropriate contexts. In order to invoke procedural due-process rights at dismissal, the public employee must prove that by law or contract he enjoys a "legitimate claim of entitlement" to the position. Where a position is by law terminable only for cause, such a claim is assertable. Where it is terminable at will, the claim is unavailing. The full extent of the "entitlement" test is evolving. For example, courts have refused to dismiss summarily an assertion by a non-tenured teacher (normally, no entitlement) that in the absence of an official tenure system at the public institution, he had relied on the security of de facto tenure earned after term of service. Even where there is no entitlement constituting the requisite property interest, due-process considerations (a hearing to clear his name, e.g.) have been found necessary where a dismissal not only damaged the person's chances of future employment, but also (through false and damaging information, e.g.) stigmatized the employee by public dissemination of damaging information said to cause the dismissal.

§ 7. Public Employee Unions. Increasingly, public employees have turned to labor unions to achieve conditions of employment which they felt helpless to achieve by other means, and to put additional muscle into the protections of the merit system. The local governments thus have faced questions of permitting union membership, elections, collective bargaining, arbitration, grievance disputes, closed or agency shops (union membership a required prerequisite to or corequisite of employment), dues check-offs, strikes and other matters common to labor relations throughout the country. At least three matters are peculiar to public employment: the relationship between collective bargaining agreements and the merit system; the authority of local government units to enter into arbitration or other binding agreements; and the nature of public employment and strikes.

a. Constitutional provisions, state statutes or local ordinances in many jurisdictions permit public-employee union organization, and many deal in specific detail with matters such as those listed

[*103*]

above.   There are some states which prohibit
public-employee unionization, a prohibition of
questionable validity.   Even in the absence of
specific public-employee organization authority,
some courts conclude that where there is no statutory prohibition, unionization may be undertak-
en and can coexist with the merit system.

Civil service statutes and statutes dealing with
public-employee labor relations present conceivable conflicts between the merit system and the
objectives of permissible collective bargaining.
The states which have attempted statutory resolutions seem equally divided among such responses as absolute priority to the civil service
laws in all matters, absolute priority to the civil
service laws on certain, specified matters, or dispute resolution left to the discretion of the local-
government employer.   The majority of states,
however, have attempted no legislative solution
and hence have left to the courts the difficult
task of defining the appropriate applicability of
the two sets of laws.

b.   When the local government employer is
asked to enter into binding collective bargaining
agreements and annual contracts which provide,
inter alia, for binding arbitration, difficulties
arise.   As we shall see in our discussion of municipal contracts, local governments may not contract away their governmental (as contrasted
with proprietary) authority or bind themselves to

[*104*]

exercise their governmental authority in predetermined ways. In addition, the governmental
employer may not have the full authority to
agree on specifics. For example, a teachers'
wage increase approved by the board of education may be subject to overall educational budget
action by the city council. Where there are detailed constitutional or statutory authorizations,
these problems may be resolved. In fact, the historical reluctance of state and local governments
to bargain collectively with public employee unions has given way to statutes in nearly half the
states requiring some form of collective bargaining, although the directive may be limited to certain groups (teachers, fire fighters, police, e.g.).
But where such authority does not exist, local
government units may be prevented from entering into binding arrangements, especially those
which purport to tie the hands of other governmental units upon which the employer units are
dependent. Likewise, courts and legislatures
have turned from suspecting arbitration in general to favoring it as a means of settling disputes.
In recent years, for example, several states have
enacted legislation providing for some form of
compulsory arbitration. Nevertheless, in the absence of state authorization, local units may be
unable to enter into blanket arbitration agreements on questions of policy although they will
generally be allowed to agree to submit such particular disputes as grievances to arbitration.

[*105*]

c. Strikes against the government by public employees have been outlawed by legislation and at common law. Such legislation may also ban work slowdowns and other strike substitutes. The prohibition is intended not only to protect against disruption of essential services, but also to protect government's ability to determine budget needs and priorities. Strike-produced gains would be the result of coercive paralysis of essential services and not the result of free, undistorted choice by the electorate's representatives.

Despite the overwhelming negative sentiment, public employee strikes abound. In a small but increasing number of states, the strike weapon is permitted by statute, with the authorization heavily circumscribed by conditions. For example, one state has permitted strikes only after exhaustion of a carefully prescribed bargaining process and concomitantly provided for injunctive relief upon proof of serious danger to the public health. In the much more likely situation where no such authority is found, enforcement of the prohibition may be left to the injunction and contempt power of the courts or may be accomplished through statutory sanctions including fines, jail sentences, suspensions and forfeiture of bargaining representational status. There has begun to be developed an intriguing theory of union intentional-tort liability to harmed private parties where the

[*106*]

unions' strikes were aimed at and damaged the public, a private remedy possible where existing statutory remedies have been held not to be exclusive.

§ 8.   Restrictions on the Exercise of Executive, Administrative, Legislative and Judicial Functions. In an earlier section, we alluded to the variety of executive-legislative forms selected by local governments. The evident possibility of a board of commissioners or council exercising legislative and administrative functions raises the spectre of the doctrine of separation of powers. For example, the board of commissioners could enact the basic governing building code, and could thereafter be the entity which grants or denies permits or considers appeals from grants or denials. The mayor may be a voting member of the legislative body, may execute legislation and may be the magistrate who adjudges violations of local ordinances. The possible combinations are limitless.

a.   It is often said that the doctrine of separation of powers is not applicable to local government. If the doctrine is understood to mean separate powers exercised by separate entities, with checks and balances, the statement is correct. It does not mean, however, that the functions which are classified as legislative, executive and judicial are so blurred as not to be separately identifiable. Even where one entity seems to possess powers

[*107*]

in all classifications, the rules governing their exercise will help to identify the separate functions and the results which accompany such exercise.

b.   The distinction between ordinances and resolutions may illustrate this. Where statutes and general ordinances are silent concerning the mode in which a municipal governing body may implement the powers conferred on it thereby, the governing body may express its will by either ordinance or resolution. For example, where a statute confers numerous powers, some by provisions expressly requiring enactment by ordinance, others by provisions silent as to the mode of enactment, the municipality may implement the latter powers by either ordinance or resolution. This choice is subject to the qualification that resolution enactments must reflect decisions which are "administrative" as opposed to "legislative" in nature. To draw this distinction, it is necessary to examine the scope and purpose of a given enactment. An enactment is "legislative" to the extent that it provides a permanent rule of government or conduct designed to affect matters arising subsequent to its adoption. An enactment is "administrative" to the extent that it deals with temporary or special matters and involves only a factual determination that conditions necessary for the operation of a statute or general ordinance have been met. Accordingly, where the appropriate statute or general ordi-

[*108*]

nance is in effect, a municipal governing body may enact resolutions to grant permits, sell particular parcels of municipal property, build bridges, establish nurseries to supply parks, order removal of specific buildings, among myriad other acts.

The most likely circumstances to be considered "legislative" and to require the more time consuming and expensive ordinance form are those where, under the rule of "equal dignity," the council seeks to amend or repeal an ordinance, or where the council seeks to regulate the conduct of persons or the uses of property and to impose a penalty of fine, imprisonment or forfeiture for violation.

c.   The determination whether a given enactment may be evidenced by ordinance or resolution is of critical importance to the municipal council.   If the council is exercising legislative power, its action may be subject to mayoral veto, if such is permitted.   If the council is exercising legislative power, it may only do so in legislative session or on charter-designated legislative days. Its action may be petitioned to referendum by the electorate.   The determination whether a matter is legislative or administrative also underlies the ability of the electorate to initiate legislation in those jurisdictions where popular initiative is permitted.

To enhance the electorate's ability to oversee legislative activity, such exercises may be required to be taken at public meetings, after legislative hearings, with appropriate notice. While regular meeting days may be set forth in the charter, notice of special meetings or special subjects may be required not only for council members but also to accommodate the jurisdiction's "open meeting" requirement. Legislative enactments will likely require a number of readings before final passage and appropriate publication thereafter.

It should be noted that municipal councils may be allowed to hold emergency legislative sessions with resultant short circuiting of the various requirements. The jurisdictions are split over who has the final say in determining the existence of an emergency, the council or the courts.

d.   Conversely, if the council's power exercise is deemed "administrative," it may be taken in executive session. The matter will not be subject to popular referendum. There will be no mayoral veto. The hearings, if any, may be investigatory. The council sessions may not be public and the enactment will not require several readings before final passage.

e.   To illustrate, let us again assume our hypothetical public disclosure law. Its councilmanic proponents may fear a mayoral veto or the law's suspension pending, and time consumption and

[*110*]

expense of, a popular referendum. The number of signatures needed to invoke the referendum process may be within reach of a consortium of influence interests, political opponents and persons who are sensitive to the law's privacy implications. Accordingly, the law has been enacted in executive session.

To the power source, preemption and constitutional challenges illustrated earlier in this text, the council has now added the possibility of attacking the resolution (it may even have been titled an ordinance) as improperly enacted. It may in fact be easier for the opposition to mount a court challenge than it would be to produce the necessary votes to win a referendum.

If a court subsequently invalidates this power exercise—a most likely result although councils continue to try this route—there may then be a long delay before the next charter-specified "legislative session" of the council. It will be necessary for councilmanic proponents to obtain the necessary, probably charter-indicated, quorum majority to declare the need for an emergency legislative session in order to avoid the delay. And the limited time allowed by the charter may be insufficient to accomplish the necessary, open legislative process so that the council is reduced to extension of the time by the fiction of not adjourning sine die the last "legislative day" for several calendar days.

[*111*]

Once again, the council may have afforded opponents the opportunity to test in court the validity of the emergency designation or the failure to adjourn so as to extend the limits. And still the opposition has not yet had to confront the law on its merits.

If one assumes that the councilmanic proponents of the many actual attempts which resemble our illustration were not poorly advised, or that the legislative-administrative characterization of the contemplated action was not really debatable, one is left with the question whether a power exercise in which so much is risked to avoid popular reaction is worth council approval. And if one believes that the council should take a leadership position despite possibly adverse constituent reaction, are not the benefits of popular education attendant upon a well run referendum worth the risk of failure and better in any event than the "back door" approach?

f. The local executive possesses only such powers as are conferred by statute or charter. In some forms of local government this may include independent powers such as administrative-department supervision, or the power to veto legislative enactments of the council subject to override.

g. Two further considerations of power separation should be mentioned. Inevitably, the courts will be separate even at the local level.

They will customarily be subject to the supervisory authority, or be actual components, of the state court system. Occasionally, the functions of magistrate will be blurred.

Even where the separate functions intermixed in one entity are surrounded by safeguards such as the above, there may be circumstances in which an individual's constitutional right to due process is affected by the compelling intermixture of responsibilities and allegiances. Illustratively, the U.S. Supreme Court invalidated a traffic-offense conviction imposed by the city's mayor sitting as authorized as judge in traffic court, not because the union of executive and judicial power in him was wrong, but because his responsibilities for the city budget and revenues to which his court's fines substantially contributed, and his participation as tiebreaking voter on the city council, placed him in a situation of virtually irresistible temptation. He was officially charged with inconsistent duties, one partisan, the other judicial. The inconsistency necessarily involved a lack of due process.

§ 9. Delegation of Implementation Authority. The local government is the recipient of appropriately delegated state authority and hence cannot redelegate it to subordinate agents, whether government employees or private entities. Two of the previously mentioned dichotomies are applicable. The local government may not delegate its

[*113*]

governmental powers, although contractual delegation of proprietary powers is possible. It may not delegate legislative authority, although it may delegate to its agents the power to administer or implement its legislation under proper standards to prevent arbitrary conduct.

a.   The general-rule-with-standards delegation is likely to be labelled administrative where the problem occurs too frequently for the legislative body to pass upon individual instances, or where it is deemed to call for determination of the existence of factual circumstances particularly described as prerequisite to the invocation of the generic legislation.   Compare legislation which delegates to the chief of police authority to set speed limits and parking regulations in the downtown business area (invalid) with legislation authorizing the chief of police to reduce speed limits to ten miles per hour and to impose parking bans when, during stormy weather, major downtown commercial events or rush hour, traffic conditions become hazardous (valid).

b.   Frequently, the determination whether delegated discretion is legislative or administrative will turn on the adequacy of the standards governing the delegated authority.   Courts are inconsistent in the strictness with which they view such standards.   The apparent inconsistency may be the result of judicial recognition of the practical realities of day to day government and the in-

[*114*]

ability of a local legislature meeting periodically, and often on a part-time basis, to cope if the distinction is too strictly enforced. Thus, the adequacy determination will be affected by such factors as the frequency of need to cope with minimally different factual situations, the need for emergency response, the social usefulness of the conduct regulated, judicial experience with local administrative responsibility, the competence and qualifications of the public official, and the inherent limitations of the language to express adequately variations to be foreseen.

c. The roles of private citizens in the exercise of local-government authority have several dimensions. In many jurisdictions, by constitution, statute or charter, the local government's citizens are accorded a legislative role in the exercise of initiative (enactment of legislation by the voters), referendum (approval or disapproval by voters of legislation enacted by the local government), or recall (mid-term removal by the voters of local officials). All processes involve similar notice, petition and election steps with attendant questions discussed elsewhere in this text. Recall may have specific requirements limiting the target offices and necessitating statement of reasons. The responsive roles of the local government during and after the processes may be specified in order to avoid the necessity of the election, if possible, and to protect the results

[*115*]

from immediate reaction. It is important to note
that by initiative or referendum, the people cannot accomplish what the local legislative body
could not achieve, whether the limitation be the
authority of the local government to act on the
matter, preemption of otherwise appropriate action at another competent but predominant governmental level, or predominance of constitutionally protected rights. The exercise of such
popular roles, if otherwise appropriate, is not an
improper delegation of authority (if it be deemed
a delegation at all).

In other contexts, local governments have attempted to allot to private citizens localized roles
in the exercise of local governing powers. On
many occasions, municipalities have given effective control over a regulatory scheme to private
citizens because the city government lacked the
political courage to regulate in the face of citizen
protest, or because the matter in question could
better be handled by those in the pertinent expert
discipline, or because the municipality deemed it
more effective to decentralize or to involve the affected electorate in the ongoing regulation.
Thus, for example, municipalities have attempted
to allow building lines to be determined by the
owners of neighboring properties, to ban billboards and gasoline service stations unless property owners within the affected area consent to
their construction, to require substantial neighbor

[*116*]

consent in the affected area for the construction
and operation of philanthropic homes for the
aged or children in a residential zone, or to involve the rental property owners themselves in
the setting of rent controls.

The rule against redelegation of governmental
authority and the necessity of adequate standards are the operative factors incident to such
apparent delegations of discretionary authority to
private citizens.   For example, where adequate
standards are coupled with the direct involvement
of municipal officers (factors governing and limits upon rent control; mayoral appointment of appeals board, e.g.) and no power is given to the private citizens to adopt or amend any ordinances,
involvement of the rental property owners to enable implementation of rent control laws is not invalid.   Where, however, delegation to private citizens of the authority to impose restrictions on the
use of others' property is not coupled with adequate standards to control discretion, there is a
high risk of arbitrary and capricious exercise.
The courts have not invalidated the delegations
simply because the delegates are private citizens
not politically accountable.   Rather, the apparent
total discretion thus delegated is deemed to constitute an invalid delegation of legislative authority because the use upon which restriction may be
placed, itself valid and not restricted or prohibited
by the city, is a matter over which the private citi-

zens have complete sway. Restriction of the use, then, is a matter of whim in the absence of controlling standards, and the private group substitutes improperly for the elected council.

Note the opposite result when the restrictions have been imposed by the government and the question is the removal thereof. Private-citizen involvement is not deemed uncontrolled where the municipalities themselves have in certain land-use zones restricted uses or banned nuisances (billboards, service stations, e.g.) properly the subject of such regulation or prohibition, but allowed the lifting of such restrictions or the location of such uses upon the consent of those who would be most directly affected by their existence, and who have a property interest greater than whim.

It does not always follow that interests of nearby property owners in permitting a restricted use necessarily substitute for standards, however. The nature of the delegates' interests may itself bar the delegation. Where the private entities were churches and schools and could prevent the award of liquor licenses for premises within a specified area, such delegation did not merit the deference normally due a legislative zoning judgment, and substituted for reasoned government action the decisions of churches which, unguided by standards, could seek to advance religious objectives. The delegation thus entangled the

[*118*]

churches in the processes of government, risking political friction on religious grounds, and hence was invalid under the Establishment Clause of the federal first amendment.

§ 10. Elections and the Fourteenth Amendment.   Having decided to tackle the thorny issues related to local governments' elections for local offices or to the exercise of initiatives and referenda, the U.S. Supreme Court and the lower federal courts have developed to a substantial extent the dimensions of the dictates of the fourteenth and fifteenth amendments to the U.S. Constitution.   The courts have thus confronted the myriad forms of local government, the occasional responsiveness of those forms to local needs, the historic disparities of voting strength, limitations frequently favoring rural interests, long-term residents, the white majority and owners of real property.   Particularly in the case of referenda, historically the elections may have been designed on other than a simple-majority basis, may have excluded some people from participation where their interests were not as great as others, and may have limited referenda to certain legislative subject matter.   Historically, popular approval or rejection of government legislation may occur only if an extraordinary majority votes to do so. Historically, the property tax has played so large a role in local revenue that property owners have been accorded the exclusive right to reject munic-

[*119*]

ipal debt which would have a direct effect on their property tax or values. Historically, on some matters referenda are mandatory; on others referenda may be conducted at the behest of the government unit or of a specified number of citizens. While the evolution is continuing, the historic patterns have been examined and some directions of fourteenth-amendment jurisprudence are clear. They relate to these questions: What is the subject matter of the election? Who can vote? How is that vote to be counted?

a.   There are local government structures which envision appointed members. The courts have reviewed election mechanisms where the governments have determined to have elections. They have not substituted their judgment for that of the local entities on whether offices shall be elective or appointive. Where local law authorizes popular approval or rejection on some issues and not on others, the alleged disproportionate impact of subject matter of the referenda may be the focal point of election challenge. The fact of the referendum, we have seen, is not an improper delegation of legislative authority. But like the legislative enactments thereby reviewed, it is subject to constitutional limits. Where the referendum's availability is not a constitutionally improper classification disadvantaging "discrete and insular minorities," making it more difficult to enact legislation on their behalf (local fair hous-

ing ordinances, e.g.), then the fact that referenda
are permitted or required on some issues (public
housing, zoning for land use, e.g.) does not of-
fend equal protection.

b.   The courts rather early in this evolutionary
period cleared away such obstacles to exercise of
the voting franchise as improper residency requirements and prohibitive poll taxes.   Also
found unconstitutional under the federal fifteenth
amendment was an attempt to reconfigure municipal lines thereby disenfranchising minority municipal voters.   Persons who are not municipal
voters cannot assert their non-voting status to invalidate state-authorized extraterritorial exercise
of municipal powers, although there is some suggestion that extraterritorial powers may be so
fully exercised as to amount to annexation in fact
if not in name.   The failure to extend the franchise might then be more successfully attacked.

When the local government has determined to
fill an office or to engage in popular review by
elections, then persons cannot be denied the vote
by classification inconsistent with the demands of
equal protection.   The right to vote is fundamental.   Denial, therefore, must be compellingly justified.   Where the asserted distinction of interests is deemed insufficiently compelling (un-
married persons who neither own nor lease property not allowed to vote to elect a school board or
approve its budget, e.g.; persons who do not pay

property taxes not permitted to vote in referenda on general-obligation and revenue bonds, e.g.; persons in the vicinity of a proposed airport improvement, but not in the city whose citizens were proposed as the only voters reviewing the airport issue, e.g.), the challenged denial will be invalidated. Where, however, the franchise is extended to all who are disproportionately affected by the operations of a special-purpose, local unit of limited functions, in an election designed to give greater influence to the constituent groups found to be most affected by the governmental unit's functions, such extension is not a denial to other potential voters. A cognate group of cases suggests that where a franchise need not be extended, but is, objections to the extension may not be successful. The apparent willingness of the courts to be responsive to peculiar needs of special-purpose units may not have been accompanied by a fully accurate appreciation of the citizen impact of these entities.

c. When the right to vote is not denied, there remains the complex balancing process demanded by assertions that the impact of the vote of particular persons or groups is diluted by lines which have been improperly drawn under equal-protection analysis. Dilution of the vote can take many forms: More votes may be needed to elect a representative than a comparable group needs to elect an equal representative. More votes may

[*122*]

be needed to uphold local-government legislation than to reject it, or the converse. Concurrent majorities in areas of unequal population may be required. The counting of units' conclusions solely as dictated by majority votes where aggregating of units is necessary to determine the ultimate result may dilute majorities or minorities in any of the individual units. The impact of minority votes may be diffused by the structure of the electoral districts.

The equal-protection commands of "one-person-one-vote" require that if officers performing local governmental functions (city, school district, local unit not having recognizable disproportionate impact, e.g.) are to be elected, their constituencies are not to consist of substantially unequal populations. When the local level is compared with federal elections, the courts appear to tolerate more leeway in achieving de minimis population differentials.

The fact that extraordinary majorities may be required in referenda is not ipso facto unconstitutional. If there are neither improper exclusions, nor disadvantages to identifiable, protected minorities, the referendum structure can validly make it more difficult to promote or prevent government action by requiring electoral approval or disapproval only upon the vote of more than a simple majority.

As above suggested, the principles designed to guard against vote dilution in the election of representatives are not as fully applicable in "single shot" referenda where a popular voice in local legislative enactments is to be given limited play. The referendum puts a discrete issue to the voters and if its adoption or rejection has a disproportionate impact upon an identifiable group, courts can decide whether it is appropriate to limit the franchise to that group or to give its votes special weight. Where there is a "genuine difference in the relevant interests of the groups," group attributes which are pertinent to its stake in the outcome, where recognition of the reality of substantially different electoral interests does not amount to invidious discrimination, a requirement of concurrent majorities among unequally populated subelectoral groups in referenda on such issues as restructuring of governmental units (consolidation, annexation, e.g.) is not constitutionally impermissible.

Dilution of majority and minority votes in the aggregation of unit votes by treating each unit as if it had voted only the way its majority voted is invalid, however, in representational elections.

An election scheme or structure is not permitted to be so designed as to minimize or cancel out the voting strength of racial minorities in the population. This aspect of vote dilution is a diffusion of minority strength. What is impermissible is

[*124*]

such diffusion as constitutes denial to a minority group of meaningful access to the political process. The intent of equal protection here is to assure minorities a fair chance to elect candidates representing their interests, not to entitle them to an election district in which they can control the election. When the electoral single, multi-member or at-large districting scheme is thus challenged as a violation of equal-protection requirements, intent to achieve this result must be shown, and the court must consider the issue in historical contexts, with "an intensely local appraisal of the design and impact." Rational justification of the electoral scheme is the preferred test.

It should be noted again that in addition to fourteenth and fifteenth amendment evaluation, there is statutory judicial and executive review under the federal Voting Rights Act of alleged local vote-abridging or retrogressive changes in covered jurisdictions. The challenged procedure may be precleared only when both the purpose and the effect of denying or abridging the right to vote on account of race or color are absent. The courts will not forbid, for example, all municipal-boundary expansions that dilute the voting power of particular groups. They may, however, insist upon modifications to the subsequent electoral plan designed to neutralize adverse impact on minority political participation.

CHAPTER III

REGULATION OF CONDUCT AND THE USE OF LAND

A. THE POLICE POWER

§ 1. **Relation to Zoning Power.** Perhaps the most pervasive of the so-called coercive powers of local government is the police power. For our purposes, we shall define the police power as the exercise of governmental power to limit, regulate or prohibit personal and business activity and property uses without government compensation in order to protect the public health, safety, morality and general welfare.

Conceptually, any such definition of the police power may be seen to include zoning. However, the municipality in question must be authorized to exercise its powers in one of the variety of ways we have earlier discussed. Traditionally, police-power authorization is separate from zoning-enabling legislation. Some municipalities possess the former authority but not the latter. Many courts will emphasize that the two, although intimately related, are not coterminous and that zoning power objectives have been customarily considered less inclusive, limited to ends peculiar to the municipality's fundamental land use program, rather than directed to a general problem common to the community at large. The dividing line of this theoretical separation is not readily discernible, especially since land use is frequently the subject of limitations originating in both the police and zoning powers. We shall explore land use regulation specifically in part B of this chapter.

§ 2. Challenges to Police-Power Exercise. The state authorization of municipal police power may, of course, relate to a specific object to be regulated. Many such detailed authorizations exist. Commonly, however, police-power authority is primarily delegated by the state in rather generic terms. Except where the question involves possible extraterritorial application of the challenged city action, or conflict with or preemption by state legislation or exclusivity, or the particular mechanics of implementation, framing of a power challenge in terms of lack of authority is uncommon. As will be discussed infra, such a challenge is more likely to be framed in terms questioning whether the object of the municipal power exercise is a proper one for invoking the police power. We shall return later to challenges to the mechanics of regulation: licensing, prohibition, nuisances, enforcement, investigations and penalties.

a. The most common challenges to police-power exercises charge that the particular municipal ordinance does not constitute a proper exercise of

the police power and thus denies due process, or
that it is violative of other federal or state constitutional provisions. When the improper-exercise
charge is made, the courts inquire whether the
ordinance is reasonable, i.e., whether the object
of the ordinance is one for which the police power
may be properly invoked, and if so, whether the
ordinance bears a real and substantial (reasonable) relation to the object sought to be attained.
In this connection, the courts are willing to invoke presumptions in the ordinance's favor and to
accept hypothetical constructions or projections
of circumstances which support the ordinance's
reasonableness. Other specific constitutional
protections which are commonly invoked include
the federal Commerce Clause, the federal fourteenth amendment, and the federal Bill of Rights
incorporated through the fourteenth amendment,
and state counterparts to the federal Bill of
Rights.

b. To illustrate, let us assume that a municipality has enacted a "Green River Ordinance," an
ordinance declaring that the practice of going in
and upon private residences by door-to-door salespersons for the purpose of soliciting sales orders
is a nuisance and as such is punishable as a misdemeanor. The ordinance has been challenged on
behalf of door-to-door salespersons for national
news and opinion magazines, perhaps as a defense in a prosecution for a violation. In addition

to the questions we have already seen, viz., whether the city is empowered to act, whether the enactment conflicts with or is preempted by state legislation, whether the city council met in proper legislative sessions observing the appropriate notice, hearing, readings and quorum requirements, and whether the enactment is in proper form, there remain such questions as:

(i) Whether preservation of the residents' privacy or their protection from uninvited solicitation when in their homes is an object for which the police power may properly be invoked;

(ii) Whether the means, declaring door-to-door selling to be a punishable nuisance, bear a real and substantial relationship to the desired objective;

(iii) Whether the ordinance impinges upon the magazine publishers' rights of free speech, or freedom of the press;

(iv) Whether the ordinance unduly burdens interstate commerce;

(v) Whether the inclusion of door-to-door salespersons and exclusion of other sales approaches constitutes an improper classification so that the group is denied equal protection of the laws;

(vi) Whether the terms of the ordinance are so vague as to allow arbitrary enforcement;

[*129*]

(vii) Whether state delegated authority to regulate for the public welfare includes the power to prohibit otherwise lawful business and whether such prohibition is confiscatory;

(viii) Whether enforcement of the ordinance is surrounded by sufficient standards so that delegation of enforcement powers is appropriately one of administrative authority; and

(ix) Whether imposition of criminal penalties is authorized.

c.   It is readily apparent that many of the questions raised about a police-power exercise are intertwined, are simply different focuses upon the same underlying problem.   For example, an improper classification may indicate that the means chosen are not rationally related to the end sought.   A provision that violates due process requirements because it is so vague as to allow arbitrary enforcement may at the same time be void under the federal first amendment requiring precision of regulation because the ordinance is overbroad in its impact upon free speech.   It may similarly violate the federal fourteenth amendment because it has classified picketers according to the content of the communication whose method is regulated.   Delegation of authority to implement such a vague provision may also be challenged as an improper delegation of legislative power because there are not sufficient standards to limit enforcement discretion to ad-

[*130*]

ministrative bounds. Finally, one might argue
that the object to be achieved is not properly
within police-power purview because it inhibits
exercise of constitutionally protected human activity.

Nevertheless, it is important to be aware of the
nature of each of these interrelated challenges.
Effective advocacy, judicial assessment and careful drafting require precision of target.

**§ 3. Appropriate Objects for Police-Power Ex-
ercise.** Is the object of the ordinance one for
which the police power may properly be invoked?
At the outset we should note that there is political reaction which serves to define rather broadly
the boundaries of regulation. Whether there be
an adverse reaction to overly solicitous government intervention in the lives of its citizens, or an
effective consortium of centers of self interest, or
a desire to engage in the conduct greater than
government can overcome, this referendum nega-
tion, political pressure or disobedience so rampant
as to overwhelm enforcement capability serves in
a real sense to circumscribe and limit the reach of
the police power. Witness public reaction to
strict residential-use codes, local gun-control efforts or public-area smoking bans.

a. The courts, of course, may reflect such political reality in their evaluation. Generally,
though, they respect the separation of powers because the state legislature has committed to the

[*131*]

municipal legislature the primary regulatory responsibility. This respect is manifested by the courts' willingness to entertain the presumption that the challenged ordinance, not on its face presenting evidence of serious constitutional implications, is reasonable. To the challenger then falls the task of demonstrating that it is unreasonable; and if there are reasonably conceivable facts to support the power exercise—even say some if the matter is fairly debatable—the challenger will lose. The challenger thus faces the heavy burden of negating every reasonable basis which might have underlain a legislative determination that there was a reasonable need for the enactment.

b. The range of police-power exercise defies accurate description. The scope can perhaps be illustrated not only by the efforts we shall see in part B of this chapter but also by the following. Municipal efforts, frequently successful, on behalf of the public health and safety have included attacks on air, water and noise pollution, smoking in public places, smoking reduction measures, restriction of the sale of drug paraphernalia, limitation of the impact of video arcades on children during school hours, restriction of headphone use while running in public streets, firearm registration and handgun prohibition, traffic-safety regulations, scientific-research laboratory controls, sanitation measures such as disease control, food

quality regulation and trash disposal, closing of
businesses on Sundays, removal of slums and
blight, school discipline and demonstration regulations, reducing crime potential (early closing
hours of certain commercial establishments, e.g.),
riot control and prevention, adult and juvenile
crime prevention and punishment.

On behalf of the public morality, municipalities
have restricted gambling and the availability of
liquor, attempted to eliminate temptation to im-
moral activity (massage parlors, prostitution,
e.g.), "protected" the status of women, and
banned obscenity on stage, film or in publication,
particularly in connection with its impact on
juveniles.

To protect the public welfare, municipalities
have sought to advance aesthetic considerations
throughout the community by such measures as
sign control; additionally to support property values by restricting uses in specific uses zones, by
specified location and dispersal of "adult-en-
tertainment establishments," and by promoting
peace and quiet through such methods as loud-
speaker control, door-to-door solicitation regulations, and limitations on telephone solicitations
("junk phone calls"); to protect the public's purse
(often matters of statewide concern) by such measures as price-sign requirements on gasoline
pumps, regulation of auctions, pawnbrokers, sec-
ond-hand dealers, loan businesses and fortune

tellers, requirements concerning scales and food weights and measurements, control on vending machines, regulation of solicitation of funds, prevention of fraud and deceptive practices, regulation of employment agencies, rent controls, landlord-tenant regulations, rate-making and franchise controls such as those surrounding local approval of cable television operation; and to protect the civil rights of its citizens through public accommodation laws and ordinances designed to guarantee fair housing opportunities and to control block-busting, panic selling and other real estate problems.

c. There are limits to the courts' receptivity to otherwise constitutional exercise of local police power. When the ordinance seeks in effect to impose "one person's morality" on the general public, or seeks to accommodate "one person's aesthetic sensitivities" by requiring public observation thereof, the courts are prepared to find that the object is not one for which the police power may properly be invoked.

In the last analysis, the city's competence to act depends upon the reasonableness of the action. There is a point, difficult to articulate in the abstract, when the reality of what is being done or the speculative or highly personal nature of what is sought to be prevented overcomes the judicial reluctance to intervene which finds its expression in the presumption of reasonableness.

d. Some courts have attempted to articulate this scope of municipal regulatory power in particular connection with businesses and occupations. These can be categorized for present purposes as follows: ordinary vocations which are pursued on private property by private means; occupations which are useful but which involve under certain circumstances social or economic evils which are offensive to the public health, safety, morality or general welfare; and businesses which involve claims of a private right in, or extraordinary use of, public streets or parks. All three categories are regulated in some degree. Obviously, the scope of municipal regulation is greatest in the last situation and certainly is sizeable in the second category. There, though, regulation is accompanied by the danger of imposition of personal morality or sense of the general welfare in the municipal determination of what are social and economic evils. This danger is most real in connection with the first category where regulation may tend to expand beyond control of external consequences to enforcement of private morality.

§ 4. Relation of Means to Object. a. Intimately related to the determination whether the matter is a proper subject of regulation is the virtually inseparable question whether the means chosen are also reasonable, i.e., whether they bear a real and substantial relation to the ends sought. Thus, for example, prescinding from the question whether specific constitutional protections have been ignored, one might ask:

(i) Whether control of incinerators and oil burning equipment is rationally related to prevention or material reduction of air pollution;

(ii) Whether reduction of phosphates in detergents will materially reduce pollution of local water sources;

(iii) Whether requirement of deposits on drink containers or additional taxes on high tar cigarettes will reduce litter or prevent smoking of the more harmful substances;

(iv) Whether closing commercial establishments on Sundays is rationally related to promotion of a day of relaxation and recreation;

(v) Whether a curfew of any use of the streets after certain hours or the closing of certain untended establishments (laundromats, e.g.) at certain times is rationally related to restoration of civil order or reduction of the potential of crime;

(vi) Whether prohibition of the administration of massages to persons of the opposite sex or of licensed taverns' hiring female bartenders is rationally related to prevention of consequences detrimental to the public morality or protection of the status of women;

REGULATION Ch. 3

(vii) Whether prohibition of "for sale" or "sold" signs on residential property bears a real and substantial relation to the prevention of racial blockbusting, panic selling and the promotion of fair housing goals;

(viii) Whether commuter, on-street parking bans and the imposition of commercial parking taxes will reduce traffic and promote the use of public transportation;

(ix) Whether prohibition of the possession of bludgeons, switchblade knives, brass knuckles, sawed-off shotguns, molotov cocktails and operative handguns will reduce accidental and intentional death and injury;

(x) Whether restrictions on group occupancy of residences advance the municipality's interest in preventing overcrowding, and in promoting traffic control, aesthetics and property values;

(xi) Whether the requirement of two attendants on duty at self-service gasoline stations is rationally related to fire prevention;

(xii) Whether prohibiting or restricting the sale or advertising for sale of implements which are known or can reasonably be known to be intended for use with law-controlled substances (drug paraphernalia) will serve to reduce illegal drug use; and

(xiii) Whether allowance of on-site, outdoor commercial advertising and prohibition of off-site,

[*137*]

outdoor commercial and non-commercial advertising on fixed structures (billboards) are rationally related to the elimination of pedestrian and traffic hazards and to the preservation and improvement of the city's appearance.

§ 5. Specific Constitutional Limitations. As noted above, the due-process question of the rational relationship of the means chosen to the end sought will not be answered by a presumption of reasonableness where the ordinance denies first amendment freedoms or imposes discriminations based upon race, color, religion or ancestry. Moreover, the presumption is rebuttable and the reasonableness of the means is rarely divorced from other constitutional considerations.

a. State constitutions contain declarations of individual rights and other provisions which may serve directly to limit police-power exercise. Indeed, these limitations (and their federal counterparts) are more strictly applied by state courts than the federal restrictions by federal courts, because the federal courts adhere to the principle that the police power has been reserved to the states and should not be interfered with unless the balancing of the federal constitutional protections with the legitimate goals of state police power so dictate. Thus, for example, while there is federal authority upholding the Green River ordinances, the majority of state courts have invalidated them as too prohibitive. Similarly, state courts have interpreted state constitutional provisions to prevent the type of municipal restrictive definition of family in a single-family-residence zone which in federal court passed federal constitutional muster. Under federal constitutional jurisprudence, however, the justification for the local power exercise must move beyond reasonableness to compelling persuasion where the impacted right is one of the fundamental rights in the federal Bill of Rights applicable to the states through the federal fourteenth amendment or where a suspect class is regulated.

b. An attempted regulation (such as the Green River ordinance or that limiting phosphates in detergents, or that approving the sending or receiving of trash, garbage or sewage to or from out of state, e.g.) may be challenged as barred by the federal Commerce Clause. Such a challenge will prevail where the police-power gain is outweighed by the undue burden which impedes the free flow of interstate commerce, or where the enactment discriminates against interstate commerce in favor of local commercial businesses. (Note that the challenge is to local-government exercise of regulatory or taxing powers, not to the government's entry into the market as a participant.)

c. An ordinance may be challenged as violating rights to freedom of speech (bans of labor picketing near schools, censorship of films, plays and books, "for sale" signs, political signs in residence yards, commercial and non-commercial, off-site outdoor advertising, uniformed paraders' permits, e.g.), freedom of association (curfews, vagrancy laws, e.g.), freedom of the press (censorship, Green River ordinances, e.g.), freedom of religion (Exercise: fund solicitations, home visits, loudspeakers; Establishment: Sunday Blue Laws, city-hall Christmas creches, liquor-license veto by churches, e.g.) or the right to travel (population limitations in land use laws, municipal moratoriums on new housing construction, durational residency requirements, e.g.). The rights thus federally preserved are not absolute but submit to the legitimate demands of the police power. The degree of recognition of the police power depends upon the balance struck between the gravity of the evil and the importance of the right (clear and present danger as against free speech, e.g.). The method of regulation may play a similar role (prior restraint, e.g.). Due process concepts of vagueness are involved in first amendment issues as well. Frequently, the question turns on not only the propriety but also the precision of the regulation. If the regulation is overbroad, it exceeds the limited area of its competence and is subject to arbitrary implementation. For example, while it may be appropriate to regulate the use of sound trucks or to avoid inflammatory "Nazi" parade activities to protect public health, safety and welfare, total prohibition together with its usual accompaniment, the potential of selective, arbitrary enforcement, encroaches unduly upon first amendment rights.

d.   An ordinance may be attacked as violative of the constitutions' due process clauses in a number of ways. (We shall refer later to procedural due process requirements in its enforcement.)

(i) The ordinance may be confiscatory. If it is a rate regulation enactment, it is not the nature of the business whose rates are regulated but the impact of the regulation that is at issue. The rates may not be so restrictive as to be prohibitory or confiscatory, thus in effect constituting an unreasonable termination of an otherwise lawful business.

(ii) Police-power regulation may also be confiscatory if the cost of compliance amounts virtually to a taking of property of the persons being regulated. State constitutional clauses and the federal fourteenth amendment will require just compensation or, failing that, invalidation of the ordinance. There is no articulable line separating proper police-power regulation from a compensation-requiring taking, and several health and safety ordinances which were understandably alleged to have crossed the line have nevertheless been upheld as valid police-power exercises.

[*141*]

(iii) An ordinance will also be deemed defective under due process requirements where it either fails to give a person of ordinary intelligence fair notice that his contemplated conduct is forbidden or encourages arbitrary and erratic enforcement, or both. For example, a curfew ordinance which prohibits loitering or remaining on the street and excepts those whose business requires being there (firemen, policemen, e.g.) may be upheld, while an ordinance which forbids citizens without exception to *be* on the street will fail to comport with reality, is incapable of total enforcement, and will both fail to define appropriately the forbidden conduct and encourage arbitrary enforcement.

e. Equal-protection-of-the-laws requirements will invalidate improper classifications. Essential to determining whether the ordinance is reasonable, whether its requirements bear a real and substantial relation to the evil to be cured, is the question of the propriety of the law's coverage. The class subject to the regulation may not unreasonably be segregated from others to whom the ordinance does not, but ought to, apply. For example, an ordinance prohibiting a person from giving a massage to a patron of the opposite sex in massage parlors, health salons or physical culture studios, but not in barber shops, beauty parlors, YMCA and YWCA health clubs was declared invalid because the class was structured arbitrarily, without rational relation to the evil attacked which could have (though apparently had not) as easily occurred in the unregulated entities.

Compare, surviving such an equal-protection classification challenge, an ordinance which permitted only municipal residents to park within the municipality. To deny parking privileges to non-residents was deemed a rational distinction reflecting commuters' heavier contribution to local traffic congestion and air pollution.

Here again, the courts are willing to invoke a presumption that the ordinance's classification is a reasonable one, with the burden of establishing the contrary on the challenger. Frequently, the challenger (perhaps with some basis in fact) will allege that the class was determined in a discriminatory manner as a result of improper city council motivation. For reasons ranging from separation of powers to the difficulty of competent proof, courts are loathe to look into the question of legislators' motivations and will frequently say so. Nevertheless, the effect of such motivation may itself be so arbitrary as to be invalid. And, of course, where the class is defined according to race, religion, color or other "suspect" status, or where the regulation applies only to some people and impacts upon a fundamental right (classification by content and freedom of speech, voting rights, e.g.), the presumption is inapplicable and

[*143*]

the virtually impossible burden is on the government to show a compelling state interest justifying the classification. The cognate equal-protection-violation charge of intentional or purposeful discrimination in the administration of an otherwise nondiscriminatory law will be discussed later.

f. Another judicial response should be noted in situations in which challengers unsuccessfully raise the equal protection clauses' classification requirements. Occasionally, the court will find that the evil sought to be cured is particularly pernicious with respect to the particular class sought to be regulated although the municipality could have expanded the scope of the evil and thus included a larger class, saying that the local legislative body need not correct all the evil at once, but may attack it step by step. For example, in upholding a fair housing ordinance applicable to owners of five or more dwelling units, whether or not contiguous, as a valid step in attacking some of the evil, the court justified the classification on the ground that an owner of five or more units who would attempt to discriminate purely on the basis of race, creed, or color in the sale or rental of such units is potentially a more dangerous threat to those who would be hurt than a like thinking owner of four or fewer units.

§ 6. **Regulation and Prohibition.** There are additional considerations relating to the enactment and implementation of police-power ordinances. Once of the most persistent obstacles to the form of the regulation is the strict interpretation which many courts are willing to give to the state's delegation of the power to regulate, holding that the power to regulate does not include the power to prohibit. Such strictness inevitably has led to regulatory attempts which are so confiscatory as to amount to prohibitions. Where challenged, we have seen that they may be invalidated. The strict interpretation, often criticized as too narrow, has also resulted in semantic exercises whereby the area of regulation is broadly expressed so that the prohibition may be seen simply as one of the limits in the regulatory scheme.

For example, our illustrative Green River ordinance may be seen as a prohibition of solicitation of subscriptions by house-to-house canvass without invitation. Or it may be seen as regulation of subscription solicitation limiting it to radio, television, periodicals, mail and local agencies. In the sense that all regulation limits, the limitations make all regulatory legislation prohibitory to that extent. Thus, in the exercise of its customary utility-regulatory responsibility to determine such economic matters as need, reliability and cost, a state has been judicially upheld in requiring sufficient interim and long-term storage capacity for spent fuel as a condition precedent to its permit-

[*145*]

ting additional nuclear-power construction. The present unavailability of such storage capacity has led challengers to view the state decision as a prohibition usurping federal nuclear-power prerogatives.

§ 7. **Licenses, Permits, Fees.** a. Regulation of activity and land use under the police power is frequently accomplished by delegating to administrators under standards the power to approve or withhold licenses and permits. Without the license or permit, the activity cannot be undertaken. State delegation of the power to regulate will usually be held to include the power to license for regulation and to impose reasonable conditions and qualifications upon the grant or renewal of licenses and permits. As regulatory ordinances, license and permit requirements are, of course, subject to the improper delegation, preemption, and constitutional challenges previously discussed. For example, an ordinance which permitted churches and schools, in effect, to veto the issuance of liquor licenses for establishments within a 500-foot radius of a particular church or school was viewed as a delegation to private entities of a power normally exercised by government agencies, and held not to be entitled to the deference normally accorded a legislative zoning enactment. Because the valid objectives of the ordinance could have been achieved in other unobjectionable ways, and because the substitution

[*146*]

of the standardless church judgments for reasoned public decisionmaking appears to have the principal effect of advancing religion, the ordinance was deemed to have risked political fragmentation along religious lines, an entanglement held unconstitutional under the Establishment Clause of the federal first amendment.

b. Fees are customarily exacted for the award or renewal of licenses and permits. While one might conceptually demonstrate that the costs of regulation are expenses of government like all others and that methods of obtaining revenues to pay government expenses constitute taxation, the power to exact license and permit fees has been considered to be within the penumbra of the police, not the taxing, power. As a result, such fee exactions cannot be intended to be revenue producing vehicles, and licensing for revenue must be distinguished from licensing for regulation. As we shall see in Chapter V, in order to license for revenue, the municipality must be empowered by state delegation of such taxing authority, and such regulation will be evaluated under the rubrics applicable to local taxation.

c. Regulatory license fees nevertheless provide sizeable amounts of money (witness the income from parking meters), largely because of judicial liberality in applying the governing standards, viz., that the fees be reasonable and not regularly or largely in excess of the munici-

pal expense of policing the function and adminis-
tering the license program. Such expenses include the costs of investigating the applicant,
expenses incurred in issuing the authorization,
costs of all supervision and investigation insuring
that the licensee conforms to the applicable rules
and regulations, and, frequently, other police
charges reasonably related.

§ 8. **Nuisances.** a. Where the municipality is
deemed empowered to prohibit, prohibition of occupations or activities noxious to the public
health, safety, morality and general welfare may
be accomplished by declaration that they constitute nuisances. It is frequently contended that
legislation cannot make that a nuisance which is
not in fact a nuisance. This cliché is frequently
voiced but has no independent significance. It
merely reflects the fact that the city's nuisance
declaration is not impervious to challenge. The
designation must be reasonable and constitutional. The list of valid municipal nuisance designations is limitless. The courts, however, have the
final determination whether the activity, condition or structure is in fact a nuisance, i.e., whether it is an appropriate object for the invocation of
the police power to prohibit.

b. The nuisances in question are public in nature. Their detrimental impact must sufficiently
affect the public or a portion thereof to warrant
prohibition. The ordinance, of course, is general

[*148*]

in nature, leaving to administration the determination that particular activity or land use falls within the generic class. Abatement of the particular nuisance will then be sought under such locally available procedures as court decrees or administrative cease and desist orders, with costs charged to the person or entity in question. Under appropriate standards, emergency summary abatement (destruction of disease-ridden or unsafe buildings, e.g.) may be allowed, so long as the citizen has an available, though subsequent, hearing to challenge the specific nuisance designation. Recovery against the public official and the municipality may be had for wrongful abatement, in the latter case because summary destruction, where improper, will be deemed a taking requiring compensation.

§ 9. Investigation, Enforcement and Penalties. Enforcement of the police-power ordinances also involves investigation and supervision to assure compliance, revocation of abused licenses and permits under applicable standards of reasonableness and appropriate procedural due process, and civil and criminal penalties for violation.

a. Frequently, regulatory investigations involve areawide, multi-building, internal inspections. The U.S. Supreme Court has held that where such inspections involve entry into private dwellings or the private areas of commercial establishments, the federal fourth amendment re-

[*149*]

quires that entry be conditioned upon judicial issuance of a warrant. Probable cause for issuance even for areawide inspection will exist if reasonable legislative or administrative standards, varying with the municipal program to be enforced, are satisfied with respect to a particular dwelling or private area, and will not require specific knowledge of the condition of that particular private area or dwelling. The Court's rulings were not intended to imply that commercial areas may not be inspected in many more situations than private homes, nor were they intended to affect licensing programs requiring inspections prior to operating a business or marketing a product, to which inspections the licensee may have consented in advance.

b. The power to impose penalties for violations of police-power ordinances must be delegated, and it is settled that the power to designate misdemeanors may be appropriately delegated to municipalities. Some state authorizations prescribe the penalties for violations of municipal ordinances and the prescribed penalties may be exclusive. There may be other state legislation, applicable to various classes of municipalities, or authorized charter provisions which make certain misdemeanor or offense penalties available for violation of a municipality's laws. A municipality may denominate the violation an "offense" or a "misdemeanor" and thus invoke the applicable

[*150*]

penalty contained in these separate general provisions. Sometimes the local ordinance itself specifies the penalty.

Clearly, a penalty which exceeds the state-delegated limits is invalid. Clearly, all violation proceedings are subject to the fundamental fairness requirements of procedural due process. Equally clearly, constitutional rights to counsel, jury, indictment, specificity of charge, confrontation of witnesses, and other due process questions involving discovery and burden of proof, and constitutional protections against double jeopardy, self incrimination, and illegal arrest and search must be afforded and observed in appropriate municipal criminal proceedings. Exploration of each of these rights and protections is beyond the scope of this text. Of significance here are the facts that absent state or charter restriction the municipality may in many jurisdictions enforce its ordinance by "civil" or "criminal" process, that, accordingly, not all municipal violation proceedings are criminal in nature, that only some rights and protections will be available in some proceedings, and that where accurate prediction can be made, municipal penalties are occasionally set to avoid the necessity of affording all rights and observing all protections.

Ultimately, it is for the courts to decide whether a given "civil" or "criminal" designation is proper. Some courts have decided that virtually all municipal violations are in the nature of misdemeanors. Others retain the traditional civil classification for some and deem others criminal. In so deciding, the courts have looked to the extent and kind of the relief and punishment sought, the degree of outrage associated with the conduct allegedly amounting to the violation, and whether that conduct is punishable under general laws of the state. Generally, as the severity of the permitted punishment increases, as the conduct for which the action is brought grows more outrageous, and as the conduct prohibited by the ordinance more closely approximates conduct prohibited by general laws, the courts with increasing likelihood will designate the proceeding "criminal." Conversely, as the relief sought more closely resembles the relief obtainable in traditionally civil actions and as the conduct for which the action is brought more approximates conduct actionable by private parties in civil suits, the designation will more likely be "civil."

Whatever designation a court decides to be proper in a given instance, the consequences which follow that decision are by no means clear. While substantial authority requires observance of basic elements of due process, the various courts have inconsistently answered questions concerning the applicability and availability of the broad range of rights and protections above mentioned.

§ 10. **Discriminatory Enforcement.** The fact
that inevitably some municipal police-power ordinance violators are penalized while others are not
often leads to a charge of discriminatory enforcement. This is particularly likely where the alleged violator suspects that political or other arbitrary considerations motivated the enactment or
enforcement of the ordinance. The courts which
are willing to consider the charge do not deem it
a defense to the allegation of violation. Rather,
it is a reason for dismissal on constitutional
grounds.

Intentional discrimination in the administration
of an ordinance violates equal protection. But
success in this challenge is rare. Selective enforcement—the fact that other offenders have
not been prosecuted—is not in itself a constitutional violation. One who alleges discriminatory
enforcement must meet the heavy burden of establishing conscious, purposeful discrimination on
impermissible grounds or an intentionally pursued pattern of discrimination. Illustratively, an
operator of an "adult" movie theater and an
"adult" bookstore who alleged, inter alia, that the
county improperly enacted a zoning ordinance
making the operations unlawful in their present
locations, prevented their status as non-conforming uses by delaying action on needed permits prior to the rezoning, permitted several businesses to bring themselves into voluntary

[*153*]

compliance by obtaining permits, but sought to abate his "adult" establishments because of the character of their business, an exercise of first-amendment rights, was required additionally to show that he was treated differently from those who demonstrated his level of chronic delinquency in seeking permits.

§ 11. **Estoppel.** As has previously been mentioned, we shall see in Chapter IV that local governments may not bargain away such governmental power as the police power. As a corollary it is frequently contended that local governments cannot be estopped to exercise their police powers. It would be more accurate to say that estoppel will be rarely applied. But the doctrine is available under traditional principles to one who is victimized by inequitable police-power application.

a. For example, where a landowner postponed his application for a particular land use permit at the behest of the city legislators who were at that time quietly preparing to rezone the area in question, the court held that it would be inequitable to permit the municipality to deny the landowner the use to which he could have obtained a vested right prior to rezoning had he not accommodated the very legislators who then rezoned.

b. The question of estoppel often arises because a citizen has relied to his detriment upon the approval of a ministerial officer which the

[*154*]

municipality now says was beyond the scope of the officer's authority. It argues that he made a mistake of fact or acted in contravention of applicable ordinances. Of course, if the official was without authority to issue a permit or approval at all, or if there was evidence of misconduct or deceit, there would be no estoppel and the city could validly revoke the approval. But where the official had the authority to issue the necessary permit or certificate, where there was no evidence of bad faith, where there was substantial expenditure and change of position in reliance, even though the official's interpretation of the applicable ordinances and regulations may have been a questionable one, though of long standing, courts have generally held the city estopped from arbitrary revocation.

B. REGULATION OF LAND USE

§ 1. Functional Components in the Land Regulatory Process. No area of local government operation is more the subject of public reaction and political sensitivity than land use regulation. At the outset, it will be helpful to identify "the players" in the land regulatory process and outline briefly the functions each performs. There is a great variety from state to state and thus the following will be typical rather than uniformly applicable.

a. The state legislatures delegate to certain political subdivisions authority to enact zoning ordinances, to create various boards and commissions, and to regulate the uses of land in myriad ways ranging from subdivision controls to such police-power exercises as housing and building codes. The federal government has not been without its role here. Many strings have been attached to federal grants and have motivated increased state attention to such matters as regional planning. Several attempts to enact federal land use legislation have been unsuccessful. Nevertheless, they have perhaps been partially responsible for state efforts to reclaim some (wetlands, e.g.) or much of the land use regulatory functions for state-level regulation or at least participation. Such efforts have raised the inevitable political outcry that land use is appropriately a matter for local control, and local government and citizen opposition has been very successful. Experience in states where comprehensive statewide land use controls have been tried, may serve as a catalyst for more statewide efforts at least in the less urbanized states.

b. Regional or local planning agencies or commissions are the repository of local and, where possible, state legislative delegations. Sometimes the planning functions are also performed by the municipal legislative body, but this is becoming increasingly infrequent. The planning

[*156*]

commission will customarily be responsible for development of the area's master plan, for implementation of subdivision control and of the necessary follow-through on planned unit developments. Applicants seeking approval of subdivision or comprehensive design plans, and frequently, those seeking rezoning, will be required to obtain the approval of the planning commission. The commission's functions are both advisory (to the municipal council) and administrative.

c. The municipal legislature will have responsibility for enacting police-power ordinances. Customarily, the council will also be delegated the zoning authority, although occasional zoning-enabling delegations are made to zoning commissions, district zoning councils and the like. These entities may simply be the municipal legislature acting under another name, or may consist of members some of whom will be municipal legislators. The council (or zoning commission) will have the responsibility of enacting the zoning ordinances, officially adopting the master plans and official maps, delegating administrative implementation functions to planning commissions, zoning boards and other administrators, and enacting amendatory zoning ordinances (rezoning). Such delegations must of course be accompanied by appropriate standards. Applicants seeking rezoning (amendment of the zoning ordinances) will apply to the council. Their application may first

[*157*]

have to be considered by the planning commission either upon referral from the council or through procedures requiring rezoning applicants to file first with the planning commission.

d. Applicants who seek to use land in accordance with the zoning ordinance or who wish to obtain exemptions from its requirements for a number of reasons will be required to seek permits, variances, special use or exception status from an administrator, often the city building inspector. This administrative entity is also commonly charged with the responsibility of compliance inspection and enforcement.

e. Appeals from administrative action concerning permits, variances, and exceptions will be considered by a board, often called the board of zoning appeals or board of zoning adjustment, created by the municipal legislature pursuant to state enabling legislation. Sometimes the city council itself will serve as the appellate entity.

f. The courts play a substantial role in the process. Under customary local procedures, persons with appropriate standing who are disappointed either in the subdivision or other administrative (as opposed to advisory) action of the planning commission, or in the permit, variance or exception decisions of the board of zoning appeals may seek review of those decisions in the courts. Persons with appropriate standing who are disappointed with the city council's amendment of the zoning ordinances (rezoning) or its rejection of the proposed amendment may challenge the amendatory ordinance or the failure to amend in the courts. In the latter case, challenge to the denial of rezoning may take the form of challenging the reasonableness of the original ordinance.

g. Implicit in the above descriptions is the matter of hearings, notice, and the due process requirements which must be observed. While there may be no federal constitutional requirement of a hearing before legislative action of the council or quasi-legislative actions of the commission, state constitutional clauses and statutory procedures deemed mandatory may contain pervasive hearing requirements. Since many of the hearings required are likely to be deemed administrative, the strictures of judicial due process beyond those necessary for fundamental fairness and substantial justice may not be applicable. The hearing and notice requirement originally caused courts in "initiative" jurisdictions to hold that the specific municipal-legislative method of enacting or amending zoning ordinances was meant to be exclusive. There is a growing number of jurisdictions, however, which permit zoning ordinances or amendments to be enacted by initiative, or to be approved or rejected by referendum, even where those processes require extraordinary majorities. As noted above in Chapter II, the initiative and referendum processes are subject to the constitutional limitations which affect the legislative power, however exercised, and are available for legislative, not administrative, matters.

§ 2. The Role of Planning. a.   Chief among the disputes incident to the land regulatory process is that concerning the role of planning. Some view planning as the primary function and consider zoning as merely one of the tools of plan implementation.   Indeed, in at least one major city, there is no zoning and the planning function is supported by land market realities and private covenants.   Others view planning as simply a means of assisting zoning to improve upon its ancestors—fire codes and the cataloging of public nuisances.   Some view zoning as the antithesis of land value protection and the free market, designed primarily to protect the residential home. Others view the planners as too remote, attempting to dictate sociological results without regard to human needs or desires.   It is no wonder, then, that consistency is not the hallmark of the planning-zoning relationship.

In some jurisdictions, the planning function is tolerated and the results have value only in providing other than adversary input and in predicting what action the city council might take.   In other jurisdictions, the results of the planning function are given almost a determinative role in the outcome of zoning disputes.

[*160*]

b.   Whatever the differences between planners and lawyers or government officials, the role of planning is undergoing a marked expansion. Strings tied to federal grants desired by states and localities to assist the development of housing, highways, sewage disposal systems, renewed city areas, pollution controls and the like, the periodic possibility of federal land use legislation, judicial insistence upon municipal recognition of the external and internal social consequences of land use policies, growing dissatisfaction with municipal balkanization, and the complex problems of growth and no-growth, availability of housing, need for more effective transportation and energy use, overtaxing of ecosupport systems—all have given renewed impetus to the role of planning in the land use process.   Results have thus far included improved scientific data for planners, expanded regions for planning, county-wide planning and related zoning in some states with substantial municipal participation, and increased municipal, extraterritorial-zoning authority.

§ 3. "Plans" and "Maps".   The terms "plan" and "map" are used so frequently in any discussion of the process that it is necessary to make certain distinctions.

a.   In most jurisdictions, zoning ordinances are required to conform to a comprehensive plan. "Comprehensive plan" may, but need not, refer to a master plan or collection of master plans. It may mean no more than a requirement that the zoning ordinance be reasonable, that it not create undesirable spot zoning, or that the city council have conformed to publicly understood municipal land use purposes.

b. The master plan (or aggregate of sectional master plans) is the published result of efforts by the planning commission, often in cooperation (if required) with affected municipalities, to guide the coordinated development of the area in question. Most plans have traditionally mapped land use locations. Recently, however, dissatisfaction with the inflexibilities of the predetermined location of use districts has led to development of plans which verbalize municipal land use objectives, with mapping of illustrative location. The newer plans are designed to guide plan implementation in the mix of uses with only necessary fixed location advice, leaving most eventual locations to the interplay of other growth determinants. In either event, the master plan will give an overview of the mix of uses (and use districts, traditionally) and will provide for various kinds of agricultural, residential, commercial and industrial uses; open space, water, forest and soil conservation; transportation and roads; public building and school locations; hospitals; parks and recreation facilities; flood control; staggered development; and building and population density. In many instances, the master plan is advisory only and serves as a persuasive and predictive resource. In some jurisdictions, it plays a greater role, as we shall see.

c.   The "official map" designation is customarily used to refer to the map of projected street extensions, and proposed parks and recreational areas. The importance of the map depends upon the land use limitations which derive from its adoption by the city council, as will be indicated infra. A cognate limitation derives from ordinances banning construction in flood plains.

d.   The term "zoning map" usually refers to the actual results of the municipality's zoning ordinances, the geographic locations of approved use districts. The graphic significance of such a zoning map will become apparent in our later discussion of floating zones.

§ 4.   Techniques of Plan Implementation: Official Maps, Master Plans, Subdivision Control, and Other Devices. It would be inaccurate to say that even the most advisory of master plans is no more than that. Techniques of plan implementation accompany planning results in almost all jurisdictions which result in required adherence to some if not all of the plan.

a.   Under appropriate enabling legislation, municipal councils have adopted official maps, often prepared by the planning commission, so as to

[*163*]

prevent land uses in the projected street extensions and parks which will increase the cost of street and park construction. It must be remembered that such land is privately owned. The thrust of the official map theory is that for a statutorily specified number of years the private owner will be denied permission to build in the bed of the proposed street extension or widening or in the area to be devoted to the park or playground. Since compensation to the owner will not accompany the denial of permits, it is necessary for the official map laws to provide a constitutional safety valve whereby the landowner is entitled at a hearing to show that his entire property cannot yield a reasonable return and that in balancing the interests of the city in keeping future acquisition costs low with his interests, justice and equity require the granting of the requested permits. If the administrator or the board of zoning appeals grants the permits, such grant may be accompanied by reasonable restrictions in the city's interest.

The courts have not favored official map ordinances when reviewing permit denials. Where street extensions are involved, the courts generally are constrained by precedent to uphold the system. But several courts have rebelled at extension of the concept to parks, where the impact upon the landowner can be significantly greater. These courts have concluded that the attempt to "freeze" the land constitutes a taking and therefore that the law as applied is unconstitutional or that compensation must be paid.

Some courts have tried to find a middle ground. One court has recommended that, during the years of the "freeze," compensation take the form of an option to purchase with the option price to include taxes accruing during that time. If the city takes up its option, full compensation is then to be paid. Other courts have ordered tax rebates during the "freeze" period.

Of course, where the denial of permit is not based on economic savings to the city, but is instead in furtherance of the public health and safety, as in the case of a ban on building in a fifty-year flood plain, courts are unlikely to find a government taking.

b. As has been indicated, in many jurisdictions, the master plan has only advisory, persuasive and predictive influence unless and until zoning ordinances are adopted which conform to it. In such localities, court challenge to the planning commission's plan is both premature (no damage until zoning) and unavailing.

But some jurisdictions have given greater sway to the plan by such techniques as forbidding the council to amend the zoning map in a manner inconsistent with the master plan, or providing that any rezoning by the council inconsistent with the master plan must be approved by an extraordinary majority of councillors.

c.   One of the major techniques of plan implementation is authority to control the manner of development of subdivisions.   There has been increased recognition of the impact upon an existing municipality of a developer's subdividing sizeable portions of land into smaller lots for the construction and sale of housing and related support uses.   For purposes of this discussion, we are assuming that appropriate zoning exists. The creation of multiple-use development zones will be treated in our discussion of planned unit development.   Such impact includes problems of traffic congestion, development ingress and egress, sanitary and storm sewers, water and utilities, safety items such as sidewalks and street lights, aesthetic and safety items such as curbs and street signs and increased burden on schools and recreation areas.

Certain assumptions have become fairly settled.   There is likely to be such an impact.   The subdivider benefits if allowed to proceed because he is able to plat the land, thus alleviating the problems of metes and bounds descriptions.   The subdivider further benefits because the approval of street access, sewers, water, utilities, and attractive plat design makes his property more marketable and hence more valuable.   The point of plat approval is a useable control point to re-

[*166*]

quire from the subdivider certain exactions to alleviate his impact upon the existing community.

Accordingly, under a variety of state legislative delegations, local units have been empowered to set conditions upon subdivision plat approval. The conditions are set in accordance with those expressed in the state delegation or those set in the resultant municipal ordinance. The administrative function is normally carried out by the planning commission (or the zoning commission or town council if it "wears both hats") to which the subdivider files preliminary plans designed to meet the guiding standards. The commission may modify the plan. Final approval often awaits final plans or performance bonds. Some of the conditions such as street construction details, lights and environmental controls are police-power requirements analogous to building lines, set-backs and minimum lot sizes. Others relate to reducing the subdivider's impact upon the existing community and it is in connection with these that much litigation occurs. A few commissions are also empowered to pass upon both the necessity for and the size of the proposed subdivision.

It must be remembered that the costs of all such conditions will be passed on to the purchaser. Certain ceilings may thus be operative. The city may have to choose between imposition of such costs at plat approval and the availability of

[*167*]

low and medium cost housing. The developer may be faced with market realities in deciding to pass on the costs. At some point, increased cost exaction may be confiscatory.

On this last point, the courts are in disagreement. Where the subdivider does not voluntarily accept the exactions and, instead, challenges them, the conditions must find their authority in the delegations of power. Even if authorized, they may be confiscatory if not attributable to his activity. The litigated issue often involves such requirements as land set-asides or dedications for schools, parks and public uses in proportion to the population density of the subdivision, or the contribution of fees in lieu of such dedications. The courts differ in their assessment of what is attributable to the subdivision impact. Some would limit conditions to those "specifically and uniquely attributable" which would otherwise be borne by the public and reject as confiscatory land set-asides and "in lieu" fees which cannot meet the strict test because they involve speculation concerning future impact, combination of existing problems and subdivision impact, or use of the exacted fees to provide city services elsewhere in the city. Other courts have been more flexible in defining the impact to include future as well as present needs, and in upholding the dedications and "in lieu" fees if the evidence reasonably establishes that the city will be required to provide more land for schools, parks and playgrounds as a result of the plat approval. Whether the substitution of private recreational areas for dedications to the public should be upheld is open to question.

Certain additional considerations deserve mention, although they are a matter of local procedure. Statutes define the minimum subdivision subject to control and it may be a division of land into as few as four or five parcels. Both the promulgation of standards and conditions and the approval or denial of the subdivision plan may be preceded by required hearings. While the due process requirements of fundamental fairness and substantial justice must be met, the hearings on approval are administrative in nature and need not observe the strictures of judicial hearings. Appeals from the action of the planning commission may be made to the board of zoning appeals or to the municipal council. Where no such appeals are provided, or after they prove unavailing, judicial relief may be sought.

d. A major problem in plan implementation is the ability of governmental units to withstand the pressures of development and land speculation inconsistent with the master plan either in location or timing, particularly if support services are governed by independent special districts not required to conform to the plan. Municipal councils have responded in a number of ways. Many have succumbed. Others have attempted to reduce the pressures by limiting times for submission of rezoning petitions, by "down zoning" (more restrictive use zones for largely undeveloped areas), by temporary moratoriums and the like. We shall see more of these in our discussion of exclusionary zoning. In addition, municipal councils have begun to study land banking plans whereby municipalities purchase land to hold for later resale in order to influence development and control land values. Opponents of land banking decry the increase of government market interference, the heavy cost to public funds, and the loss of property tax revenues. A somewhat less expensive program has involved granting to private owners of undeveloped land a virtually total exemption from property taxes in return for an option to the government to purchase the land at a future time for the price prevailing at the time of the option.

Reduction of the land speculation pressure may also be accomplished by such experiments as that imposing a tax on the gains from the sale or exchange of land other than up to one acre used for principal residence, with the rate of taxation increasing in proportion to the size of the profit and decreasing in proportion to the length of time the land is held.

§ 5. Zoning. a. Whether one considers zoning a tool of plan implementation or (the traditional view) the primary function in the land regulatory process, it is unquestionably the focal point of the political pressures associated with municipal land development and the legal point at which the plans become effective as adopted in the zoning ordinances.   Historically, zoning is the combined result of the inadequacy of its ancestors—fire codes and nuisance designations—as protections of the public health, safety, morality and welfare and the promoted desirability of protecting residential neighborhoods, ensuring maximum property values, and effectuating the many goals of planning.   While there are some who would end the process, some who would radically reform it, and some who would remove it from the province of local governments, political realities suggest that far more would agree with judicial expressions of its primacy as a local-government function, of its importance to protect the quality of life, and of the judicial deference which is necessary for effective zoning and land-use control.

Perhaps as a reaction to the futile property-by-property or block-by-block efforts of nuisance and fire code control, zoning from the beginning has been deemed almost necessarily to encompass predetermined, specified use districts.   That such districts have more recently served other goals—the "storing" of land for "foreseeable" industrial or other uses, the reduction of acquisition costs for industry, the avoidance of economic

[*171*]

and social mixes—may have served to enhance its permanence. As a consequence, more flexible techniques have necessitated additional state authorization and have been demanded by courts disturbed by the external consequences of traditional zoning.

b. Customary state zoning-enabling legislation has conferred authority for the division of the municipality into districts of such number, shape and area as may be deemed best suited to promote the public health, safety and welfare with consideration of the structures to be permitted, the agriculture, forestry, protective-greenbelt, recreation, residence, industry, trade, conservation and other uses to be permitted or prohibited according to the character of the district, its peculiar use suitability, property values, and the general trend and kind of building and property development.

c. Ordinances enacted under this authority must be reasonable and will be judicially presumed so unless a challenger shows clear and satisfactory evidence of invalidity. Among the factors influencing a determination of reasonableness are the uses and zoning of nearby property, the extent property values are diminished by the proposed restrictions (although substantial diminution of the value of the protester's property is rarely determinative standing alone), the benefits sought to be obtained, the relative gain to the public as compared with the hardship to the land-owner, and the property's suitability for the zoned uses. The ordinance will thus be tested as it relates to the particular property in question. As is the case with police-power regulation in general, judicial view of appropriate zoning objectives has expanded to include aesthetic concepts. But when the ordinance exceeds the difficult-to-articulate bounds of reasonableness, it will be invalidated as confiscatory.

§ 6. Rezoning. Rezoning, as we have seen, is actually the enactment of ordinances amending the original zoning ordinances. The power to enact includes the power to amend. As such, rezoning will similarly be accorded a presumption of reasonableness and judged by the same standards as was the original.

a. It should be recalled that occasionally local procedures will require adherence to the master plan or passage by an extraordinary majority of the council. It should also be noted that at least one jurisdiction (Maryland) applies to the rezoning-ordinance test of reasonableness the requirement of showing that the circumstances have changed substantially or that there was an original mistake.

b. The often used terms "spot zoning" and "strip zoning" refer respectively to rezonings which seem to single out a small parcel of land for use or uses different from the surrounding

[*173*]

area, seemingly on behalf of one owner, and to rezonings for commercial purposes, one lot deep, along arterial roads, both to the detriment of the public. The terms are really epithets, descriptive rather than legal. Neither rezoning is ipso facto unreasonable although it may be more vulnerable. The fact that one property or one owner is benefited is not in and of itself determinative.

§ 7. Zoning Devices: Euclidean, Floating, Conditional, Contract, and Cluster, Planned Unit Development. In addition to the question of reasonableness, zoning and rezoning ordinance challenges often raise the questions of unauthorized or illegal action. This is particularly true where modern modifications of traditional zoning devices have been used.

a. The traditional, district-and-use form of zoning ordinance most clearly conforming to the enabling legislation summarized above and to that approved in the seminal U.S. Supreme Court case, *Village of Euclid* v. *Ambler Realty*, 272 U.S. 365 (1926), is known as euclidean zoning. It envisions the specification of determined geographic areas separated according to zoning districts with the uses permitted in each district set forth in the ordinances. Thus, a property owner could from the zoning map determine in what type of district the property was located and by reference to the district's restrictions what uses are permitted.

b. Some jurisdictions have attempted under traditional enabling legislation to bypass the inflexibility of the assumed mapped-district concomitant and to avoid the vulnerability of spot zoning by creating what are popularly known as floating zones. This device envisions the creation of exceptional use districts to allow establishment of small tracts for such uses as shopping centers, garden apartments, light industry or marine recreational centers. At the time of ordinance approval of the use districts, they are unlocated but will be located upon petition of a landowner whose desire to so use his land is administratively deemed reasonable in light of the realities of land development in the community. The applicant's land will be reclassified for the floating use. These floating zones differ from traditional ordinance-approved special exceptions in that the latter apply only to a particular district. The ordinance provisions are carefully drawn to require minimum qualifying acreage and to insure through specified restrictive conditions minimal deleterious impact upon the surrounding area. Judicial reaction has been mixed. The persistent challenges to the validity of floating zones illustrate the staying power of euclidean zoning and the instinctive, alternative-limiting vision of zoning enabling authority as synonymous with euclidean methodology. Challenges to authority have been accompanied by assertions of improper delegation with vague standards as to location, of usurpation of the proper power to grant variances, and of invidious spot zoning denying equal protection.

c. Commonly, at rezoning hearings, proponents will submit descriptive materials and visual aids so as to enhance the chance of success by creating an aesthetically satisfying (even exciting) picture of what the rezoned use will resemble. Often, after rezoning is granted, the resultant use will bear little resemblance to the hearing's blandishments. Recently, two devices have been used in attempts to bind the successful applicant to the rezoning "inducements." One, conditional zoning, requires state authorization and permits very specific restrictions of the kind set forth in the statute to be imposed upon the landowner as a condition of full realization of the benefit of the rezoning.

The other, contract zoning, involves the rezoning of a property to a less restrictive zoning classification subject to an agreement by the landowner to observe certain specified limitations on the uses and physical development of the property that other properties in the zone do not have to observe. This device is used particularly in dealing with property located in a more restrictive zone but on the borderline of the less restrictive zone, for which classification the rezoning is sought. The agreed conditions would be contained in an option agreement allowing the city to

[*176*]

purchase some of the limited land, thus giving a dominant estate allowing city enforcement of the conditions for the term of the option. Again, judicial reaction has been mixed with some courts disturbed by the apparent bargaining away of governmental power or the lack of authorization in euclidean enabling statutes, while others conclude that since the rezoning can be tested in its own right, the additional conditions merely amount to a benefit to the community.

Opponents of conditional and contract zoning contend that such devices will make it easier for councils to act favorably upon rezoning applications they would otherwise (and ought to) have rejected, thereby undermining the stability of zoning. Proponents see little stability to undermine.

d. Among the more recent devices, none seems more currently popular than the Planned Unit Development (PUD) and its residential cousin, the cluster zone. The devices are popular with some jurisdictions because they may permit future development to accommodate the social and economic housing and environmental needs that would otherwise be unpalatable to, or economically difficult for, communities and developers. They are popular with builders and developers because they permit higher density use of land if open space is made available, thus allowing more rational and profitable allocation of the land available to the builder or developer.

Density zoning requires state enabling legislation. Under this device, the city council determines what percentage of a particular district must be devoted to open space on or above ground and what percentage may be used by building units. The task of mixing in specific locations in the particular district the density and open spaces devolves upon the planning commission or other administrative authority working in conjunction with the developer. The latter will submit a series of plans and seek approval to go forward at each stage.

(i) In cluster and business-district PUD zoning, the ultimate goal envisions no greater over-all density than that basic to the zoning district if no density increase were permitted. The approved density increases result in more open space. (The jurisdictions' answers to whether the open space must be dedicated to the public or can be the development's private recreation areas are not uniform.)

(ii) In the more far-reaching PUD density concept, the goal is a self-contained mini-community, built within a zoning district, under density and use rules controlling the relation of private dwellings to open space, of homes to commercial establishments and other uses, and of high income dwellings to low and moderate income housing.

[*178*]

For example, a PUD ordinance might provide for single family attached or detached dwellings; apartments, accessory private garages; public or private parks and recreational areas including golf courses, swimming pools, ski slopes, etc., so long as they do not result in noise, glare, odor, or air pollution detrimental to existing or prospective adjacent structures; public buildings; schools; churches; professional offices; certain types of signs; a theater (but not of the drive-in type); hotels and motels; and dining facilities.

The ordinance would, for example, specify that the PUD may have a maximum of eighty percent of its land devoted to residential uses; a maximum of twenty percent to commercial uses and enclosed recreational facilities; and a minimum of twenty percent to open spaces. Residential density provisions would limit the number of units per acre, height, proximity, and the number of units in permitted town house structures.

(iii) Related to the far-reaching PUD density concept is the new town, an idea as old as the original company towns, as successful as the Roosevelt administration's Greenbelt, Maryland, and the more recent, privately developed Reston, Virginia, and Columbia, Maryland, and in both England and the United States as complex as anything undertaken in response to urban housing, economic and environmental problems. The concept envisions creation in a new urban entity of a planned, all-use environment, a total live-work-recreate community. Although federal assistance has been available, the recent problems of the U.S. economy have so exacerbated the financing and other difficulties that many of these experiments have been unsuccessful. The future of the idea and of government assistance is unpredictable.

(iv) Density zoning may also be one of the elements of an employment and economic improvement package known as an enterprise zone. The creation of such zones has been authorized by several states and has been undertaken additionally by cities which perceive their customary power delegations as providing the requisite authority. Designed primarily to attract corporate investment to depressed rural and urban areas, the concept will be discussed, infra, in Chapter V.

§ 8. **Flexibility Devices: Exemptions, Accessory Uses, Special Exceptions, Variances, Nonconforming Uses, and Cumulative Zoning.** To allow necessary support services to be located in appropriate areas, and to achieve some flexibility in zoning-ordinance implementation necessary to avoid confiscatory results, there exist a number of exceptional zoning devices which permit individual land uses in apparent non-compliance with the use classifications of the surrounding zone.

a. A number of zoning-enabling statutes expressly exempt, or are interpreted to imply local power to exempt from the operation of local zoning ordinances property of paramount governmental units (as defined with the inconsistency described in the Chapter I discussion of the resolution of intergovernmental power disputes), and property of the zoning government itself, generally limiting such exemptions to property used in the performance of governmental rather than proprietary functions whether such use be by the government directly or by private parties to whom the property is leased. Sometimes, the exemption, not expressed in the zoning ordinances, will result from a judicial decree that a municipality is not subject to zoning restrictions in the performance of its governmental functions. Under such exemptions, municipalities have been permitted to construct fire houses and pollution-combatting sewage disposal plants in "Residence A" districts.

b. There are a number of ways in which permission may be obtained specially to use property otherwise governed by the zoning ordinance. The applicant may seek a permit for an accessory use, a special or conditional use or exception, or a variance. Occasionally local jurisdictions or the courts confuse the standards applicable to each such status. Frequently, one jurisdiction will list as a permitted accessory use what another will classify as a permitted special exception. Occasionally, generic standards governing administra-

[*181*]

tive determinations in the accessory and special use areas, particularly where the contemplated uses are not listed, will result in judicial declaration of improper delegation. Our present discussion will present each as a discrete device for exceptional use, recognizing that the subject of the permit or the standards governing its grant will not always be classified with the same clarity.

c. Municipal zoning ordinances regularly permit the carrying on of accessory uses. While some uses denominated "accessory" are allowed to occur as incidental to the primary use, others may be similarly labelled "accessory" but may be listed in the ordinance and require special exception permits. We shall treat the latter as special exceptions. A "permission assumed" accessory use is variously defined as one secondary to the primary use, one auxiliary to the primary use, one so customarily incident and so necessary or commonly to be expected that it cannot be supposed that the ordinance was intended to prevent it. When the use is of such a nature or extent as to impair the character of the neighborhood, it will be assumed that the ordinance was intended to prevent it. Much litigation is involved, particularly with respect to residential zones. It may be illustrative to compare doghouses, ham radio antennae and private religious, educational, cultural and recreational activities with kennels, loudspeakers, multiple person professional offices and

[*182*]

spotlight systems for night recreation, although predicting the outcome of accessory use litigation is risky.

d. For the sake of clarity, we shall refer to those "accessory uses" which are specified and defined in zoning ordinances as exceptions. For example, residential zoning will frequently permit customary home occupations (piano teaching, e.g.) and those of a recognized profession, often listing doctors, dentists, lawyers, accountants, engineers, veterinarians, etc. Such provisions will often limit the number of participating professionals to those actually residing in the dwelling. Some will limit the number of clients, patients or pupils. Some will expressly forbid medical or dental clinics. What is said here about uses also covers accessory structures such as garages and fences. What may distinguish this category of exception from the accessory uses above, may be the requirement of a permit. What distinguishes both from the exceptional categories that follow is that the former uses must be subordinate in fact to the primary use of the property. When the accessory use, even though permissible in theory, becomes the paramount use of the property, termination will be ordered and appropriate penalties will follow failure then to observe the zoning ordinances.

e. Applicants may seek special exception status, i.e., may apply for conditional use, special use or special exception permits. Such permits are designed to meet the problem which arises where certain uses, although generally compatible with the basic use classification of a particular zone, should not be permitted to be located as a matter of right in every area included within the zone because of hazards inherent in the use itself or special problems which its proposed location may present (traffic, noise, smell, etc.). Standards should govern permit approval and the ordinances frequently list the exceptional uses. Examples are churches, schools, philanthropic homes and hospitals in residential zones, gasoline stations and shopping centers in commercial zones. Exceptions may include structural conditions (height, density) as well as the type of activity. Special uses or exceptions differ from variances in that the former are compatible with, supportive of, and permitted in the zone where they will be most effective and least detrimental, while the latter are prohibited uses, allowed for undue hardship reasons.

f. The history of zoning is replete with charges of maladministration, favoritism, etc., contributing to an image local government finds hard to change. One of the most frequently criticized aspects is the grant of variances. The variance device is easy to describe but extremely difficult to administer. In virtually all jurisdictions, uses which are prohibited in the particular zone may be permitted with appropriate protective conditions if enforcement of the ordinance upon the landowner in question would cause practical difficulty or unnecessary hardship, and this standard has been upheld as sufficient guidance. The factors which govern the determination are, and the applicant is required to demonstrate that:

(i) The property could not yield a reasonable return if used only for the permitted purposes (although increase or decrease in value alone is not determinative);

(ii) The problem of the owner reflects unique circumstances and not conditions common to the neighborhood which would reflect upon the reasonableness of the ordinance in general;

(iii) The use sought will not change the nature of the local area;

(iv) The variance will be "in harmony" with the comprehensive zoning plan; and

(v) The variance will not seriously impair the public health, safety, morality or welfare.

So, for example, a variance might be possible for a residential landowner who, to meet zoning requirements, would otherwise have to build a dwelling ninety feet long by ten feet wide, where allowance of less open space would not markedly differ from houses built in the neighborhood prior to the ordinance. The court's decision (and that of the board of zoning appeals) might be other-

h. Related to the matter of non-conforming uses is the question of cumulative zoning. As we have seen, zoning principles have long been premised upon the establishment of districts—single family ("highest" or "most restrictive"), multi-family, commercial or business, light industry, medium industry and heavy industry ("lowest" or "least restrictive"). In the early years of zoning, ordinances permitted cumulative uses, i.e., more restrictive uses were permitted in less restrictive districts—a house next to the factory. In the decades following World War II, the ascendancy of planning was accompanied by noncumulative zoning ordinances which prohibited the more restrictive uses in less restrictive zones. This in turn aggravated the matter of non-conforming uses.

Recently, the pendulum has begun its reverse swing. Planners have moved beyond pure, map-located districts to statements of use-relation. Industrial and environmental-protection technology has resulted in some zoning which permits the location of industry to be determined not on the basis of what is manufactured, but rather in accordance with that industrial concern's ability to meet the "higher" district's aesthetic, health and safety standards. And the growth of use-mix and density concepts such as the PUD and cluster zoning have effected a modification in exclusive district thinking.

[*188*]

of inadequate units. Condominium-conversion
moratoriums have been enacted and new municipal regulation of the economics of income-producing land is being explored.

There are more than five thousand building
codes operative thoughout the country, with innu-
merable differences in standards. Many code enactments have adopted the proposed codes of
such organizations as the National Fire Insurance
Underwriters. But city councils have been unable, or because of the pressures of various interests, unwilling to keep pace with technological
change. The alternative of delegating to building
inspectors under generic "public health" and
"safety" standards authority to keep pace with
technological change and to approve or disapprove construction techniques and quality and
newly developed materials may, some would argue, be an improper delegation leaving too much
discretion to the building inspectors. As the
building industry expands beyond local boundaries, the variety in standards is alleged to combine with the antiquated technological burdens of
individual codes to produce substantially higher
housing costs than are necessary. In addition,
the police-power regulations have focused more
intensively on environmental protection in construction, prohibiting open burning and requiring
such measures as underground utilities, drainage,
dredging and bulkheading, safety rules, wetland

protection, grading erosion and silt control, tree
protection, storm sewers and water run-off promotion, together with the lot size and open space
requirements mentioned earlier. Although some
studies dispute the conclusion, the cost of conforming to the building codes and the environmental regulations is said to have combined with
rising labor and material costs to price housing
out of the low and medium markets. As a result,
those who need low and medium cost housing are
turning more and more to mobile homes, and municipalities have had to come to grips with the
traditional zoning pariah, the trailer park.

§ 11. Challenges to Land-Use Restrictions. a.
While there has been more involvement by the
state courts and some lower federal courts, substantial judicial deference has historically been
accorded local zoning and land-use restrictions in
large part because they are the results of the exercise of the government's legislative authority,
whether by council enactment, ordinances approved by referenda, or popular initiative (despite
some dissenting arguments that rezoning should
be considered "quasi-judicial"). The early zoning-
legislation decisions of the U.S. Supreme Court
set the tone and, while the Court generally avoided land-use-regulation issues for some time, its
recent reentry into the field has served to underscore deference (standing to challenge, necessity
of proof of intent as well as discriminatory im-

pact, one-family residence limitations, historic and
landmark preservation, urban renewal, location
of "adult" enterprises, absence of a compensable
taking, e.g.). Such judicial deference also serves
to recognize that government "hardly could go on
if to some extent values incident to property
could not be diminished without paying for every
such change in the general law."

   b. From the beginning, land-use regulation
has necessarily involved a mixture of public social
and economic values and specific-property economic consequences. Courts and legislatures
have become increasingly sensitive to the substantial social and economic impact and have a
much more sophisticated awareness of protect-
able social values and, to a somewhat lesser degree, of economic consequences and remedies.
Like the police power generally, as we have noted, the land-use power exercise will normally be
challenged on the ground that it violates such
rights protected by state or federal constitutions
as the first-amendment freedoms, the due-process
requirements of reasonableness and reasonable
means-to-ends relationship and the demands of
equal protection, or that the virtually inevitable,
substantial diminution in property value as restricted—the cost of compliance—is so confiscatory as to render the municipal action invalid. The
courts have to resolve the resultant tension

among social and economic values in declaring the action valid or invalid.

c. Where the conflict is among competing public and individual social values (in a setting of economic consequences, as with all land-use disputes), the courts apply customary, evolving police-power jurisprudence to approve or invalidate appropriate or impermissible limitations (who may and who may not be excluded from one-family residence living, e.g.). Where, however, the tension is between the social or economic value to the public and dramatic economic diminution to the specific property owner, the blurring of the local government's regulatory and taking powers and the increased understanding of the economic consequences of regulation have invoked the necessity of difficult judicial line-drawing. An attack on the validity of a police-power exercise, as noted above, is likely to be framed in terms of declaratory or injunctive relief. Increasingly, however, property owners will add an attempt to be paid for the diminution in value. Those actions, styled "inverse condemnation" (action to recover the value of property assertedly taken by the government defendant although it has not formally exercised the power of eminent domain) under local procedures or in federal courts, for example under 42 U.S.C. § 1983, attempt to "accept" the cost of compliance and seek just compensation for the property right taken (landmark preservation, e.g.). The difficulty of demarcating a noncompensable regulation and a compensable taking is occasionally increased by municipal coupling of regulatory efforts with ameliorating fiscal arrangements such as transferable development rights (see Chapter IV).

d. Judicial analysis will, of course, require that the legislative objective of the challenged ordinance be appropriate and that the means be reasonable. But this does not necessarily resolve the taking question because, as we shall see in Chapter IV, such an objective might support exercise of the government's eminent-domain authority to take formally and compensate. Otherwise legitimate government regulatory action which imposes a burden on one individual that in fairness should be diffused among the entire community will be held to be a taking and in the appropriate action the government will be required to compensate him for his loss. The courts have been unable to design a "set formula." Rather, they have favored ad hoc explorations of the facts before them. Thus, in regulatory "takings," the consequent balancing process requires a specific factual determination that the whole community, rather than the individual property owner, should assume the costs. The alleged deprivation of property may be permanent or temporary, complete or partial, affecting one or more of the bundle of rights incident to property ownership. The fact of a severe burden does not necessarily indicate a taking in the constitutional sense; the severity of the impairment begins, not ends, the analysis. The regulation must deny all use or an essential use of the property. Substantial decline in market value or loss of the highest and best use is an insufficient basis to support a taking conclusion. Resolution of the question also depends on the economic impact of the intrusion, the degree of interference with investment-backed financial expectations (but see height limits resulting in ninety-five percent diminution in value and restrictive landmark preservation, e.g.) and on the physical rather than the purely regulatory nature of the invasion. No one of these factors is determinative and none is paramount. (Compare noncompensable physical intrusion by unusual noise and truck detritus, allowed by variance, and noncompensable eighty-percent diminution in property value resulting from mining regulation, with compensable permanent physical occupation of the space necessary to wire for cable TV.)

In sum, when airport and other uses by the government of its own property and action "in an enterprise capacity" are distinguished, when irremediable, physical, trespassory invasions are not involved, the cases demonstrate that the balancing rarely results in imposing the costs of taking-compensation upon government's wide discretion in providing better balanced and more attractive communities. The courts favor declaratory and injunctive relief invalidating the regulation which is so confiscatory rather than ordering compensation for a taking; and the courts are so respectful of regulatory efforts that their status as "confiscatory" is rarely the conclusion. We shall discuss just compensation in Chapter IV.

§ 12. "Exclusionary Zoning." The issue in land use regulation may not simply be whether the individual property owner or the regulating community should bear the cost of a social objective. As federal and state courts have recognized more clearly the external consequences of local land-use regulation and the broader societal objectives thereby impacted, they have been persuaded to impose upon the regulator as well as the regulated the obligation and, hence, the cost of giving greater priority to regional considerations than to local objectives. As noted earlier, increasing housing costs have led (together with high vacation costs) to a resurgence of mobile homes and trailer parks. Ironically, it was a dissent to a decision upholding what was in effect a municipality's total exclusion of trailer parks which gave seminal judicial impetus to zoning reformers' complaints of "exclusionary zoning."

a. Although all zoning ordinances are in many senses exclusionary, the term has come to characterize ordinances challenged as unreasonable and

[*199*]

invalid in that they serve to erect exclusionary walls on the municipality's boundary, according to local selfishness for socially improper goals, beyond the legitimate purpose of zoning. In recent years, courts have become sensitive to exclusionary walls and unfavorable judicial reaction has played an increasingly great role in the growth decisions of municipalities throughout the country.

The issues involve different classes of municipalities. Some have experienced sizeable recent population growth and are grappling with the problem of increased demand on support services. Others see increased growth on the horizon and wish to assimilate the growth and support-service expansion in coordinated phases. Yet others desire to retain their existing character and resist change. Many of the desires are neither whimsical nor improperly selfish. Some are, and are masked in terms of customary police-power objectives. All, if implemented, may contribute to the present unavailability of low and medium cost housing, and deny owners' wishes to use their property. The absence of effective regional planning and land use control serves to aggravate the balkanized existing social and economic land use patterns.

b. In responding to the growth-no-growth debate, municipal legislatures have decreed rezoning moratoriums and have engaged in downzon-

[*200*]

ing of presently undeveloped land to defuse development pressures (sometimes with sale of transferable development rights for use elsewhere in the community), have enacted numerical limitations on the city's population, have retained or imposed restrictive minimum lot-size, floor-space, bedroom-component, open-space, parking, and housing-code requirements and have defined tightly the residential qualifications in single family zones.

c. The challengers frequently are the landowners (or option holders) who wish to develop the land profitably but whose profitable development (one acre homesites, medium cost garden apartments, recreational homes, e.g.) is allegedly unreasonably prevented by the ordinances. Less frequently, where rules of standing allow, challenges come from nonprofit organizations which are developing property for the benefit of minorities or economically deprived persons and from the potential beneficiaries themselves. The "exclusionary" ordinances are said to be unreasonable in that there are other solutions available for the problems they seek to resolve without depriving those who would be affected by the zoning of housing opportunities, the right to travel, freedom of association, and privacy.

d. Many courts are sensitive not only to the property rights of the landowner, but to the needs of those who benefit from the growth that

[*201*]

would otherwise be restricted, whether the beneficiaries are parties to the case or not. It would
not be unexpected for courts to invalidate
moratoriums which freeze a landowner's ability
to seek a profitable property use without some
municipal commitment to the completion of necessary planning and decision-making within a reasonably brief period of time. Nor is it at all
surprising that courts which discerned unconsti-
tutionally discriminatory motivation and effect
would invalidate denials of public housing permits which would allow such housing to be located not only in black-citizen areas but also in
white-citizen areas appropriately zoned, and a
designation of parkland and a moratorium on
subdivisions which served to block a planned low
income housing project. But the courts have also
become sensitized to the subtler and more pervasive effect of no-growth efforts. While federal
constitutional violation requires proof of intent as
well as impact, courts in urbanizing areas may
define reasonableness to include awareness of external impact. Deference to municipal legislation
is seen as abdication when the external consequences are a burden thrown on other communities by the erection of a protective wall which
"denies, rather than plans for the future." Property values, increased tax burdens, water and
sewage demands, and the customary aesthetic arguments have not overcome judicial insistence
that the wall not be built.

e. Not all exclusionary ordinances are invalid and unreasonable, however. It would appear that wall building which directly and intentionally infringes upon constitutional rights (equal protection, travel) without compelling justification and wall building in the face of imminent societal need by communities at least partially in a position to meet that need will be invalidated. The likelihood of urbanization and the imminence of societal need may be liberally determined. For example, in disapproving an exclusionary zoning ordinance under its state constitution, the New Jersey Supreme Court had defined the in-state region of suburban growth and imposed upon the locality the obligation of meeting its "fair share" of the region's low- and moderate-income housing needs. Upon reexamination of its premises in the face of a national economic downturn, the court deemed detailed explication necessary. Expanding the geographic scope to every community any portion of which is designated by the state development guide as a growth area, the court stated that good faith without results would be irrelevant. In addition to changing planning laws, municipalities must provide zoning and tax incentives, and federal-aid-request assistance to developers, must require developers to include low- and moderate-income units in upper-income projects, or must do what it takes to have such housing built. Mobile homes should not be excluded unless sound planning so dictates and fair-share compliance can be just as effectively achieved without them.

Certain state-designated, non-growth areas (agricultural, coastal zone, e.g.) are not implicated in the New Jersey ruling. Moreover, its statewide impact may not be replicated elsewhere, especially where rapid urbanization is unlikely. Thus, where a community is at least temporarily resisting the growth of recreational second homes, or is retaining the benefits of rural location and ambience and is not in the reasonably foreseeable path of marching suburbanization, the judgment of the municipal legislature will still be fairly debatable. And while over-all population growth ceilings may be seen as unduly restrictive, residence-use definitional limitations which do not discriminate among related persons and which are seen as avoiding over-crowding, traffic-producing conditions disruptive of the character of a zoned district not otherwise challenged may be upheld.

f. The burgeoning population does present real problems, however. Whatever planning and foresight were lacking in the past, more and more communities are facing development pressures likely to overwhelm existing support services, resulting in overcrowded schools, sewage pollution and the like. To resist the growth because of tax burdens is probably impossible. To forestall it through moratorium and down-zoning techniques without more will probably not be tolerated. Thus, while some have been precluded by strict, judicial, Dillon's-Rule analysis, other communities have adopted, and many more are contemplating, timed-growth ordinances which tie permitted growth to the completion of necessary capital facilities and other support services. Land in the meantime is zoned more restrictively. Recent judicial approval suggests that such ordinances will be upheld where they do not cloak no-growth intent, i.e., where the plan calls for some low and medium cost housing; where it projects completion or provision of support services according to a specified time schedule which itself does not delay all land uses or owner-preferred ones to the point of confiscation; where it permits landowner acceleration of support availability through voluntary contribution; and where property tax assessments reflect present use restrictions—where in sum the court can presently infer that within a reasonable time the subject property will be put to the owner-desired use at an appreciated value.

CHAPTER IV

ACQUISITION, LIMITATIONS ON USE, AND DISPOSITION OF GOODS, SERVICES AND PROPERTY

As with the other local governing powers, the powers to acquire, use and dispose of goods, services and property must find their source either expressly or by implication in state authorization through constitutional home-rule clauses and specific or general state statutory provisions. Exercise of the powers will also be subject to state and federal constitutional protections and to the limitations in the local governing entity's charter.

Our discussion of acquisition will focus primarily on purchase and on taking under eminent domain, both of which must serve a public purpose or permit a public use. Central to purchasing are municipal contracts. Our discussion thereof will nevertheless recognize that the contract has many municipal uses in addition to purchasing such as leases, contracts in connection with zoning and intergovernmental agreements. We shall additionally see some aspects of acquisition by gift, dedication, adverse possession and prescription and user.

To illustrate the number of limitations which may be imposed upon municipal use of property

[*206*]

by constitutions, statutes, charters and the common law, we shall focus upon nuisance uses, limitations incident to the manner of acquisition and civil and constitutional rights.

The discussion of disposition of goods and property (again often a matter of municipal contracts) will include actions affecting uses of property (franchises, e.g.) and transfers or loss of title (sale, e.g.).

It bears repeating, as noted in Chapter I, that the exemption from federal antitrust laws for state actions which are anticompetitive in nature does not, without more, apply to municipal activity which is alleged to be anticompetitive in violation of those laws. To be exempt, the municipal action must be implementative of clearly articulated, affirmatively expressed state policy. It must be authorized by something more than the often customary generic authorizations or the implications of home rule and, at least where private parties are involved, monitored or supervised. Judicial recognition of possible municipal antitrust liability for its activities or those in which it joins with private parties, whether labelled governmental or proprietary, has resulted in a rapid escalation of such claims. Illustrative of their potential reach are occupational licensing and regulation, operation of sports and convention facilities, zoning and rezoning, urban development, award of franchises, operation of garbage collection services, transportation services (including taxicab monopolies, transit systems, airports, and parking lots), and the provision of utility services. While courts have found appropriate authorization for some municipal activity alleged to be anticompetitive, and have found several other instances where the exemption could not be extended to the challenged activity, the issue of the municipality's exemption is, of course, not synonymous with the question of its ultimate liability under the antitrust laws, a much more difficult matter for the plaintiffs. If liability is found, there remains the question whether customary remedies such as treble damages are appropriately awarded against the municipality. (Federal Congressional efforts to restrict local liability are expected.) The state exemption, and where merited, the local exemption are not always applicable. For example, the Robinson-Patman Act does not exempt from its proscriptions the sale of pharmaceutical products to state and local government hospitals for resale in competition with private pharmacies.

A. ACQUISITION BY CONTRACT

§ 1. **Introduction.** a. General principles of the law of contracts govern determination of the existence, interpretation, and enforcement of municipal contracts. Additionally, customary principles of implied contracts and of quasi-contractual relief and restitution may govern municipal relationships with others. While a municipality may not irresponsibly repudiate its obligations, there are many restrictions peculiarly pertinent to municipal contracting having their source in common law, constitution, statutes and charters, violation of which may render a contract void, voidable or unenforceable in some manner. The issue will arise because an attempted municipal contract is challenged as invalid by a municipal citizen with proper standing (see Chapter VI), or, because, while the contract is invalid, either the municipality or the other party may nevertheless be seeking quasi-contractual relief or restitution.

In such situations, courts will speak of the attempted contract as being ultra vires (sometimes adding "primarily" or "secondarily"), or "specifically prohibited by law," or against public policy, or illegal, or infra vires but entered into in a defective manner. The significance of such classifications may be seen in the resultant relief that is afforded. If the original contract will not be enforced, can it have been ratified? Will the municipality be estopped to deny the agreement's validity? Is quasi-contractual relief available? May the municipality or the private party recover what it has transferred in accordance with the invalid contract? Apparently inconsistent use of these classifications or labels and answers to such questions as the availability of quasi-contractual relief may stem from the underlying judicial, requirement-enforcement objectives in the particular cases. Some courts are merely imitative in the unquestioning application of debatable precedent. Other courts are attempting to give substance to the protections which were ignored, sometimes to the point of penalizing the participants while guarding the interests of the taxpayers in general. Of the latter courts, while some will feel the necessity to label the attempted contract ultra vires or the like in order to achieve this goal, others will deny requested relief without regard to the label. Increasingly, many courts have enforced the taxpayer protections by invalidating the purported contract but have not deprived the parties of at least quasi-contractual relief.

b. For example, let us suppose that the city of Allgood had let the contract for construction of the superstructure of the domed stadium without first advertising for bids as required by its state's law. Assume that at the prescribed times for compensation of the contractor under the agreement, the city refused to pay. At some point, work would be terminated and the construction firm would sue. Its goals would be enforcement of the contract, either as initially executed or as ratified, or declaration that the city was estopped to deny its validity, or failing that, payment of such sums as would reflect the unjust enrichment of the city which gained advantage from the firm's labor and materials.

The court has a number of choices. It cannot declare the original contract valid or allow ratification of it since in both instances, the citizens would not have received the protection of the bid requirements. If work had proceeded to an advanced stage and there were other acts by the city which misled the contractor, the court might hold that the doctrine of estoppel prevented the city from denying the validity of the contract finding that the evidence supported the conclusion that the construction firm justifiably relied to its detriment. The court could declare the contract invalid but could order the city to compensate the construction firm for its labor and materials in an amount reflecting the benefit by which the city was unjustly enriched or the costs to the construction firm. If the court in so deciding the case was troubled by the labels, it could choose to find that the city was empowered to enter into such contracts but entered into the contract in a defective or illegal manner.

On the other hand, the court could be persuaded to be concerned with municipal illegality and extravagance. It could conclude that to give any relief would be to undermine the safeguards designed to protect the taxpayer. This might be especially likely if there were evidence of bad faith. It would therefore declare that those who contract with the city are charged with knowledge of the limits of the city's authority and that those who fail to observe those limits must suffer the consequences. Again, if the court felt it necessary to underscore denial of relief with the appropriate label, it could decide that the bid-less contract was against public policy, or was specifically prohibited, or that the city only had the power to enter into such contracts when they were preceded by bids and had thus acted ultra vires.

c. For those who desire predictability in this area, precedent is, of course, a significant factor. The evidentiary "smell" of fraud or bad faith is also a significant factor. While many commentators argue that there are other remedies and that the courts should not intermix principles of quasi-contractual relief and individual penalties, the degree of egregiousness surrounding the soiling of the parties' hands in failing to observe municipal limitations will continue to play a determinative role in the outcome.

§ 2. **Authority to Contract.** a. Accordingly, the basic question is whether the municipality was empowered to enter into the contract. General authority to contract is uniformly available and specific statutory authorizations abound. As in other power contexts, the courts will be interpreting express powers and those to be necessarily or fairly implied, and the outcome will often

[*212*]

turn on the court's liberality of interpretation. Illustratively, a court upheld the purchase by the city of a senior citizens' recreation and residence property in a resort city in another state, finding authority in state constitutional clauses which permitted "all works which involve the public health or safety" and public works "within or without its corporate limits," and in a borrowing-enabling statute which referred to housing facilities and public improvements within or without the city's corporate limits.

b. A contract which is declared ultra vires, because there is no authority therefor in any sense, or because the contract is specifically prohibited, or because the ignored manner of contracting is deemed central to the existence of the power to contract, will be void. Since there is no authority to contract, there is no authority to adopt or ratify the agreement and a contract in fact cannot be implied. The ultra vires determination may result as well in refusal to apply estoppel or to grant quasi-contractual relief lest the result be to enable the municipality to do indirectly what it cannot do directly.

§ 3. **Conflict of Interest.** a. Our earlier discussion of provisions designed to assure the integrity and undivided loyalty of municipal officials alluded to the invalidation of municipal contracts attended by the appearance of conflict of interest, and to laws subjecting to criminal penalty officials and employees who, while associated with the municipality or (sometimes) during a specified period thereafter, contract with, or acquire financial interests in contracts with, their local government. Such contracts are considered at common law to be against public policy and in addition are specifically prohibited by statute or charter in many jurisdictions. Prohibited are contracts in which a member of the government or an officer of the municipality is in a conflict-of-interest position, without regard to the fairness of the contract to the municipality, or the level of involvement or recusation of the member or officer, whether or not influence was actually exercised. In some jurisdictions, a conflict of interest of a municipal employee will suffice to invalidate if the employee could possibly influence the award of the contract.

b. Such contracts will be deemed either void or voidable at the option of the city. The judicial application spectrum ranges from a few decisions validating contracts where the affected person's vote was not controlling, to several decisions extending the debilitating interest to ones remote and indirect, and not necessarily financial in nature.

c. Here, as in connection with other restrictions on the power to contract, there arises the problem of an emergency. Conceivably, a municipal official might be in a unique position to ren-

[*214*]

der services or provide products needed to assist the government in meeting a sudden emergency for which, through no fault of its own, it was unprepared. Some courts have upheld municipal contracts in such circumstances. Equally conceivable are attempts by the local government to bypass contract protections by responding to debatable emergencies or to undoubted emergencies which arise because the government has negligently failed to deal with the problem until it was too late. Accordingly, to avoid multiplication of exceptions devouring the rule, other courts have ruled contracts invalid even if there were a real emergency. And even those courts which recognize the exception insist that the fact of emergency is subject to judicial review.

d. Because conflict-of-interest contracts are specifically prohibited by many jurisdictions' statutes, or will be deemed contrary to public policy, ratification and estoppel will not help to save them. Again, in many jurisdictions, quasi-contractual relief may not be given, although there are cases in other jurisdictions permitting it, especially where, under the applicable law, the contract is voidable rather than void. Here particularly, the egregious nature of the circumstances will play a determinative role.

§ 4. **Other Contracts Against Public Policy.**
a. A number of local government contracts run a sizeable risk of invalidation because they are

[*215*]

deemed to be against public policy. The municipality in defending its refusal to honor the contract or challengers with standing in seeking to
enjoin the contract's implementation or to recover
value given by the city thereunder will attempt to
convince the court that the contract will extend
for an unreasonable length of time; that it will
extend beyond the term of the present governing
body; that it has unfairly or unwisely tied the
hands of the local council's successors; that the
government has agreed to exercise governmental
powers in predetermined ways, or to refrain from
exercising them; that the agreement amounts to
an invalid delegation of legislative power to
others; that there was a conflict of interest; or
that the agreement is intended to achieve some
purpose, such as influencing state legislation,
which under that particular jurisdiction's law is
contrary to public policy. Successful characterization of the contract as being thus against public policy will result in its invalidation, will bar
ratification, will prevent use of theories of estoppel even if the other party has completely performed, and, as we have seen, will have inconsistent but increasingly less "penalizing" results on
the matter of quasi-contractual relief.

b. The question of the contract's duration
may involve a statutory limit (e.g., "no contract
shall extend beyond . . . years unless approved by the electorate at a special election

called for that purpose"). It may also involve judicial sense of what, under the circumstances, is a
reasonable duration. While perpetual agreements without specific state legislative authority
have been invalidated, some rather long durations
have been declared reasonable.

c. The governmental-proprietary dichotomy
pervades this area. Courts are much more likely
to sustain "proprietary" contracts (what are proprietary matters is a question of difficult and indeterminate predictability as we have seen) which
are alleged to contravene the above listed public
policies than they are to uphold "governmental"
ones. For example, a municipal contract contained two provisions pertinent to our discussion.
Under one, the city granted to the other party the
exclusive privilege of buying from the city all wet
garbage collected by the city, to be processed by
the other party into commercial products for his
own profit. He in turn agreed to construct an adequate disposal or processing plant. By the second provision, the city agreed "through passage
and enforcement of appropriate ordinances and
the discharge of the police power of the city" to
provide for the collection of wet garbage in separate containers from trash and other dry refuse
at the source of accumulation.

The garbage processor built the expensive
processing plant. A new city council was elected
and repudiated the contract. The garbage

[*217*]

processor's trustee in bankruptcy sued for damages which included the difference between the cost of construction of the plant and its salvage value, but not including anticipated profits.

The court upheld the first provision but invalidated the second. The two provisions offer an interesting contrast. Garbage disposal can be seen as clearly related to the public health. As such, it can be characterized as a governmental power. If it were so characterized, the court might have been disturbed that the contract was to last for fifteen years and that it was exclusive, thus extending for an unreasonable period of time, beyond the time of the contracting council, and unfairly tying the hands of the successor council.

On the other hand, there is authority for the proposition that garbage disposal is a proprietary matter, a service provided to the corporate members not in the exercise of a share of sovereignty but in lieu of private commercial arrangements. As a proprietary matter, it was an appropriate commercial understanding and did not disable the present or successor councils in their governmental role.

The second provision, however, was clearly an agreement intended to bind the present council and its successors to exercise the police power, the governmental power to regulate citizen conduct (separate trash containers) in a predetermined way. As such, it disabled the governmental function in a manner contrary to public policy.

d. Such challenges to contracts as extending beyond the government's term, tying the hands of successors, agreeing to predetermined manner of governmental power exercise and agreeing to refrain from power exercise are to a large extent different focuses on the same underlying problem. Their outcome is rarely predictable for a number of reasons. First, they may be specifically authorized by state legislation and thus valid. Second, there is the inarticulable line between governmental and proprietary matters. Thus, judicial recognition of practicalities has resulted in approval of teacher and other employment contracts, arbitration provisions, annexation and subdivision agreements, etc., which could only in the most attenuated sense be proprietary. Third, there are decisions which are premised upon the continuing nature of the local governmental entity (especially where councillors have staggered terms) thereby obviating the problem of tying hands or extending beyond the term.

Nevertheless, successful public policy challenges, as noted above, may occasionally preclude even quasi-contractual relief.

§ 5. **Bidding Requirements.** a. While the requirement that municipal contracts be preceded by bids and selection of the lowest responsible bidder is a pervasive one, it does not apply to all

municipal contracts. The requirement does not
exist at common law and must be imposed by constitution, statute or charter. The requirement is,
however, customarily so imposed to guard
against extravagance, favoritism or fraud. Nevertheless, such provisions or judicial interpretations may exempt certain contracts. Illustratively, in many jurisdictions award through the
bidding process is not required for contracts for
some professional services, for services provided
by a legal monopoly, and for particular real estate (sanitary land fills, e.g.) or other items or
services where the courts agree that it is impossible or impracticable to draft specifications which
will satisfactorily and realistically permit competitive bidding.

b. Two significant exceptions divide the
courts. One is the existence of an emergency.
As noted in our earlier discussion, while the
courts insist upon the right to decide whether
there was an emergency in fact, in many jurisdictions municipal response to a real emergency
without adherence to the prescribed bidding process will not be invalidated. In other jurisdictions, to avoid the felt problem of exception devouring the rule, courts will not accept
emergencies, real or imagined, as justification for
non-observance of the bid requirements.

The courts also divide on the question of the
power of the contracting government to arrange

without bids for the original contractor to do additional work required by unforeseen construction problems, or to make minor alterations after awarding the contract, sometimes in emergency circumstances. The statutory provision may itself speak to the matter and its dictates must be followed.

c. Efforts to evade the requirement are not uncommon. In addition to specious emergency declarations, municipalities have attempted to subdivide a large undertaking into smaller individual contracts none of which was large enough to fall within the statutory amount which triggered the bid requirement. Others have attempted arrangements whereby private parties lent funds to the city to accomplish the result desired by both, with later repayment by the city. Such evasory efforts have been rejected by the courts.

d. As noted earlier, the bid requirement may be strictly enforced by the courts and the labels chosen may predict the result of any dispute. The contract may be seen as generically authorized but specifically entered into in an improper manner. Or the generic authority itself may be held to be circumscribed by the bid requirement, and any contract in violation may be deemed ultra vires. Since there are many steps to the bidding process, determination whether the contract is invalid may turn not only on whether the re-

quirement was observed at all, but also on the
manner of compliance with each of the required
steps. Here again, many courts will deem the
procedures mandatory and require strict compliance, while others will hold them to be directory
with substantial compliance satisfactory. The
end result of the labelling will be the invalidation
of any contract found deficient, and, of course,
refusal to recognize attempted ratification. In
many cases, courts have refused to apply estoppel against the city's eleventh-hour challenge to
its contract. Here as elsewhere, quasi-contractual relief is dealt with inconsistently, although, absent egregious circumstances, courts may be
more likely to award it than they would be in connection with the ultra vires contracts, those
against public policy or specifically prohibited, or
those resulting from or accompanying conflicts of
interest.

e. Steps in the bidding process provide several
check points at which the bona fides of the municipality and the competitive compliance by bidders
may be evaluated. The process begins with the
advertisement for bids which must give accurate
notice to prospective bidders of the item or service to be contracted, the specifications to be met,
the working conditions to be observed, prequalifi-
cation of bidders, subcontract specifications and
the like. The specifications must be so designed
as to be sufficiently definite focal points for com-

petitive bidding without at the same time being
so restrictive as to make compliance possible only
by a predetermined, favored bidder. Where the
latter event occurs, it is possible, although difficult, to convince the court that the municipal end
can only be served by an item or service meeting
the restrictive specification. Whether such restrictions as patented items, union manufacture,
local business, or favorable preference to taxpay-
ing bidders may be included is a matter for which
the local laws or cases must be consulted. It is
also a matter which may involve the federal fourteenth amendment's prohibition of discrimination
(racial or alienage grounds, e.g.), impact on the
constitutional right to travel, questions of in-
fringement upon such areas of exclusive federal
control as immigration and foreign trade, the possibility of impact on interstate commerce, statutory requirements preventing use of subcontractors
which invidiously discriminate, and those urging
(or, where permitted, requiring) use of minority
subcontractors.

The bids themselves and the resultant contract
must conform to the advertised specifications.
The bidders may be required to post bonds or
submit deposits and may have to prequalify in accordance with standards governing their financial
capacity and prior experience. (This matter has
substantially hindered expansion of awards to minority contractors and subcontractors although

recent authority supports various exemptions to erase past discrimination.)

Specified procedures will govern the opening and reading of bids. The municipality will customarily reserve the right in its advertisement to reject all bids, lest all bids exceed the city's contemplated expenditure ceiling. If the municipality does not have automatic legislative authority to reject or fails to reserve this right or does not exercise it, it will be required to select the lowest (or highest if a sale of municipal property) responsible bidder, if any is responsible. So long as the municipality chooses the bidder at the lowest submitted cost, most likely in regard to skill, ability and integrity to meet faithfully, conscientiously and promptly the contract's objectives, according to its specifications, the courts will not interfere with the city's discretion.

The bidder who submits the lowest price thus may not be selected if its ability to meet specifications is surpassed by a higher-priced bidder. This low bidder may seek to challenge the award to the other as defective. In several jurisdictions, administrative procedures exist and must be followed. Absent administrative procedures, the low bidder may be unable to challenge in court unless he is a taxpayer in the jurisdiction. In many jurisdictions, only taxpayers have standing to challenge such contracts because the protections are designed to benefit them, not the competing bidder. Some jurisdictions accord standing to the low bidder who is not a taxpayer in order to increase vigilance over municipal contracting.

f. A bidder may suddenly find that its bid is mistakenly low. In the absence of a statutory provision governing mistaken bids, or provision in the advertisement excusing such mistakes, the inevitable acceptance of the bid will impose upon the bidder the obligation of performance, or, failing that, will result in forfeiture of deposits and surety bonds. Customary contract principles apply: a competitive bid is an option based upon the valuable consideration of the privilege of bidding and legally binding assurance to the successful bidder of an award as against all competitors. As such, it is both an offer and a unilateral contract. When accepted, it becomes a mutually binding contract. Some courts will not rescind for such reasons as antecedent arithmetical mistake. Others will do so only if it is shown that the unilateral mistake of fact is so great that to enforce the acceptance would be unconscionable, that the mistake is material, that it happened notwithstanding reasonable care by the bidder, that notice of mistake was prompt, and that rescission would not seriously prejudice the municipality other than by loss of its expected bargain.

[*225*]

§ **6.   Limitations to Assure Citizen Vigilance.**
There is a host of limitations designed to augment citizen vigilance against municipal extravagance.   Included are requirements that a municipal contract (often defined to be one in excess of
a certain sum) be in writing; that it be approved
by ordinance or resolution; that it be voted upon
by the electorate; that it be preceded by appropriations;   that it not exceed the cost estimates
drawn up by municipal engineers or other officials;   and that it be recorded and published.
With occasional variations in situations evoking
the suspicion of bad faith, the courts are more
likely to permit quasi-contractual relief, although
ratification is impossible when the defect involved
conditions precedent.   Deficiencies in these matters are usually deemed to be defects in entering
upon an otherwise authorized contract although
the protections themselves are likely to be
mandatory.   There is some authority permitting
municipalities to bypass such protections in responding to a real emergency.

§ **7.   Agency.**   a.   In many municipal contract
disputes, the courts have indicated that the private contractor acts at his peril and must know
the limits of the municipality's contracting power.
This is particularly the case where the question is
the extent of the authority of municipal personnel
who enter into the agreement.   Persons dealing
with agents of the municipality must be aware of

the authority of such agents; and if their actions are beyond the limits of such authority, the municipality will not be bound.

b. Such contracts may, of course, be ratified by the council or other governmental officer or entity vested by law with the appropriate contracting authority. Courts are not unwilling to find ratification and evidence thereof may include express resolution or circumstances (such as knowledgeable acceptance of benefits) from which the inference of ratification may be drawn.

c. Under customary apparent-authority principles, municipalities have not been allowed to deny authority of their agents when the municipalities have dealt before with the private contractor and others in such a way as to justify the contractor's assumption that the agents possessed the necessary authority.

d. Where municipal agents have exceeded their authority and there has been no ratification, courts are increasingly inclined to permit quasi-contractual recovery, although there remains a number of cases reaching the opposite result.

§ 8. A Note on Some Common Municipal Contract Clauses. Municipal contracts will usually contain a number of clauses to which the contractor must conform. Disputes about such clauses involve the questions whether by law they must be included or whether by law they need not be included. In short, is the municipality authorized (for example, in the exercise of its police power) to require performance in accordance with such clauses and may it waive nonperformance? Illustrative of such clauses are those exacting penalties for late performance; those setting forth labor protections, anti-discrimination provisions, applicable price controls, and contract-dispute settlement and arbitration procedures; those protecting the municipality against liability for personal injury; clauses reserving such rights to the municipality as the right to pay subcontractors; provisions requiring performance bonds and industrial compensation contributions; clauses providing for payment by municipal warrants or coupon bonds; and those limiting municipal contract-cost liability to funds derived from special assessments.

§ 9. Relief and Restitution. As noted above, where a municipal contract is not to be enforced, where an agreement is not to be implied in fact, where estoppel will not be applied, and where ratification will not be allowed, there remain several questions to be resolved. Will quasi-contractual relief be allowed on behalf of the private party? If so, what is the measure of relief? May the municipality and the private party regain what either or both have given up under the alleged contract?

a. Of course, there are many situations not involving the legality of attempted express contracts where customary quasi-contractual principles would impose a duty upon the municipality to compensate a person at whose expense the municipality has been unjustly enriched. Such situations include the wrongful taking of private property or withholding of funds and municipal benefit from another's services or from another's performance of duties imposed upon the municipality. Proof of unjust municipal enrichment is the crux.

b. Where the question involves the invalidity of an attempted contract, we have seen that the results may turn on the nature of the invalidity, on precedent, and on the courts' inclination to "penalize" egregious conduct. It is safe to say, as a general matter, that relief is more possible today than it has previously been but the case-by-case results are nevertheless rather unpredictable.

Where relief is to be granted, the traditional measure has been the value of the benefit to the municipality, however much the costs to the private party may have exceeded that value. Occasionally, the injustice of this measure or the im-

[*229*]

practicability of its determination has compelled courts to award the amount of the costs to and expenditures by the contractor (the contract price less profits), or the reasonable value of the improvement supplied or the cost that would have resulted from municipal observance of the legal requirements, whichever is less.

c. The apparent inconsistency which has accompanied other decisions in this area pervades the matter of city recovery of what it has paid under the attempted contract and of the private contractor's regaining what it has given, in circumstances where the contract will not be enforced. At the poles, results are somewhat predictable. Where an attempted contract is ultra vires, the doctrine's purpose to protect the taxpayer logically commands the return to the city of value given by it pursuant to the attempted contract. And the courts seeking to "penalize" those who fail to observe contract protections, particularly in ultra vires transactions, will refuse to order the municipality to return value given it by the private contractor. In cases where both parties are attempting to reclaim what they have given (where the city has not consumed what it has been given, e.g.), courts tend to conclude that it is unjust to permit the municipality to retain the benefits it has received under the contract and at the same time to recover what it has given to the private contractor.

B. OTHER METHODS OF PROPERTY ACQUISITION: GIFT, DEDICATION, ADVERSE POSSESSION, PRESCRIPTION AND USER

§ 1. **Public Purpose and Methods of Acquisition.** a. As we have seen, the municipal corporation may acquire goods, services and property by contract of purchase. Such purchases are limited to those that serve a public purpose. This limitation, applicable to all municipal expenditures, does not lend itself to precise articulation. Public purpose generally includes all purposes or uses specifically indicated in statutory grants of authority (although some may later be disapproved by the courts) and all those necessary to the proper achievement of the objectives for which the municipal corporation was organized.

b. The public-purpose requirement may also govern future municipal use of property obtained by prescriptive acquisition. While acquisition of property by adverse possession or prescription and user necessarily involves use by the public for the statutory period, future municipal uses may not be relevant to these title disputes. Hence, whether the property *will* be put to a public use is rarely litigated in the disputes concerning such acquisitions.

[*231*]

c. We shall see that a cognate (if not synonymous) limitation, that of public use, applies to acquisition by eminent domain. Such limitation
would also apply to acquisition by lease or by exchange of properties. It is possible that property, goods or services may be given or willed to
the municipality that it in all likelihood would
have been unable to purchase. Acceptance of
such gifts has been sustained by the courts.

d. The dedication device is an appropriation of
land to some public use, intended and made by
the owner of the fee, and accepted for such use
by the municipality. By definition, then, acquisition by this method meets a public use or purpose
requirement. Recall what public purpose must
be met where the city seeks to require dedication,
as in the case of a subdivider, discussed above in
Chapter III.

e. Customarily, municipal corporations, especially the traditional local governments, are authorized to acquire by gift, dedication, prescription and user, frequently by generic delegations.
Property obtained by gift or dedication may be
accompanied by donor conditions and reservations of rights so long as they are constitutional,
reasonable and do not thwart the municipal purposes for which the property is given.

§ 2. Illustration. Let us return to the city of
Allgood. Assume that the city is exploring con-

tingency plans in the event of failure of its extra-territorial domed stadium plan. Assume further that within its boundaries is a large open area presently used for public recreation including playing fields, adjoined by a strip of land presently used by the public as an "alley way." May the field and adjoining strip of land be used for construction of the domed stadium? The answer to this question will turn, inter alia, on whether the city has any title to the areas, how title was obtained, what title it has, and what flexibility it has in determining the uses of municipal property.

§ 3. Estate Obtained: The Fee (Directly or by Implication); Acquisition with Conditions. a. First, the city may hold both properties in fee simple. Under appropriate authority, title could have been obtained outright through purchase, eminent domain, dedication, gift or adverse possession. If the purchase contract satisfied all limitations or if the taking or acceptance of the full fee had been authorized or unobjectionable, and no appropriate conditions or reservations accompanied the acquisition, the city's plan's success would depend upon a court's view of the city's ability to change or expand the use. Whether the stadium constitutes a change in use and whether the city will be held to its original use remain to be determined.

[*233*]

b.   Second, the city may have obtained one or both properties by transfer accompanied by conditions, the effect of which may bar the plan.

c.   Third, the city may conclude that its title was impliedly obtained. Difficulties lie in acquisition of title by implication. Is there sufficient evidence to warrant proper municipal title to the property at all, and particularly title in fee simple? The courts will incline to the private owner's property rights. Accordingly, the burden of establishing title by implication is a heavy one, often expressed as requiring clear and satisfactory evidence, whether acquisition of the fee be alleged to be by adverse possession or implied dedication.

d.   In order to establish title by adverse possession, the city must show actual use by the public for the jurisdiction's prescribed number of years under a claim of right. Such use must be open and notorious. The city must show possession, peaceful control, exclusive, continuous and uninterrupted dominion, without acquiescence by the owner. Where the owner has acquiesced in the use for the prescriptive period, it would be more correct to speak of acquisition by implied dedication.

e.   Implied dedication need not always involve public use for the prescriptive period, however. It requires clear and satisfactory circumstantial evidence of the required elements of any dedica-

[*234*]

tion, viz., the owner's intent to dedicate the property to public use and the city's acceptance thereof. Use by the public alone will not satisfy the evidentiary burden. And merely sporadic city care of the property may not be enough. Of course, the owner's payment of property taxes or special assessments and the like will be detrimental to the city's case.

§ 4. Estate Obtained: Easement. a. Finally, by whatever method of acquisition, the city may have obtained only an easement. For example, it is extremely difficult to imply acquisition of the full fee if the public use to which the property has been put during the period in question could have been accomplished by a lesser estate. What the city may hope to establish as adverse possession may be judicially declared to be prescription and user of the necessary easement with the servient estate reserved to the landowner.

b. The same result may follow a dedication. At common law, dedications which did not say otherwise were deemed to have transferred only an easement. The express dedication may have specified the full fee. Or the dedication may have been accomplished by the filing of plats and maps as required by the city's appropriate subdivision control laws. If Allgood's state statute called for, or were interpreted to permit, dedication of parks and recreational areas or streets in fee simple (rather than the common law ease-

[*235*]

ment) acceptance of the dedication automatically under the statutes, or formally, as by resolution of acceptance or of approval of the subdivision plat, or informally by exercising control (repair and maintenance, e.g.) could have resulted in transfer of the full fee. In the absence of clear expression in the dedication or authorizing statutes, the full fee may not have been transferred.

§ 5. Effect of Estate Obtained and Method of Acquisition Upon Municipal Flexibility. a. What limitations accompany whatever estates the city has acquired? If Allgood had obtained the full fees by any of the means of acquisition, and had in response to the transferor or sua sponte devoted the properties to the playing-fields and passageway uses, it is nevertheless possible that some courts would hold it to the original uses, ruling that the city had "dedicated" the property to those uses, or that the property was held "in trust" on behalf of the public for the particular public uses (particularly if the passageway be deemed a public street). The more likely result, absent any other factors, would be approval of city flexibility.

b. The stadium plans would face more challenging obstacles if the city's title had been obtained in a manner signifying the imposition of a trust with conditions. If the trust is constitutional and reasonable, and the conditions allow the intended public use, and if the city's proposal will not be within the cy pres contemplation of the trust, the trust will be enforced and the city will not be allowed to change the use.

c. Allgood's title may have been the result of a transfer with conditions. In such transfers to local governments, the courts do not favor the imposition of conditions subsequent upon a fee transfer and will often attempt to interpret the transfer to be unconditional, especially where there is no defeasance clause. Nevertheless, there have been decisions viewing conveyances of property "so long as" it would be devoted to a particular use as fee determinables, with possibility of reverter the result of failure to meet or to continue to meet the condition.

d. If Allgood had obtained only an easement by dedication (or by any of the other means of acquisition), and if the stadium plan were held to be a new public use not within the terms of the dedication or the contemplation of the easement, the change would be held to create an additional burden upon the servient estate, imposition of which would be a taking of private property requiring compensation to the private owner or his successors.

e. Much, then, depends upon how the plan is viewed. If the use to which the property is *now* put is proper in light of the method of its acquisition, and if the stadium is deemed to be commensurate with that use, absent other restrictive but

[*237*]

proper conditions imposed by the grantor, it will not make much difference how the property was acquired by the city. But if the planned changes are viewed as new uses, the city's title and the court's view of municipal flexibility given the property interest acquired will be determinative. If the alley way be deemed a public street, the court's view will likely be strict. We shall see more of the limitations on municipal property use, infra.

C. ACQUISITION UNDER EMINENT DOMAIN

§ 1. **Authority.** Municipalities do not possess inherent authority to take private property by eminent domain. Such authority must be expressly delegated by the state. Such delegations are commonly made to the traditional municipal corporation and less commonly to special districts. Without express indication to the contrary, the delegation will customarily not be interpreted to permit the power's extraterritorial exercise. When eminent domain power is exercised, the taking must be only of the property and interest therein necessary for the public use unless the statute authorizes taking the fee, the taking must be necessary and for a public use, and just compensation must be paid to the condemnee, or else the taking will violate provisions of the federal and state constitutions.

§ 2. **Some Interests Subject to Eminent Domain.** Limitation to the property interest needed in the absence of statutory fee authorization suggests correctly that any property right necessary to a public use may be condemned under proper authorization. Such rights include, in addition to the full fee, rights of access, easements including those limiting the landowner's use of the land, contracts, rights to enforce restrictive covenants, leasehold interest and the like. Some deserve additional comment.

a. As we have seen, the municipality may obtain property devoted to street uses in fee or by easement. While city possession of the fee may determine the rights to underground mineral deposits and the like, and may answer the question of ownership upon closing of the street, city ability to open the street, to change or expand the use or to permit private encroachments upon the street seems to be unaffected by the property interest it holds.

Whether the landowner whose property abuts the street or the city owns the fee, the abutter has and may enforce a property right of access. While the right may not be exercised to compel opening of the street, it is defined to conclude ingress, egress, light, air, view, having the street kept open and continued as a public street, and whatever else adds to the value of the street to the abutter.

The abutter's right is commonly raised in challenges to such municipal activities as street closings, the creation of cul-de-sacs, changes of street grade, limitations of street access and such street uses as increased traffic routing, subway construction, street repair and parking regulation. The abutter's right is not absolute. It has frequently been held unimpeded by partial limitations, parking rules and temporary obstructions for repair or construction. Nevertheless, when the city's action is deemed to be unauthorized or so inconsistent with reasonable exercise of the abutter's right when considered in light of the municipal objective that it constitutes a taking (or under appropriate state constitutional clauses a damaging) of the abutter's property right, compensation for the value of the right taken will be required under traditional eminent domain principles. And there are statutory provisions which may call for compensation for certain city street actions such as changes in grade.

b.   Frequently, as is obvious from the above, municipal action will so affect individual property rights without formal exercise of the eminent domain power that the individual will bring suit under locally applicable procedures seeking to restrain the municipal activity or recover compensation for the taking or damaging. It may help to recall our discussion in Chapter III. A municipal regulatory ordinance may be challenged as so unreasonably confiscatory as to be invalid. Declaratory and injunctive relief may follow. On the other hand, where the property owner is deprived of the practical use and enjoyment of a property right, he may argue that a municipal action was intended to take his property right and did so, and that just compensation is required. His suit under appropriate local procedures or 42 U.S.C. § 1983 will be styled one in inverse condemnation: the seeking of compensation from the government as defendant where it has taken, or can be held to have taken, without the formal exercise of its power of eminent domain. It has been said that the government may act in an arbitral (regulatory) or enterprise (taking) capacity, the former to be judged for its validity, the latter to be accompanied by required compensation. The courts have said, and we have seen, though, that the line between noncompensable regulation and compensable taking is not susceptible of precise demarcation. Indeed, cities often couple what are later determined to be noncompensable regulations despite substantial diminution in property value with financial ameliorations which the courts find unnecessary to evaluate as just compensation.

c. In addition to the traditional land based easements, many cities are authorized to condemn easements which affect the landowner's flexibility in using his property. Illustrative are scenic easements which protect historic or aesthetic interests from encroachment. Often, as in the case of billboards, cities will attempt to achieve such results by exercise of the zoning and other police powers. If the action is upheld as a police-power exercise, compensation to affected individuals will not be required.

d. Occasionally, a municipality may condemn property subject to a restrictive covenant for a public use not contemplated by the covenant. Other landowners who are signatories to the covenant may contend that their right to enforce the covenant with respect to the taken property has itself been "taken." Some of the cases considering the matter have held that the right to enforce a restrictive covenant is a property right which must be condemned with compensation when the restricted land has been taken for a public purpose. Other courts disagree on the very practical ground, inter alia, that the majority position imposes too expensive a burden on the city's exercise of the power of eminent domain.

e. In a number of situations ranging from the taking of property subject to a lease to the unilateral termination with compensation of its own contract in order to expand the original public purpose, the municipality may use its delegated eminent domain power in effect to condemn a contract. Such action involves compensation and hence has been held not to impair contractual rights within the meaning of the U. S. Constitution's clause barring such impairment.

f. May a municipality exercise its delegated power of eminent domain to condemn property already devoted to a public use? The courts have held that it may not unless the power to do so is conferred in express terms, or by necessary impolication, and have further held that the rule of strict construction will be followed in making this determination. There have been a few decisions favoring the "more necessary public use."

§ 3. **Necessity and Public Use or Purpose Requirements.** We have assumed, for purposes of the foregoing, that the takings in question were necessary and for a public use. These are, of course, fundamental prerequisites to the proper exercise of the eminent domain power, even if specifically authorized by state legislation.

a. The wisdom of the municipal plan and the necessity for its implementation are questions which the courts leave to the discretion of the local legislature (and in three states no finding of necessity is required). In a few states, the question of reasonable necessity is reserved to the judicial forum by state constitutional provision. Absent such a provision (and, it has been argued, absent federal highway funds as the motivating force), resistance by the condemnee on the ground that the taking was unnecessary will likely be unavailing. This aspect of the necessity of

[*243*]

the taking should not be confused with such other aspects as when the property is needed, what property interest is needed, or how much property is needed. The courts will readily involve themselves in those determinations and sympathetically respond to municipal judgments.

b. It is essential that the taking be for a public use. The courts may frequently use the terms "public purpose" and "public use" interchangeably in this connection, although some insist that use imports more than benefit. As noted earlier, the terms defy concrete definition. By whatever name, the concept will change with the changing circumstances and conditions of society. Public use or purpose is determined on a case-by-case basis, and most courts give it liberal construction. As we said at the outset of this text, the question is largely one of the appropriateness of the activity for government. What may at one time have been thought to be a more appropriate activity for private enterprise may today withstand public use or purpose scrutiny.

Of course, takings which clearly promote the public safety or general welfare satisfy the criterion. And takings which solely benefit private interests do not. But between the poles are takings of property to serve purposes which benefit the public although the property will not be used by the public; property which is used by a portion of the public; takings which benefit the public be-

[244]

cause of public controls over later private owners; and takings to accomplish objectives traditionally within the purview of private enterprise.
These may be illustrated respectively by: condemnation of non-conforming uses; condemnation for local parks; condemnations of property
later sold to private developers in the implementation of urban renewal programs; and condemnations to build industrial plants for rental to private industry.

While there remain courts which insist upon
use by a broad segment of the public and retention of the property in public ownership, the
growing trend recognizes benefit to the public in
even an indirect manner as satisfactory. And in
determining whether there is such benefit, courts
give great, though not controlling, weight to the
state and local legislative judgment. Thus, while
each of the illustrated takings may be disapproved by some courts, the greater number of
courts would find all but the last to serve a public
use or purpose.

   c.   In one area, the courts very strictly enforce
necessity and public purpose requirements.
Where, by state statute, private persons are authorized to seek judicial assistance in accomplishing a taking to serve the public health and safety,
there must be strict legislative standards governing the actions of these "agents" and they
must be meticulously observed. Such statutes,

for example, may permit the condemnation of an easement so that a landowner may connect to a sewer across the intervening land.

§ 4. Excess Condemnation. a. The necessity and public purpose requirements are most graphically illustrated in the problem of excess condemnation. The term is used to describe municipal taking of property not strictly needed for a public use, or the taking of more property than is needed for a public use. To be distinguished is the requirement that, absent statutory authority, eminent domain should result in the taking of only such property interest or estate as is needed to accomplish the public objective. It should also be recognized that property taken in excess of that needed for a particular public use may nevertheless be justified as necessary to another public use. And finally, the city may validly consider that future expansion of the contemplated public use may be necessary and may take sufficient land to allow the later expansion, as, for example, in obtaining property necessary for an eventual four-lane road while planning at present to construct a two-lane road.

b. There remain three theories under which the city may hope to justify taking more property than is needed: the remnant theory, where takings leave remaining property remnants having little if any value to the owner; the protective theory, where additional takings would afford aesthetic benefits protecting appearance, view and air; and the recoupment theory where additional takings could be then sold to recoup sums helping to defray the cost of the planned public improvement.

While the owner of a remnant may prefer the taking, he may not mandamus its condemnation, and vigilant taxpayers may challenge the expenditure as illegal. Generally, in the absence of constitutional authorization, courts will disapprove of excess condemnation. Disapproval is most likely in response to the recoupment theory, of course. Some courts strictly interpret the constitutional authorizations which do exist in some states.

§ 5. **Quick Condemnation.** We shall see that the property's value required to be compensated in the exercise of eminent domain is measured as of the time of the taking. Where the condemnee wishes to challenge the taking, however, actual possession by the municipality may be significantly delayed. Such delay increases municipal costs (construction, e.g.) and impedes realization of the public objective. Such delay also is a detriment to the condemnee who cannot as a practical matter realize income from his property at the levels which preceded its questionable status. Moreover, in some jurisdictions, even after the delay's detriments to the condemnee, the city may abandon the condemnation.

Accordingly, an increasing number of jurisdictions are by constitutional amendment and enabling legislation authorizing the procedure of "quick condemnation," whereby upon payment in escrow of its estimate of just compensation, the condemnor immediately takes title, leaving the actual compensation amount for later determination. Quick condemnation is usually authorized for objectives whose status as a public use has long been approved and is relatively invulnerable to challenge.

§ 6.   Some Aspects of Just Compensation: Fair Market Value, Methods of Appraisal, Apportionment, Highest-and-Best-Use Factors, and Substitution.   The procedures for determining just compensation and the other procedures for the exercise of eminent domain and judicial review thereof are heavily statutory and the statutes must be strictly followed. There are, however, some common aspects of just compensation which deserve limited discussion in this text.

a.   The basic standard for determining just compensation is fair market value: what a willing buyer who did not have to buy would pay a willing seller under no compulsion to sell for the property or property right in question at the time of the taking, though without reference thereto. In determining fair market value, there are three recognized methods of appraisal:

(i) The most common is the market data approach utilizing recent sales of comparable property. Obviously, other condemnation compensation awards are not relevant. The courts do allow evidence of comparable sales and rentals even if reported as hearsay evidence as substantive proof and as bases for expert opinion on the subject. This method is virtually always used for land and property rights and frequently for structures thereon. Difficulties include property for which there is no recognizable market, selection of comparable time periods, differences in dollar purchasing power, zoning, different construction materials, gaps between value and assessed value for tax purposes and the like.

(ii) Where the subject property is specialty property for which there is no market and the value as a specialty outweighs its value for other purposes, courts frequently allow appraisals based upon the costs of reproducing less depreciation as evidence of value to be considered, adding the resulting value determination to the value of the land. The difficulties of determining construction and labor costs and estimating depreciation are obvious.

(iii) Income-producing property is frequently valued by adding to market data appraisal of the land a figure capitalizing the net income which the property would have produced during its remaining useful life. Difficulties include projecting rent schedules of relevant comparison properties, vacancies, taxes and insurance and discounting to present day value.

b. Where there are several interests in the property to be compensated, procedures will call for the apportionment of the award according to the measure of the value of the interest. The leasehold interest may serve to illustrate. The value of the leasehold interest is the difference, if any, between the lease rent and the fair market rent (market data approach) for the term of the lease. Some differences of judicial opinion occur on whether the term of the lease should include its option period and whether the result should be discounted to present value.

c. In determining the fair market value of property taken under eminent domain, the property's highest and best use (whether it is actually put to that use presently) is a valid measure. The phrase "highest and best use," taken at face value, can be misleading. It does not mean the imaginative conclusions of unsupported speculation. If damages are sought on the premise that property has a more valuable use than its present one, the condemnee must establish by competent proof not only the property's physical adaptability to the suggested use but also the need and the demand in the market at the time of condemnation for such use in the area.

d. Zoning in the area, of course, plays a substantial role in affecting what can be posited as the property's highest and best use. While the condemning government may not place property within a street bed on an official map, condemn it and pay only compensation for its depressed value as so limited, it may validly raise existing zoning as a limitation upon projected uses of the property. But rezoning in the area may be probable and this fact would be of price-influencing interest to a willing buyer. Thus, the condemnee may show, and the jury may consider, not value of the property as rezoned, but value of property subject to a relatively probable rezoning.

e. So too, in measuring the value of property with mineral deposits, it would be inappropriate to measure the value of the property and add to it the full estimated value of the mineral deposits (which when mined and sold will bring their own price). Rather, the "willing buyer" should appropriately be put in possession of information which would influence the price he would offer. What would he offer to pay for land with mineral deposits of specified estimated worth?

f. Where under appropriate authorization one governmental entity exercises its power of eminent domain in taking from another governmental entity property already devoted to a public use, some (but not all) courts will agree that just compensation requires costs of substitution. In such cases the courts may deem the reproduction-less-depreciation method insufficient. Additionally, by statute, many government properties (such as water and sewage facilities, schools and roads) are required to be replaced. Since substitute acquisition (perhaps by condemnation) will then occur, the just compensation amount for the original condemnation is allowed to include a sum permitting duplication of the facilities taken. Indeed, there is some authority permitting the original condemnor to take additional property necessary to replace the disrupted public use, or to take such property interests as are necessary to make whole even a private condemnee (whose right of access had to be replaced, e.g.). Again, it should be noted that other courts will refuse to apply the substitution rule where replacement is not required, particularly where the government property taken consists of land without structures thereon.

g.   Preceding sections of the text have noted that municipalities have coupled land-use regulation with ameliorative fiscal arrangements. Examples include zoning with compensation and restriction of development capability of specific property with purchase of the development rights or permission to use them elsewhere (transferable development rights in landmark preservations, e.g.). In the context of regulatory ordinances not considered takings, such ar-

rangements may, but need not, be germane to judicial assessment of noncompensable regulatory
reasonableness and constitutionality. As possible
compensation for takings, however, such arrangements may be of insufficient value or may be so
incapable of valuation as to be deemed unsatisfactory.

Transferable development rights (TDRs) are a
case in point. When, in order to require preservation of a landmark, for example, the municipality severely restricts development of that property, it may proffer to the property owner the
opportunity to transfer what development potential the property would otherwise have had (or to
sell these transferable rights) to parcels located
in designated transfer development districts of
the local government, which parcels may then be
more intensively developed than would otherwise
be permitted under the zoning laws applicable to
that district. But the value of these "floating
TDRs" is difficult to determine. Until the use of
TDRs becomes so extensive as to provide sufficient evidence of market value, valuation of
TDRs will be considered speculative and their
worth as just compensation very questionable.
Accordingly, some local governments have adopted a plan whereby they purchase the restricted
property's development rights, thus attempting
to compensate the owner if the regulatory effort
be deemed a taking. The purchased rights are

then "banked" and later sold to developers in the designated transfer-repository districts, thereby recouping in whole or in part the cost of compensating the original owners of those rights.

§ 7. Consequential and Severance Damages, Offsetting Benefits. In addition to just compensation for the property taken, payment may have to be made for special damage to nearby property or to the portion of property remaining in the hands of the owner from whom part was taken.

a. We have already seen the possibility that the taking may have to be accompanied by compensation to other signatories of restrictive covenant whose rights to enforce them against the taken property are deemed expropriated. Similarly, the courts have been willing to award consequential damages to owners of nearby properties whose properties are specially injured in a manner peculiar to them not suffered by the public as a whole, if the damages rise to the level of a taking under the applicable constitutional provision, or if the provision calls as well for compensation for damaging.

b. When there is a partial taking, the landowner is to be compensated for the part taken in an amount reflecting the difference, if any, between the fair market value of the entire property before the taking and the fair market value of what remains after the taking. However, the condemnee may be able to show to a reasonable certainty that by virtue of the taking, damages also resulted to the remainder. While such damages may not be remote or speculative, they need not be peculiar to that property as is required in the case of consequential damages to a nearby owner's property. These severance damages to the remainder must result from the taking and include injury due to the use to which the part appropriated is to be devoted. The measure of damage is commonly the fair market value of the part not taken before and after the taking. Some elements not to be valued in and of themselves may nonetheless be evidence relevant to diminution in value of the remainder. For example, one such element may be the remainder's loss of seclusion resulting from the taking. Under a "unity of use" theory, courts have awarded such severance damages where two separate properties are treated as one because they are so inseparably connected in the use to which they are put that injury to one will necessarily and permanently injure the other.

c. It should be noted that if all evidence of the fair market value of the remainder is considered, an award which is based upon the value of the entire tract and the value of the remainder should logically include both damages for the taking and severance damages to the remainder, and some courts so hold. Where, however, the severance damages to the remainder are measured solely by *its* before-and-after valuation, the courts frequently allow the award or some portion thereof to be offset by benefits to the remainder convincingly proved by the condemnor. Some courts allow a set-off for any benefits and some allow a set-off against the total award. There are many variations, but the most frequent result is to allow the condemnor to prove special benefits to the remainder, the value of which will be set off against the taking-resulting diminution in value of the remainder only. Here the benefits must be special, i.e., while not necessarily unique to the residue property, substantially greater in degree than those accruing to the other properties in the community. Since just compensation is a judicial question (court or jury), what are special benefits is a matter for case-by-case determination.

d. An additional matter must be noted. Some public improvements which are local in nature and which specially benefit particular properties may be funded by special assessments imposed upon those properties to the extent benefited. The concept "special benefit" in the severance-damage-offset context may be considered much narrower than its counterpart in the special-assessment context, because the latter includes, as "special", benefits peculiar to the entire improvement district. Nevertheless, there is substantial overlap especially where the taking is for street purposes. Accordingly, in street condemnations,

[*256*]

the courts have been reluctant to allow benefit offsets because later construction of the street could be a local improvement for which a special assessment might be imposed and the condemnee would then have to pay twice if he suffered a deduction in connection with the taking.

§ 8. Comment on Extent of Just Compensation. The matter of compensation is fraught with problems which raise serious questions concerning the "justness" and increase the coercive nature of the eminent domain power. The volume of takings at the federal, state and local levels defies imagination. There has been a commendable increase in statutes providing compensation for previously uncompensated factors such as business losses, relocation expenses, experts' and attorneys' fees, and losses resulting from last-minute reductions in the size of the taking, and from eleventh-hour abandonment of the taking. In addition, states have attempted to remedy the unfairness incident to negotiations at value levels determined by government "captive" appraisers.

Nevertheless, by far the greater number of eminent domain exercises do not compensate for moving expenses, replacement-property financing differentials, replacement of tenants' housing, business dislocation expenses, loss of profits, good will (some courts allow compensation for loss of location good will), experts' and attorneys'

[*257*]

fees, and losses between the announcement of
condemnation plans and the actual taking (there
is some liberalizing movement). For example, it
has been estimated that more than half of the
businesses dislocated in urban renewals in this
country suffered partial or fatal damage from
consequences which were not required to be compensated. It is submitted that while the power of
eminent domain is admittedly necessary, its coercive impact should be reduced by legislation recognizing that *just* compensation requires more
than the provable fruits of a forced "voluntary"
sale.

D. SOME LIMITATIONS ON MUNICIPAL USE OF ACQUIRED PROPERTY

Briefly, the municipality's use of its property
may be limited by common law, legitimate private
restrictions, the constitutions' protections of individual rights, trusts, judicial or statutory policy.

§ 1. **Nuisances.** A municipality will not be allowed to use its property in ways that will be
deemed nuisances. At the behest of persons injured by municipal nuisances more than speculative in nature, judicial relief will be available.
Many courts will apply this restriction even to
property held in the city's governmental capacity.

§ 2. **Inconsistent Private Uses.** The municipality has no power to permit private uses of proper-

ty held by it "in trust" on behalf of the public (streets, e.g.), which uses are inconsistent with the public objectives. Such private uses are frequently termed "purprestures," a form of common law nuisance constituting an encroachment upon lands or rights and easements incident thereto, belonging to the public or to which the public has a right of access or enjoyment. Thus, while the city may permit temporary private activities or structures on, above or beneath the streets, it cannot allow permanent uses which are not deemed customary street uses.

§ 3. **Constitutional Limitations.** While the city has reasonable discretion in the management of its properties, it cannot use them, permit them to be used, or lease them to others who will use them, in violation of the federal and state constitutions or of constitutionally protected rights. Illustratively, it cannot discriminate on the basis of race, creed or nationality. It may not restrict use of its property in a manner violative of first amendment rights (unclear and too discretionary restriction on dissemination of religious information in airports, e.g.). Its limitation of use to its own residents may be valid if it does not impact upon others' constitutional right to travel. It cannot in the use of its property violate the federal first amendment's Establishment Clause (Christmas creche on city hall steps, e.g.), or ignore the notice and hearing requirements of due process in the face of a legitimate claim of entitlement (eviction of public housing tenants; termination of utility services, e.g.).

The constitutional restrictions are applicable even where the violative use comports with the expressed intent of one granting the property to the city in trust. While, as in the case of other property held in trust by the city, reasonable construction will be given to the conditions and the cy pres rule is available, the failure of such efforts will result in a determination of unconstitutionality.

§ 4. **Holding City to Present Use.** If the municipality has acquired property subject to legitimate and reasonable private reservations and conditions, we have seen that it must abide by them. Our earlier discussion of the city of Allgood's stadium plan and the city's estate in lands possibly to be used for that purpose indicated that the stadium plan might be thwarted if the court were to hold it a change in use for the properties presently used as playing fields and as an alley way. Such result could follow a court ruling that the city had "dedicated" its property to that use (although the city held the fee) or that the city held the property "in trust" on behalf of the public, or that the city had received the property in trust or by transfer of a terminable fee. Such result might also follow a decision that the city's estate was no more than an easement. If

[*260*]

the city were to use its eminent domain power to acquire the necessary interest to go forward with its plan, or if persons were to challenge the city's change of use, it is important to know who may enforce the above limitations upon the property.

It is possible that any taxpayer with appropriate standing (see Chapter VI) might enforce the limitations especially if they resulted from the "city dedication" or "in trust" interpretations. The actual trust may be enforced by the grantor or his successors, as may the terminable fee. The easement limitation will be enforced by the owner of the servient estate. It is thus possible that one who abuts the street where a city holds only an easement may be attempting to assert servient-estate rights and the conceptually independent right of access of an abutter.

In many instances, a number of persons will purchase property from a plat showing land reserved for streets, parks and public squares. On a theory of restrictive covenant or estoppel, the original purchasers from the plat may hold the city to the limited use, and even where the city has not accepted the plat, may nonetheless hold the developer to the reservation. Subsequent purchasers who abut the restricted property retain the right to enforce the restriction against the city.

Those of the above challengers who claim return of title because the city has failed to honor their restrictions may be estopped if they have sat by while the city made large expenditures in accomplishing the change of use. In addition, courts will decline to order reversion so long as there is a reasonable possibility of restoration of the original use.

§ 5. Change of Use of Property Held in Fee. As noted earlier, courts may hold that property held in fee simple, however acquired, may nonetheless be held "in trust" for the public. This is particularly true of streets. In such cases, changes of use will customarily be barred. Of course, all streets need not be open to all street uses; conversion of a street to a pedestrian use is not a prohibited change of use. It should be noted that statutes occasionally bar a change of some uses (schools, e.g.) even where the full fee is held. And there are courts which have expressed resistance to changes by concluding that the fee-owning city had "dedicated" the land to a particular use which it was not now free to change. Absent these statutes or judicial restrictions when the full fee has been obtained by eminent domain or by purchase, or when the property is otherwise free of trust, or when a fee-dedication's use has been fully complied with, the municipality may change the use in its discretion.

E. DISPOSITION AND LOSS OF
MUNICIPAL PROPERTY

In discussing restrictions which attend, and results which follow a municipality's disposition of its property, it may help to consider, first, municipal actions affecting the property's use and, then, municipal actions involving a transfer or loss of the title to the property. The two overlap since, as we have seen, some municipal actions affecting the use will work a title transfer or reversion. Those actions which affect the use are abandonment, leases, franchises and vacation. Those which raise the question of title transfer or loss include gifts, sales, mortgages, adverse possession, estoppel to claim title, reversion, eminent domain and compulsory transfer. The entire area is heavily affected by statutes.

§ 1. **Abandonment.** a. The municipality, absent statutory direction to the contrary, may abandon the use to which property is put, including street uses, with little interference by the courts in this area of municipal discretion. Abandonment is especially unremarkable where the city owns the fee. However, when the city's estate in the property is less than the full fee, and where a claimant is asserting an ownership interest therein, difficulties may arise in determining whether abandonment has occurred and, if so, what results will follow.

[*263*]

b. Abandonment needs no formal action by the city. Its elements, including intent to abandon, may be shown circumstantially. The burden of proof is upon the claimant to show that the use has entirely failed. Courts have not been persuaded by evidence of non-use or misuse, or of city acceptance of tax payments from the claimant.

If the grant to the city was acompanied by conditions subsequent or reversionary clauses intended and interpreted to work a forfeiture upon total failure of the use, abandonment may achieve that result. But the courts do not favor conditions subsequent and will not divest the city if the intended result of use-failure is unclear or if there is the possibility of resumption of the determinative use.

§ 2. **Lease.** a. Authority must be found in order for the municipality to lease its governmental properties or those held "in trust" for the public. There are many such statutes among the most interesting of which are those permitting abutting owners to lease air rights over city streets for specified building purposes. Any doubts concerning city authority are resolved against the city and the courts take a very broad view of what properties are governmental in this connection.

b. There is case law inferring authorization from the power to acquire, own and control property for leases of governmental properties for private, temporary uses not inconsistent with the public rights. Some uses, such as concessions in public buildings, will not be deemed leases and thus will be approved. And there is authority permitting leases of governmental property no longer needed for the governmental purposes.

c. No specific authorization is needed for the leasing of proprietary properties although the courts take a restrictive view of what properties fall within this class.

d. Leases will often be required to be preceded by bids, and other contract protections such as those discussed earlier in this chapter will frequently be applicable.

§ 3. **Franchises.** a. As has been noted, some state constitutions commit the granting of franchises to local, politically accountable bodies. Even without such clauses, local involvement is frequent. Cities award franchises to utilities and others for use of public streets (transit, power, water and sewage, cable television, e.g.) below, above and on ground level.

b. A franchise is a right or privilege, essential to the performance of the primary purpose of the grantee, which can only be granted by the government. It is a contract conferring upon the grantee a property right, analogous to an easement between private parties. As a result grantees can be protected against such incursions as

[*265*]

municipal impairment. A city must have both the
authority to require the grantee to seek it and the
power to award it. The constitutional or statutory sources of this authority may circumscribe it
by limitations prohibiting exclusivity, perpetual
franchises, irrevocable grants, unreasonable time
periods and the necessity for voter approval. Because many municipal franchises are sought com-
petitively, in the award to one or more grantees
and in the subsequent city actions in relation to
the franchise, the awarding municipality must be
careful of such local-law matters as the bid-speci-
fication considerations mentioned earlier, the impact of "sunshine" requirements in its proceedings and the like, of the possibility of antitrust
liability under federal law, and of constitutional
equal-protection and due-process requirements.

c. Where constitutions are not interpreted to
require exclusive local control, state involvement
varies, some requiring approval by state commissions, some retaining sole power in the state, and
others refraining from any involvement.

d. Municipal grants may, in the sound discretion of the city, be accompanied by such conditions as city ability to prescribe or regulate rates
and fees, to require a public utility to pay to the
city a percentage of its dividends, to require the
grantee to collect city service charges, in the context of cable-television franchises to specify the
number and variety of television channels, to

[*266*]

have some television channels allocated to public use, to insist upon constitutionally valid control of access to "adult" programming, and to require other reasonable benefits. (There are pending Congressional efforts to assert federal authority to establish a consistent national policy for regulation of the cable industry. The federal role would not displace that of the cities, but would spell out municipal and federal authority.)

Terms of the franchise, particularly those relating to exclusivity, will be strictly construed against the grantee. The contract will terminate in accordance with its terms, or if not specified therein, then in the reasonable discretion of the city.

§ 4. Vacation of Streets. a. Statutes and charter provisions exist virtually everywhere authorizing the vacation of streets and occasionally of other municipal properties under specific procedures which must be followed. While the courts give deference to municipal discretion, they insist that the power to vacate streets be expressed or necessarily implied; that vacations serve the public interest; and that, if there are benefits to private interests such as the abutters who petitioned for vacation, those interests be incidental to predominant public interests. The municipality will be allowed to impose conditions upon uses of the property after it is vacated.

[*267*]

b. Abutters upon streets which are vacated may seek damages for special injuries (to rights of access, e.g.) different from those suffered by the general public. Non-abutters who can demonstrate special injuries may also recover damages. Special injury to a non-abutter is a difficult matter to prove although street closings can be shown peculiarly to affect his right of access.

When streets are vacated and the city possesses only the easement, title to the property will then likely be held by the abutters, and not (if not an abutter) the original grantor, unless he provided for reversion. When the city holds title in fee, upon vacation it should be free to use the property as it sees fit, although there are statutes and authority which nevertheless pass title to the abutters.

§ 5. **Gift, Pledge, Mortgage.** a. Turning now to transfer of title, property held "in trust" and governmental property cannot be given away by the city. In addition many state constitutions contain clauses prohibiting gifts or the lending of municipal credit to private interests and in those states gifts may not be made. There have been decisions approving gifts even of governmental property when made to another public body for the governmental use.

b. Absent statutory authority, which some courts find in the power to sell, the city may not pledge or mortgage its property. Some courts have found implied authority to pledge income from city business ventures and proprietary assets.

§ 6. **Sale.** a. Sale of municipal property, like other methods of disposition, requires statutory authorization. Statutes, charters and ordinances set forth procedures which must be honored, including notice and bid requirements, electoral approval, council approval, and others discussed above in our exploration of municipal contracts. Commonly, the city may impose reasonable conditions on the subsequent use of the property to assure beneficial tax revenues, maintenance of existing characteristics, income of citizens, and the availability of additional housing, and to ameliorate the effect of the proposed use upon other municipally owned lands. It is the imposition of conditions of this sort which has enabled urban redevelopment resale of property to private owners in the face of lending-credit and public-purpose challenges.

b. There are additional difficulties. Cities cannot sell property obtained through dedication to public uses or held in trust even if statutorily authorized to do so. A city may not sell its governmental properties and particularly its streets without specific statutory authority. The power to sell its proprietary properties is readily implied, and there is some approval of sale of gov-

[*269*]

ernmental properties no longer needed for governmental purposes, or of sales where conditions do not permit accomplishment of trusts.

When the city does have the power to sell, courts will not interfere with municipal discretion except in cases of fraud, illegality, or clear abuse even if a better price could arguably have been obtained.

§ 7.   Adverse Possession, Estoppel to Claim Title.   a.   A city cannot lose title to its governmental property by adverse possession. Such property as is deemed proprietary may be acquired from the city by adverse possession but "proprietary" in this connection is probably limited to vacant or "private" lands and many statutes exist which bar any adverse possession of municipal property.

b.   May the city be estopped to claim title to what was once municipal property alleged now to be owned by a private owner? The courts have applied estoppel in connection with clearly vacant or "private" municipal land, and with the exception of a few decisions, have refused to do so in cases involving governmental property. To be successful the private claimant must show abandonment (including intent to abandon), prescriptive private use, inequitable conduct by the city approaching fraud, and reliance upon the conduct to the detriment of the private claimant. Where the above are present and there is every indica-

[*270*]

tion that the city has in the past treated the land as private property, courts may estop the city to claim title.

§ 8. Reversion. As we have seen in connection with acquisitions of and limitations upon the use of municipal property, municipalities may lose properties under reversion clauses for failure to satisfy restrictions or by changing the use specified in a dedication containing a reversion clause. The courts will be liberal in allowing the city the opportunity to meet unfavored conditions subsequent and other restrictions and to restore the dedicated use. They may further refuse to set aside a dedication accompanied by private reservations and conditions unless failure is specified as a condition of forfeiture or reconveyance.

§ 9. Eminent Domain, Compulsory Transfer. a. Municipal property may be taken by higher governmental entities in the exercise of their power of eminent domain. There is authority suggesting that compensation must be paid for proprietary property and there are occasional statutes requiring state compensation in all cases where it takes municipal property.

b. The state may compel municipal transfer of governmental property to another public body unless limited by restrictions surrounding the city's acquisition of the property or constitutional provisions.

[*271*]

CHAPTER V

MUNICIPAL REVENUES

The several local governing powers which have been explored in preceding sections of this text depend, of course, not only on authority so to act, but also on revenues necessary to support the power exercise. The considerations incident to the several methods of municipal revenue raising, whether by licensing, taxation, assessment or borrowing, include questions of authority, procedures, purposes and state and federal constitutional implications. This chapter is intended to illustrate a number of sources of municipal financing and in connection therewith to explore some of the limitations and considerations incident to those methods. While the scope of this text does not permit exploration of applicable considerations in the context of each revenue source, such considerations will be identified in discussion of at least one revenue method with full realization that they may be applicable to others as well. Our discussion will also highlight some salient considerations concerning expenditure of municipal revenues additional to those which have been mentioned in earlier chapters.

A discussion of municipal revenues cannot be divorced from prevailing political and economic

realities and the consequent tensions. The fiscal
burdens on municipalities are increasing dramatically. Among the contributing factors to the revenue gap are inflationary increases in the cost of
services, increased citizen expectations derived
from better economic times, the imminent demands of long postponed capital maintenance, the
consequences of inadequate, unsophisticated
management, the increased cost of over-extended
borrowing, and such broadened municipal expo-
sure to liability for damages as that under state
tort doctrines and federal civil-rights and antitrust laws. At the same time revenues are not
keeping pace because intergovernmental transfers have decreased, because voters have imposed
restrictions on the property tax and have shown
other indications of taxpayer "revolt," because
other governmental levels compete for customary
incidents of taxation, and because national and international economic crises detrimentally affect
tax bases and citizen employment and income.
The results include near bankruptcy of major and
small municipalities, creative development of new
and expanded sources of revenue (lotteries, user
fees, increased licensing for revenue, increased
use of revenue bonds, e.g.), and the accompanying major policy debates concerning the "intrusion" into local governing affairs by other governmental levels, the economic effects of vastly
increased municipal debt, the social effects of
gambling and of greater use of regressive taxa-

tion, and the wisdom of political limits on the major tax source.

Our discussion will somewhat arbitrarily divide municipal revenues into groups according to their contribution to a "typical" city's total revenue picture. It should be remembered, however, that a revenue source characterized as minor may nevertheless involve sizeable sums.

The reader should recall several state constitutional clauses which will have particular applicability in this area: clauses which accord or authorize home rule to municipalities; provisions which are deemed to commit to the state legislature exclusive authority to impose certain taxes; clauses which prohibit the state from levying taxes for municipal or corporate purposes; state equal-protection and uniformity-of-taxation clauses; clauses prohibiting municipal lending of credit to private enterprises; provisions imposing the public-purpose or municipal-purpose standard; and provisions imposing limits upon municipal debt.

A. IMPORTANT SOURCES OF REVENUE WHICH GENERALLY ARE NOT MAJOR CONTRIBUTORS TO THE MUNICIPALITY'S TOTAL REVENUES

§ 1. **Licensing.** The city obtains sizeable revenues from fees paid by those whose activity is required to be licensed or permitted, whether it be on-street parking or the practice of nursing. The source of the city's power to require the fees dictates the limitations upon the city. License requirements imposed solely for the purposes of raising revenue are a form of taxation and must be authorized. License and permit requirements imposed not as taxes, but as manifestations of the police power need no taxation authority but may not command fees largely in excess of the costs of administration of the regulatory program.

a. The municipality may not levy, assess or collect taxes without a delegation of taxation power from the state. Such delegation may be accomplished by inclusion within the attributes of home rule as interpreted by the courts (constitutional home rule) or delegated by the legislature to the city (legislative home rule) or by a legislative grant of power to levy a particular tax. Determination whether the power has been delegated will be a matter of rather strict construction and the power will not be found by implication. The state possesses the power not only to determine the incidents upon which taxation may be permitted, but also to specify when and by what means such taxes shall be exacted. Authorized licensing for revenue may occur even where regulation of the licensed activity is preempted by the state.

b. Without, then, the delegated power to license for revenue, the city cannot impose such licensing requirements in the guise of regulatory measures. But there is no question that in the exercise of its regulatory powers the city may impose license-fee requirements assessing sums to be paid in return for the granting of a privilege. In many instances where the city grants a license, the city incurs such expenses as the costs of registration and inspection. The courts have held that it is proper that those who seek the privilege should defray the costs of administration. Thus, where the license fee is required in the exercise of regulatory authority, the fee cannot exceed that which is commensurate with the expense incurred by the city in connection with its program of issuance and supervision of license or privilege of that type of business.

This limitation is rather liberally applied by the courts with the result that substantial sums are realized through the regulatory process (parking fees; license fees on each mechanical device used to depict sexually explicit materials, e.g.). Recall that regulatory licensing may be upset on a number of other grounds: lack of authority to regulate the activity, unreasonable regulatory scheme, improper classification, improper delegation, etc.

c. Where the city has with authority enacted revenue licensing measures, such ordinances must observe reasonable classifications. Additionally, state constitutional clauses requiring uniformity of taxation within appropriate classifications must be observed. In some states, if the

[*276*]

revenue license is, as is customary, deemed a tax on privileges rather than property, the uniformity clause may be held not to bar selectivity.

d. The tax imposed in licensing for revenue cannot be confiscatory so as to suppress the business taxed. Thus, imposition of a daily business privilege fee upon door-to-door salespersons (and others properly within the class) of fifteen dollars, where the business revenues barely exceed that, would be confiscatory. Assume that the salespersons represent firms in interstate commerce. Imposition of the taxation is likely to be challenged as confiscatory but also as improper under the federal constitution's Commerce Clause.

e. Recall that in our discussion of the police power, we said that municipal power exercises which unduly burden and impede the free flow of interstate commerce and those which discriminate against interstate commerce will be invalidated. Since so much that is taxable moves in interstate commerce, and so many occupations and activities relate thereto, some balancing between local (state) and federal interests has to occur if city taxes are to be allowed at all.

Are there points at which the otherwise appropriately taxable interests in the property or in the business dealing with the property may be taxed by municipalities without running afoul of the commerce clause? Three such opportunities present themselves: before the property begins to   .

move in interstate commerce; after its movement has come to an end for intrastate disposition thereof; and at a point where there has been a cessation of movement for an indefinite period with ultimate destination undeterminable. Where the cessation is in issue, the courts will look to see whether the property has come to rest, being held or stored at that point at the pleasure of the owner for later disposal within or outside the local jurisdiction as the owner's interests dictate. In determining that there is not an intended continuity of transit, despite a temporary interruption, the courts will be persuaded to uphold the tax if, at the date on which the tax is to be determined, the ultimate destination of the property cannot be discerned, the duration of the cessation is indefinite, and the goods are fungible so that those originally sent into the stream of commerce are not the identical goods which may finally (after cessation) arrive at the ultimate place of consumption. If such factors are present, it is not what finally happens to the goods, but the occasion and purpose of the interruption which will be controlling.

Thus, an ordinance which forbids carrying on the business of storing goods for hire except upon the payment of an annual license tax may be upheld in the face of a challenge that it contravenes the commerce clause because the nature of the business was interstate. Note that the out-

[*278*]

come of such balancing of the federal and local interests may in fact be that goods later moving in interstate commerce will be locally taxed and that citizens in another state will pay prices therefor based upon costs including those of earlier taxation. Such balancing will occur without distinction between a tax on the property (i.e., the sum of all the rights and powers incident to ownership) and the taxation of the exercise of some of its constituent elements, such as sale or storage.

If, however, the municipality were to apply our above hypothesized privilege tax only to salespersons for out-of-state enterprises or were to differentiate in amounts charged (by whatever device) between intrastate and interstate business so that, for example, a gross receipts tax applicable to the former were likely to impose less of a financial burden than an annual privilege tax imposed upon the latter, or were to prohibit the taxed entity's passing on the tax as a cost to local customers in a manner likely to increase the costs to out-of-state customers, the municipal actions would be forbidden as having a substantial exclusory and discriminatory effect upon interstate commerce.

f. License taxes are not held to be income taxes. Even though the municipality may lack the authority to impose local income taxes, it may nevertheless be able under license-tax authority to require payment of the more regressive business and employee occupational privilege taxes, with the accompanying judicial approbation of withholding requirements readily given to many types of tax programs.

§ 2. Local Income Taxes. a. A primary example of the tug-of-war for revenue sources between the state and its political subdivisions is the local income tax. Challenges to a municipal attempt to impose such a tax may be upheld because there has been no state authorization, because there has been state preemption, because provision for tax credits or deductions violates federal first-amendment (private-school costs) or state uniformity (home improvements) clauses, or because the constitutional home-rule clause must be read in conjunction with another constitutional clause deemed to commit income taxation to the exclusive jurisdiction of the state legislature. Nevertheless, many municipalities are able to impose local income taxes. Some are progressively graduated. Others are flat percentages. In some situations, state income taxes include a surtax for transmission to, and use by, the localities.

b. One of the major disputes in this area involves the earnings tax. Several cities are enabled to impose a local income tax upon earnings at their source (the taxing municipalities) no matter where the income recipient is resident. There are attendant political, intergovernmental problems of reciprocity and crediting, but the availability of reciprocity and crediting is not crucial to the validity of the earnings tax. The validity of the tax and its amount is upheld if it affords due process, i.e., if it bears a fiscal relation to the protections, opportunities and benefits given by the municipality to the nonresident earner for which it can ask a return. In multistate metropolitan areas, a municipality which sought to impose an earnings tax solely upon nonresident (out-of-state) commuters would run afoul of the federal Privileges and Immunities Clause designed to assure that in-state residents and out-of-state non-residents are treated alike by authorities accountable only to residents.

c. Income taxes imposed upon domestic and foreign corporations present complex problems which are largely beyond the scope of this text. The interstate-commerce and other constitutional implications and the scope of the income reachable by state and local taxation present such myriad issues as appropriate nexus, immunity of interest on federal obligations, problems of multinationals and subsidiaries, the curbing effect on local power, if any, of international tax agreements, and access to needed income data. State and local taxation of net income from what may be interstate operations of foreign corportions must be nondiscriminatory and fairly apportioned to local activities that provide a sufficient

nexus to support exercise of the taxing power.
One method of assisting states in determining the
necessary information is the work of the Multistate Tax Compact Commission. The compact
has been upheld as not impermissibly enhancing
individual state power at the expense of federal
commerce supremacy.

§ 3. Sales, Use and Gross Receipts Taxes.
Here again, taxes imposed upon the sale of interstate goods for intrastate consumption, upon the
intrastate use of goods purchased out-of-state,
and upon gross receipts of businesses which may
or may not be involved in interstate commerce
will be challenged as contravening the Commerce
Clause. Again the courts will respond that the
Commerce Clause does not relieve the taxpayer
of the just burdens of city taxes merely because
they add to his costs so long as the taxes do not
unduly burden interstate commerce, or do not discriminate against it in favor of intrastate commerce, or do not operate in such a way as to prohibit it under the guise of taxation.

a. Thus, sales or use taxes upon the sale for
consumption to the local consuming purchaser,
imposed upon the consuming purchaser, with that
sale or use as the taxable event, imposed on all
such class of goods whatever their source, are
valid if authorized. Imposition upon the seller of
the duty to insure collection of such tax from the
consuming purchaser is an appropriate collection

method which does not change the nature of the tax so as to make it violative of the Commerce Clause.

b.   While the municipality may not tax the gross receipts of a business engaged in the city exclusively in interstate commerce, it may impose such a tax upon receipts properly attributable to business done within the city by a largely interstate enterprise, roughly approximating a just allocation.   If the court can be persuaded to view the gross receipts tax as a valid business privilege tax, however, it may permit the tax to be applied to gross receipts whatever the source.

c.   As in other areas of taxation, the city is subject to federal and state equal protection requirements and state constitutions' uniformity-of-taxation clauses (sales-tax exemptions for food, e.g.) may also apply.   Nevertheless, wide diversity in taxing distinctions is tolerated.   Equal protection clauses may not require equality of burdens upon taxpayers.   The burden of establishing that a classification is unreasonable is a heavy one because courts frequently conclude that the wisdom of taxing one class and of not taxing another, distinguishable class is a matter within the exclusive jurisdiction of the local legislature.   As has been seen in our discussion of the police power, the chosen class may implicate other constitutional considerations, however.   Thus, a use tax on the cost of paper and ink products used in publishing was held to violate the federal first amendment.

d.   Conceivably, such taxes as gross receipts taxes may be imposed at levels so high as virtually to destroy the business taxed. While the state courts are by no means uniform on the subject, there are a number of decisions invalidating prohibitive, confiscatory, arbitrary, capricious or unreasonable local taxes under state concepts of due process. The burden of establishing that the local tax is to be so characterized is very heavy. Reaching a similar conclusion under federal due process concepts embodied in the fourteenth amendment is even more difficult.

The decision of the Supreme Court in *City of Pittsburg* v. *Alco Parking Corporation*, 417 U.S. 369, 94 S.Ct. 2291 (1974), is instructive. The Pennsylvania Supreme Court had invalidated as violative of federal due process a local ordinance imposing on local parking lots a substantial gross receipts tax. Some of the parking lots were run by the municipal parking authority. It could absorb this tax and, with its advantages as a public agency, charge less for parking than private-lot owners who deemed the tax so excessive as to make future operations approach unprofitability. The Pennsylvania Court concluded that the tax was excessively and unreasonably high. It reasoned that use of public funds for the parking au-

thority and the imposition of the tax benefited the
competing government at the expense of the private taxpayer. The unreasonable burden of private operation at a loss in competition with the
parking authority was a special and rare instance,
said the court, in which federal due process might
be invoked because the taxing ordinance was so
arbitrary as to constitute not an exercise of the
authorized taxing power, but the exercise of a
confiscation of property without just compensation.

The U. S. Supreme Court reversed, finding that
the circumstances, even in combination, were not
sufficient to invoke federal due process. The
Court preferred to adhere to its policy of refusing
to undertake the task of passing upon the reasonableness of an authorized tax, or to hold the tax
unconstitutional because it rendered a business
unprofitable or destroyed particular businesses.
Analogous to other courts' reactions to challenges to health objectives of cigarette and liquor
taxes, the Court indicated that federal due process affords no objection to the exaction of a "discouraging tax as the alternative to giving up a
business." The ordinance in question gave every
indication to the Court of being a revenue measure. Even if the expected revenue had been in-
substantial or only a secondary objective of the
ordinance, the Court expressed the likelihood that
it would nevertheless treat the ordinance as a tax

[*285*]

measure entitled to the customary presumption of validity. The judiciary should not infer an attempt to exercise a forbidden power under the guise of taxation from the sole fact that the tax appears to be excessive to the point of threatening the existence of a business or occupation. Nor should the courts attempt judicial oversight of the terms or circumstances of governmental competition with private enterprise. (Query, in light of later antitrust rulings.) The fourteenth amendment, said the court, does not prevent a city from competing with private business or preclude taxation to help the public competitor succeed. The Court saw the record-demonstrated fact of a shortage of parking spaces in the city as indicative that private business would suffer losses not to cheaper spaces but to citizens' decisions that they could no longer afford downtown parking at all. This, said the Court, amounted to a "discouraging [tax] rate as an alternative to giving up [the] business," a policy to which federal due process affords no objection. In light of the traffic and other problems and expenses incident to nonresidential offstreet parking, the city was constitutionally entitled to put the automobile parker to the choice of paying more or changing to other modes of transportation.

e. In the wake of voter efforts to reduce the real-property tax burden, municipalities have made, and will continue to make, increased use of sales, use and gross receipts taxes to lessen the revenue shortfall, sometimes, indeed, with results which have analogous impact on the real property owner (commercial-rent and business-occupancy taxes, e.g.).

§ 4. **Other "Minor" Revenue Sources.** It has been indicated that the state legislature plays a significant role in controlling the city's ability to impose taxes, even if the city has home-rule authority. As the major sources of municipal revenue fall farther behind the demand for expenditures and the erosion of inflation, ingenious governments realize that additional services, actions and relationships so benefit from municipal protections and services that new taxes may be imposed on these incidents. But the states also need new revenues. Consequently, cities and their states are in constant political conflict over newly devised tax schemes with the result that cities may not be authorized to impose taxes which the state seeks to use or reserve for its own benefit. The compromise which has seen a "piggyback" surtax for local use appended to state income taxes, while helpful where adopted, has ended neither the search for new tax revenues nor the state-local conflict.

Nevertheless, there are a number of taxes imposed by local governments in addition to those previously discussed which are not major revenue sources but which in the aggregate give sizeable assistance to local revenue needs. They include: admission and amusement taxes; cigarette, tobacco and alcohol taxes; deed transfer taxes; poll or capitation taxes (not preconditions to voting); gasoline and motor vehicle taxes; public-utility gross receipts taxes; fines and penalties; a parking tax; hotel and motel room taxes; a tax on the percentage of increase in value of property as the result of rezoning; and an enplaning tax.

In addition, states and municipalities, appropriately authorized, have turned to user and service fees (which cannot exceed costs) for previously tax-supported services, lotteries and other forms of gambling, and the encouragement of gifts to avoid the reductions of services which would otherwise accompany reduced revenues. One response to property-tax limitations, upheld against a limitation-avoidance challenge, has been intensified and creative use of special assessments which more directly match burdens and benefits.

§ 5. **Special Assessments.** Special assessments are here classified as "minor" revenue sources because the return is virtually entirely consumed by the cost of the improvement and the collection of the moneys, although sizeable sums may in fact be involved.

a. The theory of special assessments is that, where properties are enhanced in value by a local improvement which specially benefits them, the

[*288*]

owners of such property may be required to bear all or a portion of the cost of that improvement.

b.   In order for a municipality to be able to determine that the cost of some or all of an improvement such as street construction, lighting, repaving and repair, sidewalks, sewers, water drainage, etc., should be borne by the properties specially benefited thereby, it must have both the power to make the improvement and the power to impose special assessments to pay for it.   Improvement districts created under state legislation and local general governments customarily possess such powers, many of the latter under the general grants of home rule. In fact, much new legislation is being enacted broadening the concept of special-assessment improvements to include parking facilities, pedestrian malls, downtown business improvement districts, condemnation of non-conforming uses, and other projects reflecting more refined and subtle views of what may constitute factors affecting property values and responding in part to the revenue restrictions of voter-enacted, property-tax ceilings.

Special assessment authority cannot be implied from taxing delegations because such assessments are not viewed as taxes. The imposition of two or more assessments on one property does not therefore violate constitutional bans of double taxation and assessments are not subject to other taxation clauses such as those mandating uniformity of taxation.

c.   Special assessments and the procedures incident thereto are for the most part matters quite specifically dealt with in constitutions, statutes, charters and local ordinances. Such procedures are commonly viewed as requiring strict compliance. While local law must therefore be consulted, there are common elements which may best be set forth in the context of a chronology of the process, a brief discussion of the likely challenges by affected property owners, and considerations applicable to all interests.

d.   In viewing the chronology of the process, it is important to note that in particular jurisdictions, the initiation of the project, the city engineer's cost estimate, the scheduling of hearings, and the completion of the improvement itself all precede the assessment bill to the property owner and may affect the property owner's later ability to challenge the necessity for the improvement, to seek court review and to make certain arguments in seeking to overturn the assessment. Unfortunately, the first time many think to begin their protest is upon receipt of the assessment bill.

(i) The process will frequently be initiated by petition of a specified percentage of property owners directly affected by the improvement, followed by notice to all potentially affected of the proposed resolution of the necessity of the improvement.

(ii) Alternatively, the municipal council or the board statutorily authorized to do so may initiate the process by enacting a preliminary resolution of necessity or intention. Such action occasionally requires the approval of an extraordinary majority of the council or board.

(iii) Often at this time, the cost estimate will be prepared. Payment for the project may later be limited to this amount with little if any allowance for increase.

(iv) Local procedures will customarily require an opportunity for protest of the necessity of the improvement by those who did not petition therefor. In some jurisdictions, if more than one half or two thirds of the affected property owners protest, the plan may go no further.

(v) Before a determination that the improvement will be constructed, hearings may be required. Absent such requirement, federal due process dictates will not be violated so long as there is an opportunity to be heard before the individual assessments are imposed. Most state due process concepts will similarly be construed, particularly where the state legislature has created the improvement district, it being assumed that the legislature has made an improvement-necessity inquiry.

(vi) Plans, maps, specifications and cost estimates will be filed and open to public inspection, as notice to the public will have indicated.

(vii) After the above steps have been completed, the council or board will enact an ordinance or resolution ordering that the improvement be constructed and defining the bounds of the improvement or assessment district where such is authorized by law. This action will sometimes require enactment by an extraordinary majority.

(viii) Administrative personnel will then begin the construction process, advertise for bids and let the contracts.

(ix) Construction of the improvement will occur, and after necessary inspections, the improvement will be accepted for the local government entity. Payment may be made to contractors from improvement moneys borrowed from banks in return for city improvement certificates or warrants. Frequently, the contractors may themselves be paid with improvement certificates which they in turn will transfer to investor companies.

(x) Administrative personnel and assessors will then determine the amount of the individual assessments, and prepare a plat and schedule setting forth the various lots subject to assessments, the names of the owners and the amounts of the assessments. Sometimes caution will dictate that some portion of cost be borne by the general treasury—for example, that amount reflecting the improvement's incidental general benefit to the city at large. Sometimes, such cost sharing will be required by statute or by the courts. The proposed individual assessments or the more formal assessment roll, if required to be filed by law, will be confirmed by the council or board statutorily authorized to impose assessments.

(xi) Notice will be given to listed owners announcing the assessment and indicating the time fixed for filing objections thereto.

(xii) A hearing will customarily be afforded on objections to the individual assessments. An opportunity to protest individual assessments before they become final is generally thought to be a due process requirement, although the method of accomplishing this result may vary. For example, court confirmation is required in some jurisdictions, and the opportunity to seek judicial review is available at this juncture in some others.

(xiii) When the opportunity to protest has been afforded, the council or board will then adopt a resolution levying the individual assessments as corrected after protest, and will certify the levy to the proper assessment-collecting official.

e.   A property owner who wishes to resist the special assessment will challenge the improvement itself, as conceived and as constructed; the power to specially assess therefor; adherence to mandatory procedures; the inclusion of his property in a defined improvement district; and the excessiveness of the assessment in relation to his property. It should be noted that local procedures will indicate the manner of challenge including judicial relief, and that unjustified failure to follow them is fatal to the property owner's case.

(i) Generic challenge to the power of the municipality to make improvements or to levy special assessments is customarily unavailing in the face of universal state authorization.

(ii) Nevertheless, it is possible to challenge the improvements, as conceived, as unnecessary. Necessity is a discretionary determination of the local body which will be overturned only when it is clearly arbitrary, unreasonable and oppressive. The ordinance will be presumed valid and the challenger's burden will be very heavy. There has been successful attack where, for example, the unimproved utility system clearly met current state standards.

(iii) But the improvement as conceived may not be local in nature, in almost all jurisdictions an absolute prerequisite for imposing special assessments. To be local, the contemplated improvement must specially benefit properties in a local area in a manner and degree different from any incidental benefit which may accrue to properties in the community at large. The presence of general benefit will not be harmful so long as it is not deemed primary. The judgment of the local body is almost foolproof, but courts will listen to the challenge. Special assessments avoid use of scarce (or nonexistent) general tax revenues. It is not inconceivable then that cities' attempts to perform their functions by means of special assessments will occasionally be attempts to achieve general benefits (bridges, e.g.) and will be disapproved by the courts.

(iv) The procedures set forth by law will, for the most part, be deemed mandatory. Failure to comply will invalidate the assessment process. Such procedures may include hearings on the cost estimates and necessity of the improvement, and on the individual assessments. Notice of pending resolutions or hearings must be sufficient to disclose to persons of ordinary intelligence what is proposed (the nature of the improvement and the property to be affected), and how, when and where they may be heard. Unless the property owner is contending that the entire process is void as unauthorized, or can rigorously justify his failure to do so, he must have exhausted all appropriate procedures for protest before seeking the aid of the courts.

(v) The property owner may contend that the property should not have been included in the im-

[*295*]

provement district or on the assessment rolls because it will receive no benefit or because it is not
subject to assessment. We have seen earlier in
this text that a property owner whose property
obviously received no benefit from the improvement (hill surrounded by swamps in a water
drainage district) successfully invoked federal
equal protection requirements in his favor. So
too, one who is able to show by the exclusion of
comparable property the absence of any benefit,
particularly where aided by a state constitutional
clause commanding equal burdens on similar
property, may successfully contend that the property was unlawfully included.

In many jurisdictions, property owned by
higher governments, particularly federal and
state, may not be subjected to special assessments. In some states, however, the courts, in
measuring benefit by envisioning future property
uses, conclude that even county and state highway property within the local jurisdiction may be
assessed. Property which is exempted by law
from taxation, whether on governmental, charitable or religious grounds, is not by that fact necessarily exempted from special assessments.

(vi) In directly challenging the amount of the
assessment, the property owner may contend that
the amount of the assessment exceeds the special
benefit, if any, received by the property. While
there is occasional statutory language affirming

the finality of municipal determinations in the area, the power to determine that certain properties have been benefited and by how much is subject to judicial review. The courts are receptive but grudging in reacting to individual-assessment challenges.

A special assessment can be levied only to the extent the property is benefited specially by the local improvement. In addition, some courts require that the property bear only a fair share of the cost of the improvement, which may be less than the extent of the benefit. Where such further ceiling is not imposed, and where statutes do not limit the assessments (frequent), assessments exceeding even the preexisting market value of the property have been upheld.

The special benefit is measured by comparing the value of the property before and after the improvement, taking into account not only its present use but any use which might reasonably be made of it including its probable zoning status. The reader should recall the discussion of market value in eminent domain cases in Chapter IV of this text.

The assessment must be distributed among the benefited properties in accordance with the benefits each receives, but the courts frequently indicate that precise accuracy is not required. Where there is a substantial disproportion, the courts may conclude that there has been a taking of property without compensation under the guise of taxation, or that there has been unreasonable action amounting to a "fraud at law." Where there is a statutory method of allocating the improvement cost to be borne by the properties, it must be followed. Where the choice of the method of apportionment is made by the municipality, it will generally be presumed correct. Such methods include "front foot" (sidewalks, e.g.), "square foot" (storm sewers, e.g.), and "value" of the benefit. The courts will disapprove the use of any method which results in substantial disproportion between allocation and projected benefit. Disproportion arguments will not rise to federal equal protection status unless there has been manifest, invidious or unreasonable discrimination.

f. There are additional considerations of importance to the city, the property owner and the businessman who deals with the municipality in financing or constructing the improvement.

(i) When local procedures provide for publication of a notice to property owners and for subsequent hearings at which the owners may argue that the improvement is unnecessary or that their property will be unlawfully included in the improvement district, or would not be benefited, or that they would bear an unjustly burdensome share of the total being assessed, such objections can then be dealt with and matters remedied before the expense of construction has been incurred. Accordingly, one who, with notice, fails to attend such hearings and to protest, who sits by while the work is completed, so that contractors have accepted certificates of payment reposing faith in the unchallenged record of the regular proceedings, will not be heard to object (estoppel or laches) in later court review.

(ii) Those who originally petitioned for the improvement and who in the allotted time did not withdraw their names, and successors to their titles, with notice, will be estopped to deny at least the necessity for the improvement if not the validity of the assessment itself. Notice to successors is accomplished by filing the special-assessment information in the required public repository (Register of Deeds or City Tax Collector Office, e.g.).

(iii) Typically, once the individual special assessment has been levied, there is a lien on the property for the amount of the assessment and collection may entail foreclosure. Such liens will be prior to private contract liens but not to tax liens. The right to enforce such liens may follow the assignment of certificates or the revenue bonds in some jurisdictions or may be retained by the municipality to be enforced on behalf of appropriate creditors. If the property owner fails to pay the assessment, there will be publication of default followed by a brief period of redemption. Then the property will be sold as it would be for taxes. Due process requires that tax-sale notice include posting, publication, and mailing to owners and reasonably ascertainable mortgages.

In a growing number of jurisdictions, in addition to the above in rem liabiliity, there may be personal liability sometimes extended to non-resident owners. Of course, personal liability will attach for failure to pay under contracts permitting payments to be spread over a longer time.

(iv) In most states, such installment-payment contracts are authorized. But the owner who takes advantage of this opportunity will typically assume personal liability for the debt and the contract will contain clauses waiving any and all objections to the improvements, procedures, amount, etc.

(v) The property owner may resist enforcement of a payment-certificate lien by showing that notwithstanding city acceptance, there was no substantial compliance by the contractor, the improvement was not made or was made so improperly as to give no benefit. Success in this contention is rare and the burden on the contender is very heavy.

(vi) Where the original assessment is insufficient to cover the costs of the improvement, authority frequently exists permitting municipal reassessment. Reassessment is not permitted where the inadequacy is caused by the failure of some to pay the original assessment. Reassessment statutes are sometimes construed to permit reassessment where the original assessment was defective, although the new assessment must conform to all mandatory requirements. Occasionally, curative statutes will validate defective assessments.

(vii) In determining the total cost of the improvement, the city may include construction costs, and such incidental costs for services performed by city employees or others as the cost of plans and estimates, determining the assessment rolls, levying the assessments and sale of warrants, and attorneys' fees. There is some authority for including the cost of sale of municipal paper at discount (below par), brokers' commissions and the interest to be paid on improvement certificates.

(viii) The existence of the assessment lien and the cost of any required connection to improvements present problems in the sale of property. While liens may be recorded, assessments about to become due may not appear in the customary title search unless the search includes the city tax collector's office. After the improvement is constructed, the city may by law require connection to it (sewers, e.g.). Such requirement may not be enforceable by lien and thus may not be discoverable in a title search. These matters should be carefully handled in the contract of sale.

[*301*]

(ix) Other matters of significance include the manner in which contractors are to be paid; the negotiability of city paper; whether payment is limited to revenues acquired by the special assessment; whether this municipal debt is affected by a constitutional debt-limitation clause; and what statutes of limitations apply to challenges to the process. The question of the availability of other municipal resources may be significant if the city fails to reserve revenues from the special assessment solely for the creditors who hold the payment certificates or warrants, or fails to undertake the necessary efforts to ensure full payment of the individual assessments. A number of avenues of relief exist whereby creditors may enforce city adherence to its contracts or may seek recompense from other city funds.

B. IMPORTANT SOURCES OF REVENUE WHICH CONSTITUTE MAJOR CONTRIBUTIONS TO THE REVENUE PICTURE

Because there is widespread evidence that the property tax has reached or will soon reach its political ceiling, and because its use to support education has been found to be vulnerable to attack under several state constitutions, the increased search for, and use of, other sources of revenue may change the major-minor classifications adopted for this text. Such increases may occur, for example, in local sales taxes and in lo-

cal, "piggyback" surtaxes on state income taxes.
Nevertheless, at the present time, three prime
sources of municipal revenue contribute the major share: intergovernmental transfer, property
taxes and borrowing.

§ 1. Intergovernmental Transfer of Revenues.

a. Municipal efforts had been increasingly successful in obtaining transfer from governments
with broader revenue raising power of funds to
support continuation and expansion of local services. To a large extent, the impact of these
funds has been diminished by inflation and the
erosion of the local tax base, particularly in large
urban areas. The future will see reduction of
such support with possible realignment of the
levels of government responsible for particular
services. Nevertheless, substantial revenues
have been realized from state grants for education, capital construction and other purposes,
from federal categorical grants and tied grants
and now consolidated block grants with the inevitable debate over misplaced priorities, restrictive
strings, and matching funds, and from the federal revenue sharing program. At least one state
legislature, with judicial approval, has insisted
that the federal revenue-sharing funds be included in the state's general funds for it, not the executive, to appropriate. Many contend, with
some support in fact, that increased intergovernmental transfer of revenues which are not un-

[*303*]

restricted have served to distort proper municipal priorities and to erode municipal power by subtly transferring ultimate decisional functions to state or federal officials. Nevertheless, large urban efforts in renewal, transportation, and pollution control, and in some cases the continued fiscal ability to exist have depended heavily upon such revenues.

b. Although reduced or eliminated and partially replaced (consolidated block grants) as a state revenue source and vulnerable to replacement and reduction for localities, the federal revenue-sharing program has provided, through a series of complicated formulae, moneys collected through federal taxation for locally determined uses by state and local governments. The formulae are the means of passing through to the local governments a sizeable share of the revenue pie without intervention of states which until recently received approximately one third of the revenues.

Space does not permit exploration of the formulae in detail. It is important to note, however, that individual governmental shares reflect that government's tax effort. Proponents of the program had also sought to give greater impetus to the desirability of non-regressive taxation. The objective was realized to a greater extent in those provisions of the legislation concerning ceilings on allocable amounts than in the provisions defining tax effort.

The relatively unrestricted grants have reduced federal intrusion at the local level but have received much criticism charging that remiss enforcement has undercut the anti-discrimination restriction in the law. While there has been at least one notable instance wherein transfer of revenue sharing funds has been held up by a court pending a large city's attempts to end discrimination, the criticism may have some basis in fact. Commentators upon the program's effectiveness have urged that the restriction can work if there is a large civil rights enforcement staff.

c. As the federal and state governments attempt to reduce deficits by reducing transfers to local governments, the obvious fact that intergovernmental transfers have become integral parts of the localities' resource pool suggests that reduction will inevitably result in severe curtailment of expenditures and services or a fiscal crisis of substantial dimensions.

§ 2. **Property Taxes (Real and Personal).** a. A property tax is imposed on real estate in virtually every municipality in the nation. Indeed, it is very likely that an individual landowner's property taxes will include a portion for his local general government, portions for special authorities

and districts—school, library, water, fire, parks—
serving his property, and portions for his county
and state. In nearly all states there is authority
to impose property taxes on at least some specified types of tangible personal property. While
the significance of property-tax revenues has
been diluted by tax limitations and shifts to other
revenue sources, the scope and pervasiveness of
property taxation which still accounts for thirty-
two percent of local and increasing portions of
state revenue cannot be overstated.

At least forty-three states have traditionally
imposed a variety of limitations upon their local
governments' property tax rates. The ceilings
accompanying the recent "taxpayer revolt" will
be discussed later in this section.

b. Typically, the aggregate of state and local
rates is applied to the assessed value of the property as of a certain tax day. Assessed value may
be based on the cost of the property, its market
value at the time of assessment, or its income
value, a method of income capitalization for commercial property. Personal property may be valued by the taxpayer or by assessors. Personal
property taxes may be imposed on all tangible
personal property, on inventory at a certain date,
or on some types of personal property such as
motor vehicles.

c. If the taxpayer wishes to challenge the assessment, he is customarily faced with specified administrative procedures for so doing, by protests required to be filed within a short time after notification. If the administrative protest proves unavailing, the taxpayer's burden in court is a heavy one. Judicial inquiry into the propriety of property assessments made by the assessor and confirmed on administrative review will be restricted to whether the assessor performed his legal duty, i.e., whether the evidence viewed in a light most favorable to the taxpayer, amply discloses that the assessed value was so out of line with other similar or comparable property values, or with actual cost or value, as to give rise to an inference that the assessor failed properly to discharge his duty. For example, the jurisdiction may require property to be assessed at one hundred percent of its true value. (Other jurisdictions may permit assessments at less than one hundred percent. In yet others, the assessors may be able to take into account an "inflation factor" with the result that the percentage of present market value is less than full.) The full-value jurisdiction will nevertheless require that the assessment be equitable as compared with other similar property. So, the complaining taxpayer will try to show the existence of similar properties, their actual values, their assessments, the actual value of his property, its assessment, and the conclusion that his property is assessed at a

[*307*]

higher proportion of its actual value than the ratio of assessed and actual values of the comparable properties.

d. While the share of revenues resulting from the property tax has in many jurisdictions been reduced by more than one third, it remains a potential source of substantial revenue. In actuality, however, its revenue effectiveness has been hampered by the "taxpayer revolt" and by such inefficiencies as poor administration, questionable operational premises, and historic or modern exemption choices.

(i) In many states and localities, perceiving that state and local government budgets combined, as a share of personal income, had risen dramatically in the years following World War II, taxpayers promoted a host of provisions designed to limit tax burdens and reduce expenditures. These included reductions of, and inflexible limits on the growth of, property taxes, tax (all forms) expenditure limits keyed to inflation, population growth or a percentage of personal income (with legislative safety valves for emergencies), "sunset laws" leading to automatic termination of programs unless reexamined and renewed under specified conditions, and specific relief for certain groups of property taxpayers (circuit breakers, homestead exemptions, e.g.). Several such attempts were successful. As noted earlier, there

[*308*]

has ensued a growing use of whatever alternative revenue sources were unrestrained by the
limits. There have also been threatened or actual
reductions of expenditures for basic services,
with attendant reductions in the number of government employees. There are some signs of
change, but voters who have been asked to restore some flexibility have declined to do so.

(ii) At the operative level, loss of potential revenues may occur as a result of inadequate or infrequent assessments, inefficient or understaffed
assessor offices (some assessors are elected), and
unwritten accommodation of commercial interests.

(iii) The operational premises may also be
counterproductive. For example, it is common to
assess real property by according one third of the
value to the land and two thirds to the improvements thereon. The frequent criticism that such
division undercuts the desire to improve property,
particularly in areas of urban density, and increases "slumlordism" may be supported by the
increasing frequency of the so-called, slumlord
"endgame" wherein the property owner remains
in default of his taxes for as long as the over-
worked, delayed enforcement mechanisms allow,
thus increasing his profit, and then abandons the
unrehabilitated, near-worthless property before

the tax collection process can be fully implemented.

(iv) Substantial amounts of property are exempted in whole or in part from property taxation
by state law or by state-authorized local ordinances. Some of the exemptions are designed to
attract and retain industry and commerce in order to achieve other municipal purposes. A modern equivalent promoted at federal and especially
state and local levels is the "enterprise zone," a
mixture of property and other tax relief measures and regulatory (land use; building code,
e.g.) incentives designed to attract otherwise un-
available corporate investment and expansion to
specially targeted, depressed rural and urban areas with resultant economic and employment re-
juvenation. A majority of states authorize "free-
port exemptions," whereby property stored in the
state but destined for interstate commerce is exempted from inventory taxation. In several
states there are "circuit breaker" provisions protecting for the most part senior and low income
citizens from the regressive impact of property
taxes by authorizing a tax credit or rebate when
the covered persons' property taxes exceed a
specified percentage of their income. Several jurisdictions provide "homestead exemptions"
which reduce property taxes for residence purchasers. In all localities there are exemptions for
non-profit, charitable (sometimes on the theory

[*310*]

that they are performing the public's business) and religious institutions. In toto, the exemptions represent a substantial reduction in available, taxable property.

e. On the other hand, the system is slowly undergoing some reform. For example, administrative improvements have been made by standardizing assessment procedures for performance at the state level on behalf of the state and its local governments. Administrative reform has been spurred by court decisions requiring annual reassessment, and reassessment of all property within a particular jurisdiction. Decisions have disallowed reassessment and resulting tax increases for only a portion of a jurisdiction while the remainder undergoes no tax increase until its turn. (The possible heavy impact of assessment reform and high inflation has motivated some jurisdictions to achieve "full value" in multi-year stages.) Communities are rethinking the value of commercial exemptions. More care is being used in determining whether property owned by a tax-exempt institution is used for the purposes which underlie the exemption.

Reform of operational theories is also under discussion. Altering the division of value between land and its improvements so as to reflect more accurately the potential of the land and to motivate further improvement is being explored.

Measures are also being developed to increase the accuracy of the assessments of presently undervalued apartment properties.

f.   Like other taxes, the property tax raises federal constitutional questions and the answers are similar to those we have already seen. Thus, property deemed to be in continued transit in interstate commerce, even though the journey has been temporarily interrupted will be immune from local taxation. If the journey has come to an end, or if the interruption is indeterminate in length, purpose and eventual destination, taxation which is not discriminatory will be upheld.

Similarly, the federal constitution's Import-Export Clause limits municipal property taxation to imported property which loses its imported character by being subsumed into the general aggregate of otherwise taxable property within the municipality and to otherwise taxable potential exports which are held for shipment in federal duty-free storage or which have not yet been shipped, entered with a carrier for actual shipment, or started on a continuous journey for exportation.

Local property taxation of the interstate-and foreign-transportation units of carriers domiciled in the local taxing jurisdiction will be upheld so long as an identifiable segment of the taxable corpus (average number of fungible units, e.g.) has not been continuously present in an out-of-

state taxing jurisdiction throughout the taxable
year and therefore, not having acquired situs in
the latter jurisdiction, could not be subjected to
an apportioned tax thereby. Non-domiciliary jurisdictions may impose an apportioned tax upon
carrier units which have acquired situs therein so
long as the tax bears a reasonable relation to the
opportunities, benefits and protections provided
by the jurisdiction. Fair measures of such apportionment have included those which result in reasonable compensation for the use of local roads
and highways (mileage, passengers, e.g.) and
those which relate benefits to the average number of vehicles stored in the taxing jurisdiction
throughout the year.

g. Two unsuccessful federal constitutional
challenges deserve mention. The U.S. Supreme
Court has rejected the contention that tax exemptions of property owned by religious institutions
violate the Establishment Clause of the first
amendment's religious-freedom guarantee in language which raises the question whether a statute or ordinance abolishing such an exemption
would itself be unconstitutional.

The comparative inadequacies of the property
tax bases of local governments have for a number of years motivated equal-protection challenges seeking to overturn the customary method
of supporting local public education largely
through property-tax revenues of the particular

locality or school district. Some districts have
and spend more than others. The school-support
challenge began with an aborted attempt to seek
a requirement of equal per-pupil expenditures.
Attention then turned to overturning the local
property tax as primary support by showing discriminatory disparities among school systems.
After initial success in some state and lower federal courts, the attempt failed in the U.S. Supreme Court. The Court ruled that education
was not a fundamental right and poverty was not
a suspect classification giving rise to strict scrutiny requiring compelling state justification. The
Court then found the reasons supporting local
control and local property-tax support to be a rational justification for the present system under
the federal fourteenth amendment. (It is interesting to note that, in subsequent cases involving
the same state school system, the Court invalidated a law denying tuition-free public education to
children of illegal aliens, and upheld a law denying tuition-free public education to minors who
live apart from parents or parent-substitutes for
the purpose of attending free public schools.)

h. The system of local property taxes as primary public-school support is not invulnerable to
challenge, however. Using state constitutional
clauses requiring equal protection of the laws,
mandating a complete and uniform system of
public instruction, or requiring that the state pro-

vide a thorough and efficient system of public education, some state courts have overturned the traditional system, even where state legislative equalization efforts had occurred (and at least one has declined to do so). There has been evidence of state legislative difficulty in settling upon the school-support replacement—income taxes, statewide property taxes, or the like. There remain the difficult problems of relating capital and operating expenditures to urban-density or rural areas of higher need, to the desire to retain veteran faculty, to areas of higher cost of living and to a host of other legitimate factors affecting the costs of education.

§ 3. Borrowing. a. If it is authorized to do so, the local government may borrow funds for the short term in anticipation of the particular year's tax revenues or of the immediate collection of special assessments. It may borrow for long term repayment from the general treasury or from revenues generated by one or more specific enterprises. It may accomplish the borrowing by issuing bonds and other paper and may issue such obligations in payment of existing debts. For example, we have seen the local-improvement contractor compensated by improvement certificates. A number of considerations accompany the nature of the municipal paper issued and the sources from which the obligation is to be paid.

b. Illustratively, our hypothetical cities may have to issue bonds to obtain the revenues necessary to construct the airport and domed stadium. After revenues have been obtained, individual contractors and subcontractors may be paid by check or by warrants payable from the city treasury. The bond issues themselves may be payable over a period of years from airport and stadium revenues, from the general treasury (the full taxing authority) or both. If tax increment financing has been employed, repayment will be made from targeted tax revenues traceable to the increased investment in real property spawned by the projects. Purchasers of the bonds and holders of the warrants may face obstacles to payment if authorization questions, extraterritorial problems, public-purpose and land-acquisition difficulties, local debt limitations, failure to realize projected tax-revenue increases, or city fund diversions encumber the projects or exhaust the funds. Such obstacles (and others) may be raised by the cities seeking to avoid payment or may be the basis for taxpayer suits seeking to stop the projects, unless the obstacles are removed by the negotiability of the paper or the completion of existing bond-validation procedures.

§ 4. **Warrants.** a. A municipal warrant is a written order from a local officer or board to the city treasurer or comparable official directing payment of a specified amount of money to a

named person or bearer sometimes from a specified fund. Warrants are payable upon presentation when funds are available. Similar municipal
paper may sometimes be called improvement or
tax-anticipation or revenue-anticipation certificates or certificates of local government indebtedness. Accurate understanding of the paper of a
particular local government requires consultation
of the customary plethora of governing statutory
provisions.

b. Warrants are frequently used for fund disbursements and short-term, anticipated-revenue
borrowing particularly from banks. Authority to
issue them is customarily implied from borrowing, bond-issuing and taxation authority. Regis-
tered warrants may also be used to pay tax re-
funds, bills and wages when the government is in
deficit. (At least one state has ruled that such
warrants may then be used by holder taxpayers
to pay their sales and excise taxes.)

c. Warrants may bear interest, although demand warrants usually do not until the warrant
is presented and payment is refused because of
lack of funds which should be available.

d. Since warrants are assignable, their negotiability would be an added attraction. Absent
statutory allowance, they are not negotiable and
defenses available against the original recipient
(fraud, want of consideration, illegality, e.g.) are
available against bona fide purchasers for value

except in the rare instance in which a court might apply estoppel. Occasionally, statutes do permit issuance of negotiable "unconditional," warrants even though payment is limited to a particular fund or source.

e. While warrants frequently are payable only from specified funds with the attendant risk that the holder may find the funds inadequate unless he can hold the city liable for wrongful diversion or failure to create the fund, statutes at times make the warrants general obligations of the local unit. The municipality itself can agree to do so if within, or not covered by, the debt limit so as to make the warrants more acceptable.

§ 5. **Bonds.** a. When authorized to borrow, and to issue bonds (by specific grant, home-rule basic authority, or implied authority) of either the general-obligation or revenue type or both, the local government may issue bonds for a public purpose. Some states limit local bond issues to "municipal" or "corporate" purposes which terms may for this purpose signify public purposes of particular benefit to the local inhabitants. Some states may impose by constitution or statute such additional restrictions as those limiting issuance to capital expenditures and excluding internal improvements.

b. As noted above, "municipals" (the trade name for bond issues of both state and local governments) may be general obligation bonds, payable from all revenues, backed by the full taxing authority, or revenue bonds, payable solely from the revenues of a particular enterprise. In the latter case, local governments frequently enter into covenants agreeing to use the facilities, to charge adequate and uniform user fees or to take other measures designed to assure that the revenue source will be productive. Such covenants have been sustained as authorized by revenue-bond delegations and as valid in the face of challenge as improper delegations of governmental powers, although an occasional covenant to use the police power in a predetermined way has caused difficulty. Subsequent, mid-payment, statutory attempts to modify bondholders' contractual expectations of revenue and project realization and completion will raise serious impairment-of-contract questions under the federal Contract Clause.

A particular type of revenue bond has been seen more frequently in the rapidly spreading municipal use of tax increment financing, whereby bonds issued to obtain funds for municipal-redevelopment improvements designed to attract private investors are to be repaid from the tax increments resulting from the enhanced assessable value of the improved property which such investment encouraged. Authorization for such financing necessarily permits the issuer to capture traceable tax revenue increments which might otherwise have accrued to overlapping taxing districts. Because bondholder risk is greater, higher interest must be paid.

c. As in the case of other municipal actions, the issuance of bonds everywhere involves constitution-, statute-, charter-, or ordinance-required procedures many of which will be deemed mandatory. Illustrative are the bond-referendum provisions governing resolution-publication, notice and elections. Failure to comply substantially with directory procedures or to adhere strictly to mandatory procedures renders the proceedings for the issuance of the bonds invalid.

d. The process of borrowing through bond issues depends, of course, on the marketability of the bonds. Underwriters will bid upon advertisement therefor and will offer to purchase the issue at a sum reflective of the face amount (par) less discount (below par) where and to the extent that discounts are allowed and will specify the lowest interest rate which in their judgment will allow the bonds to be marketed given the source of payment, the length of time until maturity and the credit rating of the city. At times bids may not be required. The interest rate is a composite of many factors in addition to the source of payment and city credit rating: the narrowness of the municipals market, the tax deductibility of

[*320*]

the interest, and the purpose for which the money is borrowed. (Compare bonds issued to build a plant to be rented to a major, profitable corporation with bonds issued by a nearly bankrupt city to pay daily operating expenses.) A bond issue with serial maturity dates for segments thereof will bear different interest rates for each such segment reflecting the length of time to maturity.

e. The bonds of a local government may be negotiable if issuance of such negotiable securities is authorized. Nevertheless, the fact that under negotiability statutes questions may be raised concerning governing constitutional provisions such as debt ceilings, the nature of the consideration or substantial compliance with governing legal requirements, and the authority of the municipality makes both underwriter syndicates and potential investors skittish and hesitant. Accordingly, a number of additional steps may be available to enhance the issue's marketability. Constitutions and statutes often dictate that municipalities must provide in advance of a bond issue for annual taxes or other revenues sufficient to pay the principal and interest. Frequently by statute or the bond contracts, local governments may be required to make regular payments into a sinking fund which will be protected against diversion or inadequacy and available ultimately for the redemption of the bonds.

In a number of states, local government bond issues require (automatically or upon citizen protest) approval and supervision of issuance and
sale by state administrative boards or officers.

f.   There are other protections for investors
(diversion-of-funds rules, receivorships, e.g.) and
for taxpayers (allowance of taxpayer suits, often
by statute, e.g.).   One system of increasing us-
age, protecting both, is the statutory provision
for pre-issuance judicial bond-validation procedures.   How the procedures are invoked, whether
by the local entity, state officers or taxpayers,
whether they must be invoked and whether they
are exclusive are matters for local law.

g.   Recognizing that municipal default on bond
issues is not impossible, and indeed has appeared
likely on several recent occasions, with possible,
widespread repercussions in the bond market,
state and federal legislators have attempted to
augment financial-market bond ratings with more
elaborate municipal disclosure of financial information, akin to that required of corporate bor-
rowers, to enhance potential bondholders' knowledge of the risks associated with their
investments.   Such disclosure can be required by
law (to the federal Securities Exchange Commission, e.g.) or voluntary (Municipal Finance Officers Association, e.g.).   The fact that failure to
apply sound fiscal management is a fundamental
cause of local fiscal difficulty has also prompted

observers to urge more states to join those already active in adopting such reforms as uniform accounting standards for all local units, controls on budgetary practices (to prevent capitalization of current operating expenses, e.g.), required, periodic financial reports, and creation of state agencies to provide technical assistance.

Fiscal crises have occurred and local governments have attempted to stave off default and the breakdown of city services. The courts have looked with disfavor upon local-government attempts to ameliorate financial crises by such steps as: suspension of repayment and unilateral extension of the time span of short-term, tax-anticipation notes (notes' repayment constitutionally guaranteed); delay in making required payment of tax revenues into a tax-anticipation-note retirement or sinking fund (mandamus lies to require payment); and unilateral alteration of bondholder protections set forth in the debt instruments (possible violation of U.S. Constitution's Contract Clause).

In the event that such crises cannot be resolved, federal law provides the possibility of municipal bankruptcy at the behest of the municipality without advance approval of creditors. A stay of ancillary actions against the petitioning governmental unit is envisioned. The petition to the court must be accompanied by notice to the federal Securities Exchange Commission, the state, and all creditors. The court is enabled to issue certificates of indebtedness to maintain essential city services.

§ 6. Debt Limitations. a. As noted earlier, state constitutional provisions prohibiting borrowing for later private investment and lending municipal credit to private enterprises, and requiring a public, or a municipal or corporate purpose circumscribe somewhat the flexibility of municipal borrowing. Such provisions were repeatedly raised, with little lasting success, in challenges to urban renewal programs. One of the most persistent constitutional and statutory problems, however, has been the existence in a majority of states of clauses governing municipal debt. In some states, constitutional or statutory debt limits are not applicable to home-rule cities (although their charters may contain similar provisions) and their applicability to special districts and authorities is a matter of interpretation.

b. The type of limit or ceiling varies. Some are expressed in terms of a fixed amount. Others impose a ceiling based upon a percentage of the assessed value of property within the local entity. Yet others limit debts to income for the year or require approval of the electorate. Some limits are interpreted not to bar certain debt purposes or debts necessitated by emergencies. Earlier debts within the limits will not be invalidated by subsequent excesses. While involuntary obli-

[*324*]

gations may be included in computations to determine whether the limit has been reached, ceilings
will most likely not be applied to bar assumption
of involuntary obligations such as those imposed
by state authority (unfunded pension liability,
e.g.) and tort judgments against the municipality.
And bonds issued to refund existing debt do not
create new debt.

c.   The reader should recall that the bond referenda electorate may not be limited to property
taxpayers, whether the bonds be general-obligation or revenue, without substantial justification.
The results of debt-limit invalidation cannot be
avoided by attempted municipal "ratification" and
although results are predictably inconsistent,
quasi-contractual relief may not be available to
holders of the invalid obligations.

d.   There exist means whereby municipalities
have, with frequent judicial approval, avoided the
impact of debt limitation.   Illustrative are long
term lease arrangements with options to purchase, bonds payable from special funds or revenues, and creation of special districts or authorities.   Combinations of these methods are
frequent.   For example, in order to obtain the
revenues necessary for construction and operation of the airport and domed stadium, our cities
may issue bonds with repayment limited to the
revenues of the two projects.   Alternatively, they
may avail themselves of state legislation permit-

ting creation of special authorities which may lease the stadium and airport to the cities, or after construction thereof, may operate them, and which in either event will finance the projects through bonds payable from their revenues and not includable within the sponsoring cities' limited debt.

At the outset, it should be noted that there are a few court decisions which view present assumption of long term lease obligations or issuance of revenue bonds as debts of the city of the type to which the limits apply. And the majority of courts feel that installment-payment purchase arrangements where the city now receives the property should be computed at the full amount eventually to be paid and considered debts to which the ceilings are applicable. Finally, when the courts conclude that a city's general faith and credit in some manner stand behind what purport to be bonds payable from special funds or revenues, the debt limits will apply to such obligations. There is room, nevertheless, in the majority of jurisdictions for avoiding the appearances of installment purchasing or general faith and credit obligations.

e. If the lease arrangement is entered into in good faith and creates no immediate indebtedness for the whole amount but confines liability for payment to consideration actually furnished in a given year, the full projected cost will not be computed as debt in determining whether the limit has been reached or exceeded. If the court finds evidence that seems to allow no conclusion but that the arrangement is a subterfuge, in actuality a conditional sale with installment payments, it will conclude that debt subject to the limit has been assumed and, if the limit has been exceeded, that the contract is void. Such evidence may include immediate indebtedness for the aggregate of rentals, "options" for eventual purchase whereby, for little or no additional consideration, the property will be conveyed to the city upon completion of the "rental" payments for the term of the lease, or annual payments in excess of reasonable rentals.

f. The debt limitations are not ordinarily held applicable to bonds or other obligations payable from special funds such as the revenues from municipally owned utilities and other facilities or from special assessments, so long as creditors can only look to the special fund or the revenues of the specified undertaking, and not to the general credit of the municipality. As noted earlier, city covenants to assure successful revenue production by the undertakings, including agreements to maintain sufficient rates do not convert revenue obligations to general credit obligations. Such municipal revenue and special-fund obligations are authorized in almost all states.

(i) There are matters of some difficulty for which the cases supply inconsistent answers. There is authority permitting several undertakings to be financed by the revenues which only a few of them will produce. A few courts insist that the revenue producing entity be a new or at least a related one and look with disfavor upon the pledge of revenues from enterprises already in existence to support new endeavors. When either the property being financed or other municipal property is encumbered as security for the obligations which are payable solely from special revenues, the courts may conclude that because general city credit may be called upon to satisfy liens in the event of default, the mortgages convert in whole or pro tanto an otherwise special-fund arrangement into a general obligation debt subject to the limitations.

g. Normally, the debts of coterminous or overlapping special districts, authorities, boards or commissions created under the plethora of state authorizations will not be added to that of the coexisting city to determine whether its debt has exceeded constitutional or statutory limits. To the extent that the debt limitations are applied at all to such special districts, debt within the limit will be available to each as an individual quasi-municipal corporation, so long as each was properly created in the manner permitted in the unquestioned wisdom of the state legislature for a

proper purpose. As a result, separate authorities
have enabled sponsoring cities to achieve many
goals including housing, sports facilities, public
buildings, sanitation, recreation, transportation
and flood control.

(i) But this ever-proliferating limit-avoidance
technique is not foolproof. In addition to the few
jurisdictions which do not subscribe to the inde-
pendent-debt conclusion, courts in other jurisdictions are becoming more circumspect, and receptive to the contention that creation of a special
authority to perform a vital public function, one
long within the province of local general governments, must be justified on grounds other than
financing (ease and efficiency of management,
separate accountability, isolation from politics,
professional expertise, e.g.) to escape rejection as
a subterfuge to evade the debt limit.

§ 7. Illustration: Industrial Revenue Bonds.
a. No device better illustrates flexibility in the
face of constitutional limitation, the evolution of
the concepts underlying public purpose, and the
expansion of judicial recognition of the appropriateness of government initiative than the industrial revenue bond. At the same time, no device
better illustrates the priority distortions and municipal overextensions which result from innovation and competition unchecked by confrontation

with strict judicial views of the commands of the state constitutions.

b.   The device envisioned the use of state or local authority or local general government revenue bonds to finance construction or expansion of industrial or commercial facilites to be leased to private industry for the rentals necessary to pay off the bonds. Because the bonds bore lower interest rates as tax free municipals, industry could be enticed to come or remain and expand at costs which themselves were tax deductible and were in any event lower than the costs to industry of itself raising the necessary capital. Begun, not surprisingly, in industry-starved areas during the Great Depression, the concept spread throughout the country as the objective expanded from community economic improvement to defensive efforts to retain industry which was being enticed to leave. (If it departs, will it reimburse?)

c.   The device in its broadest sense has undoubtedly had beneficial results in bringing economic and cultural improvement to a number of states and localities. Indeed, it is presently serving to provide pollution control facilities purchased through municipal bonds for rental by private industries required to meet increasingly stringent pollution control standards, enabling them to do so less expensively. Nevertheless, the growth of the industrial revenue bond has im-

[*330*]

pacted heavily on the narrow municipal bond market and consequently has served to defer more important city borrowing ventures or to make them more expensive because the competition required higher interest rates to attract buyers. Query, for example, which is a more attractive investment, the local bridge authority revenue bonds or the revenue bonds of whatever municipality backed by rentals obligated to be paid by a nationally known, major, sound and successful industrial corporation?

d. As industrial revenue bonds proliferated, the primary challenges were, of course, lack of authority to borrow in this manner, or if authorized by the state, violation of such state constitutional clauses as those requiring a public purpose and those prohibiting the lending of state or municipal credit to private enterprise, forbidding delegation of municipal power to special commissions, and banning gifts to private entities or debt in excess of specified ceilings. In many states, the courts resolved these questions in favor of the concept's validity. There have been impressive decisions to the contrary, however, some extending the approving majority's public-purpose rationale to municipal use of eminent domain to benefit private industry, in order to demonstrate the possible horrors of continued, unchecked public-purpose evolution and expansion. It should be noted that some such decisions have been overturned by voter-approved, state constitutional amendments.

e.   Related, authorized expansions of the use of municipals have included such revenue bonds as those issued to build facilities for tax-exempt institutions (universities, e.g.), those issued to fund student-loan programs, and mortgage bonds which provided capital for housing at costs lower than prevailing high mortgage interest.

Spurred by the Treasury Department's continued effort to reclaim the revenues "lost" through non-taxation of municipal bond interest, the U.S. Congress has dampened the investor enthusiasm somewhat by withdrawing from tax free status industrial revenue bond interest for issues which do not meet such conditions as legislatively specified priority purposes and which in the aggregate do not exceed rather restrictive amounts. Subsequent revenue rulings have adhered closely to the objective of limiting tax-exempt issues. Recent federal legislation has further restricted available projects and somewhat liberalized the aggregate ceiling.   Whatever a critic may think of some of the exceptions, one cannot deny that there has been a major change.   The industrial renters frequently also benefited by purchasing the bonds themselves.   The Congressional legislation taxes interest earned by such bondholders even if the bond issue is otherwise within an exception.

While tensions remain unresolved between the revenue-enhancing objectives of the executive and the intentions of the Congress, the IRB's cousins have also been subjected to limitation which may reduce market enthusiasm. For example, the tax exemption for the interest on mortgage bonds faces a sunset provision (although there are efforts to extend) and in the meantime, new issues will be available only for veterans housing, or for housing conforming to certain yield, volume, homebuyer, purchase-price, target-area, low-income use (if rental), and other restrictions.

§ 8. Practical Considerations: Borrowing Restraints. a. In discussing borrowing as a revenue-producing power, it is appropriate to comment that few, if any, local governing powers are so inconsistently and inefficiently restricted. The amount of the debt owed by local governments is massive. Less than half of it is owed by local general governments with the remainder split between school districts and other special districts and authorities.

These facts alone are not necessarily bad. Borrowing, after all, is necessary and provides the means whereby improvement can be related to future economic growth. But history shows that local governments may borrow excessively and may borrow to achieve objectives not as necessary as others which go unattended. Restraints are few and ineffective.

b. Political restraint is a sometimes thing. The mobility of populations, desire of present generations for present improvements with costs to be "postponed," and frequent public apathy are such that municipal borrowing is not forced to withstand cost-benefit and priority scrutiny. And the electorate is at best an inconsistent superintendent, venting its wrath in financially difficult times upon proposed bond issues for education and sanitation while funding dreams such as major sports facilities which turn out to be nightmares of wildly inflating construction costs and minimal annual revenues. If our city of Allgood were to succeed in building its stadium, its annual debt costs (if it stood behind the bonds) might have an impact similar to the experience of one American city which reportedly had to give up a new major fire station, downtown aesthetic renovation, physical improvements in libraries and cemeteries, lighting for safer streets, recreational improvements for two city parks, needed street and sewer improvements, and other plans including preliminary engineering for a new civic center—all to pay the annual debt cost for a stadium which would not have a major sports user for at least another year.

c.   In fact, political restraint may promote borrowing.   As the politically tolerable levels of municipal taxation have been reached, major cities
have been issuing general credit bonds to pay the
daily expenses of government (and are threatened with bankruptcy).

d.   The constitutional and statutory restraints
typified by the debt limitations are ineffective because the inflexibility of their somewhat archaic
ceilings and standards has been met by the avoidance methods previously described.   Repayment
of special district and revenue bonds is limited to
the undertaking's revenues.   Although the quality of revenue bonds varies widely, they tend to be
a more suspect investment, with good reason giv-
en the riskiness of some turnpike, bridge and stadium endeavors.   Accordingly, they require a
higher interest cost than the debt-ceiling-limited
general obligation bonds.   Municipal borrowing
has intensified because tax revenues may have
reached a political ceiling, because creative ideas
for providing local growth capital have been developed, and because the borrowing objectives of
one locality necessarily cause competitive reaction in another, even if its local priorities be dis-
torted.   Interest rates necessarily reflect not only
the risk inherent in the revenue source (some cities' credit generally; others' venturesome tax increment financing, e.g.), but also the competition
in individual-issue yield necessitated by the

proliferation of massive borrowing in a narrow market. Thus the result of debt limitations and their avoidance techniques is not less borrowing but more expensive borrowing—hardly the desired objective.

§ 9. Practical Considerations: Federal Taxation. a. A significant intergovernmental political factor in municipal borrowing is the federal tax law's exclusion from gross income of interest on the obligations of the states and their political subdivisions. We have noted above the continued modifications of this exclusion in the case of industrial revenue bonds and their cousins. There are significant pressures to end the exclusion altogether. But the U.S. Congress may feel that direct federal taxation would be such interference with a major revenue source as to affect the sovereign rights of the states thus raising federal constitutional difficulties. Moreover, major lobbying efforts by state and local governments are premised upon the belief that the exclusion enables government borrowing which would otherwise be thwarted by competition with private industry bonds and other investments, and would necessarily involve even higher interest costs.

b. Proponents of taxation argue that the result would be an increase in federal revenues and an expansion of the market for investment in municipals. The municipals market has been relatively narrow, consisting for the most part of

[*336*]

commercial banks, casualty insurance companies and individual federal taxpayers on the average in the higher tax brackets, investors who need the tax benefits of such an investment. Even this market had been further limited to those who could invest sizeable sums until the growth of municipal-bond funds selling in $5,000 and even $1,000 lots.

c. Legislative changes have so far been only partially successful. Suggested attempts to avoid the constitutional risk have included federal taxation of preferential income with such income including municipals interest (not enacted) and the establishment of a minimum tax to be paid by those who earned largely tax-free income. Proposals designed to retain the lower interest cost for local governments while increasing federal tax revenues have included those creating an Urban Development Bank and those combining federal guarantees and interest supports. For example, one suggestion advocated a fifty percent federal interest subsidy to be paid to municipalities issuing taxable bonds. The cities would be permitted to ask underwriters for bids on issues both as taxable and as tax-exempt, and to accept the bid with the lowest cost to the city. Advocates of the status quo have successfully forestalled such attempted solutions fearing that they would result in federal control of municipal borrowing. Nevertheless, continued tax-exempt sta-

[*337*]

tus for municipals is at best an uncertain prediction, and IRBs and their cousins are the most
vulnerable.

C. SOME ADDITIONAL CONSIDERATIONS RELEVANT TO MUNICIPAL EXPENDITURES

§ 1. Constitutional Restrictions on Expenditure Objectives. a. Local governments must
have authority to spend for particular purposes.
As we have seen throughout this text, the expenditure authority will be restricted to a public purpose, and in some jurisdictions to a corporate or
municipal purpose. Again, if there is any distinction between public and corporate or municipal
purposes, it is that the local government action or
expenditure must reasonably promote the public
health, safety, morality or general welfare of that
municipality's citizens somewhat more substantially than it does other residents of the state.

b. Recall that other constitutional restrictions
include those prohibiting the lending of municipal
credit to private enterprise, barring gifts to private individuals and corporations, forbidding investments, and banning the paying of additional
compensation to municipal officers and government contractors.

c. In the face of such constitutional prohibitions, would the courts uphold expenses incurred
[*338*]

by officials of a port authority for meals and entertainment of shippers designed to promote increased shipping use of the port facilities in the face of heavy competition? Would courts uphold municipal expenditures by our illustration cities designed to persuade voters to approve any bond issues necessary for the airport and stadium projects?

§ 2. Expenditure Method Restrictions. a. We have noted that in many states local-government fiscal procedures could be much more detailed and sophisticated. While much improvement is needed, localities do not operate totally without controls, however. In order to foster taxpayer knowledge of proposed expenditures and resultant taxation, and to insure that the priorities determined by the political process be observed, constitutions, statutes and charters set forth mandatory specific restrictions governing expenditure methods. The requirements may include statutory limits upon annual spending increases; presentation of revenue and expenditure estimates and budget recommendations by an administrative officer; adoption and publication of annual and biennial budgets and appropriation ordinances by the local governments after notice and hearings; reasonably clear disclosure in the budget of the purposes for which money is to be expended; and post-spending audits and published annual reports. Enforcement of the restrictions includes voiding expenditures in excess, or in violation of the prerequisite steps; forbidding enactment of interim taxation ordinances increasing the taxation during the year; and prohibiting intra-budgetary, permanent transfer or diversion of funds for purposes other than those for which they were originally budgeted.

b.   The restrictions may not be totally inflexible, however.   Some jurisdictions permit intrabudgetary, temporary borrowing of funds. Some charters permit appropriation and budget amendments by ordinance during the year.   Some courts will uphold emergency appropriations, although in such emergencies approval of the electorate or of a state agency may be needed and judicial agreement that the emergency was real is not a foregone conclusion.   In some localities, unexpended and unneeded funds in one budget category may be diverted to another purpose.

c.   A number of certifications and permissions may be necessary prerequisites to municipal spending.   For example, spending may have to be preceded by the comptroller's certification that appropriately budgeted funds exist, or an expenditure above certain levels may require specific approval by the local governing body.   In some states, in addition to state-prescribed procedures, there may be state administrative supervision, review and final approval authority over borrowing and expenditures.

§ 3. Officer Liability for Unlawful Expenditures. a. Municipal officers who are responsible for the loss of public funds or who make illegal disbursements may be civilly (and in some cases, criminally) liable for their conduct and reimbursement by them or, if bonded, by their sureties may be required. Personal liability for the loss may depend upon negligence or upon value received by the city. Personal benefit by the officer or by an employee will result in personal liability for the return of the funds.

CHAPTER VI

CONSIDERATIONS PERTINENT TO CITIZEN LITIGATION WITH LOCAL GOVERNMENTS

The questions discussed throughout this text reach the attention of the courts in a variety of ways. Challenges to local governing actions or failure to act are raised by individuals, groups, governmental entities and classes affected by ordinances and administrative implementation thereof. Such challenges may be raised directly or through attorneys general in actions quo warranto, questioning the authority by which an officer or a governmental entity purported to hold or create office or to act; in court reviews following upon the exhaustion or denial of administrative review procedures, either upon the administrative record or by such procedures as mandamus to compel the performance of an allegedly non-discretionary duty; in declaratory judgment actions; in individual actions seeking injunctive relief or damages; in taxpayer suits on behalf of or against the local government seeking to recover illegal expenditures, compel or restrain action; and in defenses to the proceedings brought by the local government to assert its contractual or other rights or to enforce its ordinances and regulations. Often, suits will add ei-

ther the local government or its officers as
defendants to avoid the restrictions of the respective immunities. Sometimes, relief will be denied
because another remedy is adequate and more appropriate. Indeed, the area is so circumscribed
by local procedures that no summary can adequately substitute for consulting local statutes
and ordinances.

Nevertheless, there are some aspects common
to citizen litigation with local government which
deserve brief consideration in this chapter. Municipal immunity, restrictive statutes of limitations, and notice and claim-filing requirements
will be viewed in the context of citizen suits in
tort against the municipality. The chapter will
conclude with some observations on standing in
individual and taxpayer actions against the local
government, primarily in state and local courts.

A. CITIZEN TORT CLAIMS AGAINST THE LOCAL GOVERNMENT

§ 1. **Customary Theories.** Our purpose here is
not to review tort theories of recovery. Rather,
as noted above, our focus is upon those matters
which are peculiar to a tort case against a municipal corporation. At the outset, the reader should
recall inverse condemnation suits which seek
damages reflecting just compensation for property taken or damaged under applicable constitutional clauses on the theory that, although no for-

[*343*]

mal exercise of eminent domain has been attempted, the governmental entities have in effect exercised, or should be held to have exercised, eminent domain power. Such suits may involve municipal negligence, nuisance or trespass. Under this theory, for example, it was held that residents in close proximity to a municipal airport who complained of its expansion of facilities and uses with demonstrable property damage had stated a sufficient claim for relief to withstand a motion to dismiss.

The tort actions against local government run the gamut from assault and battery, trespass and malpractice to nuisance and interference with business relations, seeking customary damages for injury to person and property under the traditional intentional, negligence or strict theories of liability and applicable agency principles. For example, plaintiffs may allege that the city permitted lake waters to escape and trespass upon their private property with the result that electrical wiring shorted and their buildings caught fire. Or, a farmer may argue that the city's open-burning, public dump constituted a nuisance with resultant impact upon the quiet use and enjoyment of his property. It should be noted that the dump, although outside city limits, was on municipal property. Or, plaintiffs may assert a claim for special damages (economic losses) against an illegally striking, public-employee union, under an

[*344*]

intentional-tort theory, urging that the strike caused the damages and was directed against the public, and that statutory government strike remedies were not to be exclusive.

§ 2. Ultra Vires. Where the municipality is engaged in ultra vires activities in the sense that the activities are beyond the powers of the municipality under all circumstances, it will successfully plead that recovery in tort for injuries caused by such activities should be denied. Despite the apparent injustice to the injured party, the ultra vires doctrine's protection of the taxpayer's interest in proper use of municipal funds, though unspoken, will predominate. Perhaps because of the apparent injustice, recovery will not be denied where the ultra vires status results from a determination that the municipality's activity was not barred in all circumstances but was undertaken in an improper manner.

§ 3. Statutes of Limitations. Tort actions against municipalities are frequently governed by limitation periods significantly shorter than those governing actions between private individuals. (The statutes of limitations governing other actions against the city will also involve much shorter time periods.)

§ 4. Notice Requirements. Except for suits to enjoin municipal torts, tort actions against municipal entities are customarily barred unless the claimant has met notice requirements imposed by statute, charter or ordinance. Such notice requirements are generally upheld by the courts, even against constitutional, equal-protection challenges. Some legislation has attempted to ameliorate possible harsh results, while retaining the requirements' valid objectives, by providing that actual notice of sufficient facts reasonably alerting the government or its insurer to a possible claim be construed as compliance, or that no claim be defeated by lack of post-injury notice unless the government shows substantial prejudice thereby. Generally, such notice requirements are of three classes:

a. Where the city's liability is alleged to result from breach of a duty imposed upon the city to exercise due care so that persons are not injured by defects in property supervised by the city, such as streets, the city must have received actual notice of the defect's existence, or the circumstances must amount to constructive notice, and then there must have been a reasonable opportunity to take remedial action, before liability will be imposed.

b. The injured party must give notice of the injury to the appropriate government officials within a specified time, so that the municipality may investigate while the facts are fresh and may make appropriate budgetary plans. Some courts allow the notice period to be tolled because of the unsupervised infancy or comatose condition of the injured person or permit such conditions to be raised in defense to a charge of notice failure.

c. The claimant must submit the claim either to administrative entities or to the city council itself in order to afford an opportunity for settlement before suit is filed. Denial of the claim or failure to act at this level does not serve to bar or delay suit and attempts by ordinance to add that suit can only be filed with permission of the city have been ruled invalid.

d. Illustratively, a city charter provided that notice of injury must be served upon an officer of the city within four months of such injury, setting forth the time, place and manner of injury, the act or defect complained of, the nature of the injury, and the identification of known witnesses. In addition, no suit could be brought unless the claimant had first presented to the city manager a claim in writing and under oath setting forth specifically the nature and extent of the injury and the amount of damages claimed.

A person injured when a metal rod he was holding came in contact with a city power line gave notice of the injury more than five months after the occurrence. He alleged that during that time he was totally physically disabled, was for much of the time vague and confused in communications with others, had severe pain, poor memory and unclear ideas about the passage of time, was partially paralyzed, and underwent seven operations and daily therapy. The trial court's decision that suit was barred was reversed on appeal. The appellate court adverted to the disagreement among courts concerning whether excuses for delayed filing should be permitted, chose to excuse a filing delayed by disability, and remanded for a determination whether the claimant's injuries were such that he was reasonably incapacitated from giving timely notice and, if so, whether notice was presented within a reasonable time after the incapacity ended.

§ 5. Municipal Immunity. a. Until statutory and the more recent judicial abrogations of immunity, municipalities had enjoyed immunity for the results of at least some of their torts. There have long been exceptions. Where municipal liability has been founded in trespass and in nuisance, the courts have been loathe to uphold any claims of immunity even if the municipal function is classified as governmental. So too, cities have traditionally been held liable for injuries caused by defects in streets and sidewalks at common law and by statute. The tradition of liability is not without its exceptions, however, as decisions immunizing cities where injuries were caused by "trivial defects" or by snow and ice attest.

b. With respect to torts other than trespasses, nuisances and those involving street defects, the history of municipal immunity has followed the classic course of the various immunity doctrines: It was judicially created and in the beginning was absolute. In time, new theories of justification were developed (though commentators differ on whether the doctrine preceded the justifications). Compelling cases presenting manifest injustice were accompanied by (caused?) judicial creation of exceptions. With the growth and expansion of the insurance industry, municipalities were able to insure against liability (although it was sometimes difficult to prevent insurers from raising the immunity defense). Recent decades have seen geometric growth in criticisms of the doctrine by commentators and even reluctant courts. Today, the trend is clearly judicial abrogation, and the number of such decisions has grown rapidly. Such abrogation is inevitably followed by state legislative responses.

c. Thus, municipal immunity (to be distinguished from public officer immunity) began in response to the inability of English unincorporated "citizens associations" (Hundreds) to respond in damages to tort suits. The rule was carried into the jurisprudence of this country on the strength of overeager subservience to debatable precedent. Soon, the weakness of its origins and the demands of justice compelled modern justifications, first on the basis of "a sharing" by political subdivisions of the state's sovereign immunity, and then on the basis of the financial disruptions which increasingly large damage awards would cause. (One commentator insists that the sovereign-immunity premise was the source of municipal immunity from the beginning at least in one state.)

d. Exceptions inevitably developed. If the activity could be classified as "governmental," the municipality remained immune where that activity caused the injury. If not "governmental," the causative activity was termed "proprietary"—one of those functions which, as we have seen, were not locally performed as state "agent" for the benefit of the general public, but were functions of particular benefit to the corporate member-citizens, which perhaps earned profits, which perhaps could be performed by private enterprises, and desire for which may have constituted motivation for the city's initial incorporation. There would be no immunity for torts resulting from proprietary activities. While the dichotomy neatly fitted a sovereign-immunity basis, it has been, and, where still operative, continues to be very difficult and unpredictable in its application. What determines whether an activity will be labelled "proprietary" may include the profit and private enterprise factors mentioned above, precedent, and arguably the justness of the plaintiff's cause.

Other judicial exceptions included liability for active but not for passive tortious conduct, liability for voluntary activity but not for duties mandated by law, and liability for ministerial functions but not for those determined to be discretionary.

e. State legislatures enacted a number of statutes abrogating immunity for specified types of municipal activity (fire and police vehicles, e.g.) and more rarely for broad categories of claims (mobs and riots, safe places, torts and contracts, e.g.). Judicial reaction to the latter served at times to limit the impact by strict views of the scope of municipal duty, or by interpretations permitting immunity for quasi-legislative and discretionary activities.

f. Criticism of the immunity doctrine grew. Many courts moved from the way-stations of exception to abrogation. They recognized that the judicial origin imposed upon them, not the legislatures, the duty to remedy what they had come to believe was an unnecessary and unjust rule. Several courts have relied upon the availability and acquisition of municipal liability insurance to decide that immunity was ended or had been waived. Some states have enacted liberalizing legislation. As a result of this broad judicial and legislative action, the "piece-meal" liability provisions mentioned earlier have been overtaken by events. A minority of courts continue to uphold the rule with its exceptions (at least absent municipal waiver by purchase of insurance) because it has so long been a settled principle of the law that any change should come from the legislatures, which are better equipped to assess the financial impact of change upon the local governments.

g.   Where judicial or legislative abrogation has occurred, it has not resulted in the rule's total demise for a number of reasons. First, courts have generally retained immunity for judicial, quasi-judicial, legislative and quasi-legislative functions. These somewhat amorphous classifications and the discretionary-ministerial dichotomy chosen by some of the abrogators permit immunity even for executive or power-implementative activity intimately related to the core functions of government.

For example, in a jurisdiction where the courts had abrogated immunity, courts rejected the contention that negligent failure to inspect or negligent inspection by the city, pursuant to its building code of a private store's mezzanine was an actionable wrong to persons subsequently injured by the faulty construction and resultant collapse. The act of issuing a building permit was deemed quasi-judicial. The enactment of a building code was classified as legislative and the enforcement thereof was labelled quasi-legislative. The court concluded that to hold that the negligence was actionable would exceed the broadest boundaries yet established for government liability to its citi-

[*352*]

zens. Another court characterized a government failure to raise the divider between the east- and west-bound lanes of a highway after its resurfacing as a "policy or political decision" (discretionary) rather than a ministerial task of highway maintenance, thus immunizing the city.

Second, post-abrogation holdings to the effect that abrogation removes immunity but does not create any new liability not traditionally recognized in tort bring a reluctance to a field of law more accustomed to evolutionary growth and revive the "no-duty" theories which constricted the municipal waiver of immunity thought to be accomplished by statute, as noted above. Such reluctance may be understandable in view of the pervasive role played by local government in the lives of its citizens (claims of educational malpractice, e.g.). For example, one court has held that a city which passed favorably on the safety condition of what was in reality an unsafe place violated no duty to the injured plaintiff. The building code did not create duties to individuals; rather, it imposed a duty owed to the general public. Another court has ruled that where blatant motel fire and safety violations existed, the town breached a duty to those with whom it had a special relationship (the motel owners and operators) when it failed to perform the non-discretionary task of refusing to issue a certificate of occupancy. A court has imposed liability for negligence

[*353*]

when police undertake protective responsibilities
to particular members of the public, thus giving
rise to a special duty (wrongful death held caused
by failure to respond to a "911" emergency call,
e.g.), although it would not extend such concept
in the absence of the special relationship. In a
governmental-proprietary jurisdiction, similar
facts were held to be the exercise of a discretionary policy and hence, a governmental function.
(The commingling in some opinions of "discretion" language in connection with "governmental" conclusions may suggest either that the former is becoming a subset of the latter, or that a
potential abrogation of the latter and replacement
by the former is evolving.)

h. Finally, despite the availability of insurance, state legislatures found or feared major
detrimental, financial consequences of unlimited
tort liability and moved to follow judicial abrogation with responses ranging from restoration of
immunity to moratoriums, to complex statutes
permitting but governing tort recovery, to a variety of ceilings on amounts of recoverable damages. The courts in turn have responded by complete acceptance of the statutes, liberal or
restrictive (duty; discretionary-ministerial, e.g.)
interpretations or invalidation of some provisions
under the state and federal constitutions.

i. To the extent permitted by such state constitutional clauses as that requiring that the

courts be open to every citizen and that an expeditious remedy be afforded, or to the extent that the alternative remedies are available, there remain statutes which may exempt particular local government activities from liability (airports, street defects, snow and ice, e.g.). Illustratively, such a statute immunized municipalities from liability for personal injury from the use of any public grounds, buildings or structures. Suits were brought on behalf of two boys, ages eleven and three, to recover for injuries incurred on play equipment in municipal parks. In a consolidated appeal, in a state which had virtually abolished the judicial rule of immunity by court decisions, the court decided that municipal parks and playgrounds were covered by the statute. The court reiterated the judicial interpretation that the statute immunized only *governmental*-function buildings and grounds and concluded that parks and playgrounds were governmental. Accordingly, what it viewed as possibly a harsh result it deemed required by the statute.

j. It is important to distinguish immunity of a state's political subdivisions from immunity of the state itself, regardless of whether "sovereign immunity" provides the basis for both, in determining what has been abrogated. Some courts have abolished both. Some have abolished only municipal immunity. And some responsive statutes have reiterated state immunity so that the abrogating decision may not be interpreted to arrive at a contrary result. Quasi-municipal corporations such as counties, townships and special function districts will not be immune if immunity of the state of which they are "agents" has been abrogated. Even if state immunity is retained, however, abrogation of municipal immunity will commonly include the quasi-municipal entities as well. Different treatment of states and their political subdivisions is not uncommon, as we have seen in other contexts (unavailability of the federal eleventh amendment, state protection for municipalities; no automatic state-action exemption from federal antitrust laws for municipalities, e.g.).

As noted earlier, immunity of the governmental entity must be distinguished from public-officer immunity under state law. The latter doctrine may provide absolute immunity for particular functions (judicial, e.g.), thus requiring close examination of the circumstances in multiple-role positions (see Chapter II). It may provide immunity for discretionary but not ministerial acts. Thus, in jurisdictions retaining government immunity for governmental actions, public officers may be more amenable to liability if discretionary and governmental are not synonymous. The respective immunities would seem coterminous if the discretionary-ministerial test governed both government and an officer acting within the scope of his employment. Liability of public officers is at times more likely because municipalities have provided insurance and the likelihood of indemnification for those acting within the scope of their employment. At the same time, in several jurisdictions, courts have recognized the need to protect those serving the public from the burdens of undue litigation with the result that public-officer immunity may be more extensive than that of the government itself where its immunity has been substantially abrogated.

k. Attempts are often made to seek damages or equitable relief against a municipality and its officials for violation of the plaintiffs' civil rights in state or federal courts under 42 U.S.C.A. § 1983. Because many of the rights asserted may also be protected by common law tort doctrines, and because the violation of constitutionally or statutorily protected rights may be classified as "torts," it is important to note here an exponentially increasing area of municipal "tort" liability. Municipalities, counties, special districts, even interstate-compact authorities whose actions are held to have caused a deprivation of plaintiff's federal rights under color of state law, whether by legislation, official policy, custom or tradition, are subject to compensatory-damage (and punitive-damage) or equitable awards under § 1983. This is an evolving area of liability and in the recent flood of litigation its dimensions and any municipal-entity immunities are not yet clearly developed or demarcated.

The extent of public officers' immunities in this area is not clear. Immunity appears to relate to the function being performed, with absolute immunity for local government officers acting in legislative, judicial, prosecutorial, public-defender or state-court appointed attorney-defender capacity. Qualified immunity is possible for officers in other capacities where their actions were taken in good faith (no injurious intent) and in circumstances wherein the official did not know or have reason to know that he was acting illegally. Officials may thus act appropriately pursuant to official policy, authorization or custom, and thereby may be entitled to at least a qualified immunity. Their government entities, "persons" under § 1983, may nevertheless be liable. Public officials may, on the other hand, act in ways that deprive plaintiff of federal rights but may not have done so pursuant to official policy, authorization or custom. In such circumstances, respondeat-superior theory will not be applied, and their governments will not be liable under § 1983. (A theory of direct constitutional cause of action against municipalities, applying respondeat superior, has had substantially less receptivity since the U.S. Supreme Court declared them potentially liable under § 1983.)

The scope of possible § 1983 liability, while not unlimited, is immense. It includes all actions under color of law (except, under principles of comity, state tax laws) which may harm federal constitutionally protected personal and property rights (employment; inverse condemnation, e.g.) and all rights accorded by federal statutes except those which were intended to exclude § 1983 enforcement. Section 1983 liability envisions both intent and negligence theories, although the U.S. Supreme Court has indicated that in some, but not all, circumstances, the availability of due process in state procedures would bar assertion of rights under § 1983 by a plaintiff who failed to take advantage of the state remedy (prisoner had a state cause of action for negligent loss of his hobby materials at the hands of state prison officials, e.g.).

§ 6. Some Notes Concerning Damages, Execution, Contribution and Indemnity. a. If the person suffering special injury seeks to enjoin municipal tortious conduct, traditional equity principles will apply. In actions seeking damages, it was traditionally likely that only compensatory damages would be awarded from the city. A series of arguments had been persuasive in avoiding the imposition of punitive damages in the absence of authorizing statutes. It was felt that their principal goals, punishment and deterrence, would not thereby be effected. The citizens would bear the burden of the award and are the same who would benefit from its deterrent effect. The size of the award, if related to the wealth of the tortfeasor, would perforce be based on the unlimited taxing power of the municipality. A large award against the city would not necessarily deter city employees who would not have to pay it, and the compensatory award would probably motivate city deterrent disciplinary procedures in any event. While for these reasons, the majority of courts have held that public policy precludes punitive damages, some courts in the absence of statutory prohibition have recently reached the conclusion that punitive damages should be available against the city where in similar circumstances they would be warranted against a private defendant.

   b. When a judgment is obtained against the city, we have seen that recovery will not be barred because the judgment debt pro tanto exceeds constitutional or statutory debt limitations. Such a debt will be included in determining the total debt of the city in evaluating other borrowing, however. When funds are borrowed to pay the judgment, the bond issue or other form of borrowing does not constitute a debt additional to the original liability under terms of the debt limits, although both are in a sense "outstanding" after borrowing and before payment is made.

c. In some jurisdictions, attempts to obtain satisfaction of judgments by execution upon municipal property or the garnishment of funds in the hands of debtors and depositors of the city will be met by rulings that the only available remedy is mandamus against the appropriate city official to obtain the necessary funds by the appropriate taxation methods. In many jurisdictions, where no constitutional or statutory provision prohibits, attachment and execution may be had against proprietary assets of the government entity, although its governmental assets may not be reached. The courts adhere to a more inclusive concept of what assets are governmental than is common in other uses of the dichotomy.

d. Where the municipal entity and a private individual are co-tortfeasors, customary principles of indemnity and contribution (where available) may allow eventual recovery by one against the other of all or some of the tort judgment, subject to the usual difficulties. The private tortfeasor may face the additional difficulty of governmental immunity. On the other hand, indemnity awards against the city in several jurisdictions are made more possible by laws requiring the municipalities to indemnify specified employees against whom tort liability has resulted from actions in the performance of their duties. Indemnity awards for the city have been more likely (the general trend toward comparative negligence may affect the likelihood) than in private co-tortfeasor situations in cases where duties, such as the prevention of street defects, are imposed upon the city, which will then more likely be found "passively" or "secondarily" negligent within the meaning of indemnity doctrines, warranting recovery against the defect-causing co-tortfeasor deemed "actively" or "primarily" negligent. Indemnification of the city by its co-tortfeasor contractors is also more frequent because many municipal contracts will contain clauses providing therefor.

B. STANDING

§ 1. **The Requirement's Rationale.** We have seen a number of challenges which might be raised in appropriate actions attacking the city of Allgood's domed stadium, another city's airport and a third city's public disclosure ordinance. Each such challenger would face an initial hurdle: does the plaintiff have standing to bring the action? There are a number of general policies served by the requirement that the suing plaintiff have the necessary standing to bring the action. Among them is the policy that legal rights should be presented by such parties as to assure that there will be the "specificity," "adverseness" and "vigor" of advocacy best designed to enable proper resolution by the courts. The requirement is also intended to serve the public interest in a judicial system unencumbered by an inundation of litigation which saps the courts' abilities to give reasoned, considered resolution to important legal and social problems—the judicial administration or convenience objective. So, insistence upon proper standing is intended to isolate and serve parties specially aggrieved in lieu of attempting to provide a platform for voicing a multiplicity of felt grievances common to the public at large. It is intended to protect interests which are societally significant without dissipation of judicial energies upon a host of challenges to government activity which do not rise to this level.

The challenges here discussed may be raised by individuals, groups or classes who claim standing because they suffer the adverse effects of government action, and seek to uphold personal, property or contractual rights alleged to have been violated. Or they may be raised in a taxpayer action on behalf of the taxpayer class either because it is suffering an injury peculiar to its taxpayer status or because it is serving as watchdog to see that important legal rights and protections are not bypassed by otherwise unchallenged municipal activity.

§ 2. "Adverse" Effect of Government Action; Illustrative Questions. a. Where standing is to be based upon the "adverse" effect of the municipality's action upon persons and groups, the courts will insist upon a personal injury in fact, a

[*363*]

direct impact, one that is special to them, that gives them a "personal stake in the outcome" which assures the desired adversity. Are their personal, property and contractual rights such that the common law, the statutes or the constitutions provide that they shall be free from this type of injury?

b. So, may one who is injured by construction at the stadium site sue to recover from Allgood (prescinding from questions of indemnity or immunity)? Does a property owner who lives one half mile from the stadium site have standing (come within the statutory label "aggrieved") to challenge the rezoning ordinance permitting the site to be used for a stadium or the surrounding area to be used for the inevitable commercial satellites? Does a nearby property owner have standing to assert that stadium access and traffic regulations have damaged his right to ingress, egress, etc.? May an unpaid contractor sue to recover money allegedly owed under a contract to construct the airport? Does an association of surrounding landowners have standing to challenge the airport plans because the eventual construction on land created by filling in wetlands will disturb important breeding grounds for animals, fish and birds? May one who has submitted the lowest bid for construction of the airport challenge the award of the contract to one whose bid was higher? Do citizens or candidates or public officers have standing to contend that the public disclosure ordinance constitutes an unreasonable intrusion upon the right of privacy, an unjustifiable limitation upon the right to seek or hold public employment and an ambiguous and vague affront to the dictates of due process?

c.   Whether each of these challengers has the necessary standing will depend on whether the courts conclude that there is a right to be free from such injury contemplated by the law which the challengers seek to assert (the low bidder, e.g.); whether, in light of the nature and gravity of the municipal action and the degree of its impact upon the plaintiff, the courts are receptive to the asserted interest sought to be vindicated (rezoning effect one half mile away, e.g.); and whether the courts see the injury as special, different in kind and degree from that which affects the general public interest in the outcome (the wetlands challenge, e.g.).

d.   It should be noted that in addition to the broader recognition of assertable legal interests resulting from court liberal standing decisions, statutes will often promote judicial review of particular municipal actions by according "standing" to (giving legal recognition to the interest of) specified individuals (the low bidder, e.g.).

§ 3. **Taxpayer Suits.** a.   The balancing process which weighs the importance of the legal right's vindication and the significance of the societal interest against the desire for the honing process of adversary advocacy and the goal of restricting judicial-forum invocation has led the jurisdictions to inconsistent results in deciding whether taxpayers have standing to bring representative actions in connection with municipal activity. Is it more important to allow general-citizen oversight of municipal activity or are the judicial-facilities overtaxing and municipal inconvenience of citizen vigilance sound reasons to leave citizens to remedies at the polls and the rights in question to review only where such is sought by someone adversely and specially injured?

b. May one or more taxpayers of our illustration cities bring representative actions to enjoin payment by the city of Allgood of extra compensation to the construction contractor at the stadium, or to recover from the airport contractor extra compensation wrongfully paid by the city? May a taxpayer sue to require the city to zone the area around the airport to avoid unsafe conditions for residences? Does an Allgood taxpayer have standing to seek on behalf of all taxpayers to enjoin the city from entering into an ultra vires contract to build the stadium? May a taxpayer suit be brought to compel recalcitrant city officials to enforce the public disclosure ordinance?

c. One can see how the convenience-vigilance balance is struck in the prevailing attitudes of the courts to questions such as the above. In many jurisdictions, a taxpayer has standing to bring a taxpayer suit on behalf of his municipality if taxpayers in general would be exposed to financial harm because the city failed to bring the action itself. Where such standing is recognized, the right being vindicated (recovery of funds and property wrongfully disposed of, or of funds wrongfully retained by public officials, e.g.) is deemed to outweigh the fact that the plaintiff has suffered no special injury.

d. Similarly, in many jurisdictions a taxpayer, no matter what his motives, may bring a representative action against the municipality and its officials when the class of taxpayers would be exposed to financial loss (increased taxation) to enjoin illegal expenditures, or contracts which would have such result, illegal disposition of property, waste, assertedly illegal levy of taxes or creation of tax-exemptions (even though ending the exemptions would not affect plaintiff's taxes). These courts insist, though, that the municipal action result in actual financial loss to the taxpayers. Some other courts insist on a greater interest before the plaintiff and the class have standing, viz., special injury different from that suffered by taxpayers in general. A few courts are wary of any of these actions. Yet others would allow them only with respect to funds derived from general taxation (insisting that actions

[*367*]

involving water revenues be brought by ratepayers, e.g.). For example, in a suit by a city taxpayer seeking declaratory and injunctive relief from the city's issuance, pursuant to statute, of industrial revenue bonds for a solid-waste central processing facility, the court held that, to have standing, he must show that the bonds would constitute an indebtedness of the city, or would be a charge against its general credit and taxing power, and that he has suffered at least an "infinitesimal pecuniary loss." Because in that state revenue bonds do not create such an indebtedness and are not a charge upon city credit or taxing power, because municipal bonds are not exempt from that state's taxation, and because the plaintiff could not, therefore, show that he suffered a pecuniary loss which bond-buying taxpayers could escape, he lacked standing to bring such a suit.

e. A sizeable body of authority supports the proposition that municipal nondiscretionary duties imposed by law are of such significance that standing should be accorded to a citizen or taxpayer who invokes mandamus to compel performance of such duties. This concept of citizen vigilance and the importance of deciding significant legal questions and matters of public interest has been extended by some provisions in constitutions, statutes, and charters and by some liberal judicial standing determinations to permit representative actions by residents or taxpayers, whether or not the class will suffer financial harm, seeking to require power exercise or to restrain waste or illegal expenditures, disbursements, and contracts.

§ 4. Note on Federal Cases. a. Because the rights invoked against municipal action so frequently flow from the federal constitution and from federal statutes and administrative implementation, the challenges are frequently brought in federal court. The specific details of standing requirements in the federal forum are, of course, beyond the scope of this text. It is important to note, however, that they are designed to achieve the same goals as those described above, with the special underpinning of the federal constitution's case or controversy requirement.

b. Where a state court might require measurable financial injury in a taxpayer suit, the federal requirement per taxpayer might be significantly less demanding. Where a state court might require no demonstrable financial injury in a taxpayer suit, the federal court might be somewhat more stringent, seeking to be assured that the plaintiff has a "sufficient stake in the outcome." Where a state court might allow a taxpayer suit to restrain or compel the exercise of a non-expenditure, non-taxation power, the federal court will allow only such challenges as relate to the expenditure and taxation powers of Congress. In fed-

[*369*]

eral court, then, a taxpayer must challenge an exercise by Congress of its taxing and spending power and must allege that the challenged action exceeds specific constitutional limits on the exercise of such powers. (A group dedicated to the separation of church and state which challenged the executive's exercise under Congress' property power did not have taxpayer standing to enjoin the transfer of surplus government property to a private church group, e.g.) The U.S. Supreme Court's restrictive view of federal and state taxpayer standing to challenge allegedly unconstitutional uses of tax dollars does not seem intended to overrule the long line of cases which establish that municipal taxpayers, as opposed to federal and state taxpayers, have standing to sue to challenge such alleged use of their tax dollars.

c. Individual standing in federal court requires that the plaintiff have personally suffered actual or threatened injury which is fairly traceable to the challenged action and is likely to be redressed by a favorable decision. The alleged injury must be to personal or property rights which are federally protected (customer's interest in continued utility service is such property interest as constitutes a legitimate "claim of entitlement" protected by the federal Due Process Clause; city's interest in stopping realtors from steering black purchasers to a particular neighborhood so as to avoid increased residential segregation and property-value disruption, and residents' interest in an integrated neighborhood support standing to enjoin violation of the federal Fair Housing Act, e.g.). They may sue if a private right of action can be implied from a federal statute, because they are one of a class for whose special benefit the law was enacted, because there is legislative intent to create or no legislative intent to deny such a remedy, and because the cause of action is not one customarily relegated to state law and the private remedy is consistent with the purposes of the legislative scheme. (Recall the evolving § 1983 jurisprudence allowing claims of deprivation of federal statutory rights.)

d. Prudential considerations may be significant in federal standing determinations as well. Thus, courts may require a party to assert his own legal rights, not those of third parties. Although prudential considerations weigh in favor of standing, the Article III requirements must nevertheless be met; and although Article III requirements are met, prudential considerations may move the court to avoid adjudicating "abstract questions of wide public significance" amounting to "generalized grievances."

e. The area of alleged exclusionary zoning offers interesting illustrations of the impact of the standing doctrines in federal courts.

Would two non-profit corporations, the sponsor and the developer of planned multiracial, federally subsidized, moderate and low-income housing, and eight individuals suing as a class, who would be possible residents in the housing, have standing to sue the city and its officers challenging the validity of a zoning ordinance which prohibited the construction of all apartments, including such housing, within the city? The city was incorporated and the ordinance was enacted after plans and location had been announced, and initial funding steps had been completed. The challenge was based upon property rights secured by the fifth and fourteenth amendments, and upon individual rights protected by the federal civil rights acts and the thirteenth and fourteenth amendments.

The federal court found that the developer had expended sufficient time and money to have an injury in fact and a specific stake in the outcome. Both the sponsor and the developer were held to have such an economic interest as to have a "personal stake in the outcome of the controversy" of satisfactory proportions to permit litigation of constitutional violations. The history of the city-project dispute assured the necessary adversity. Invalidation of the zoning ordinance was not a difficult remedy and the matter was thus capable of judicial resolution. The corporate plaintiffs were held to be able to assert the constitutional and statutory rights of future residents because the latter group's interest in protection against

[*372*]

the city's alleged discriminatory zoning was sufficiently close to the sponsor's and developer's interest to fulfill their purposes to provide integrated housing. Both the corporate and the
individual plaintiffs had standing to litigate the
civil-rights and fair-housing acts questions. Finally, as to the eight individuals, the matter was
ripe for determination. The issues were fit for
judicial determination, involving a remedy traditional in nature, and there would be great hardship to the parties (continued poor housing and
rising construction costs, e.g.) if consideration
were now withheld. The requirements of case or
controversy were met.

The United States Supreme Court subsequently
emphasized that, in the above described case and
others like it, the plaintiffs attacked zoning restrictions which were applied to particular
projects which would supply housing within plaintiffs' means in which they intended to live.
Where plaintiffs' challenges to "exclusionary"
zoning restrictions are seen as less specifically
harmful, where there do not appear to be allega-
tions of "specific, concrete facts" related to a particular housing project constituting harm to the
plaintiffs personally, and where no tangible, personal benefit to the plaintiffs (or members of
plaintiff association) will result from court relief,
the Court has held that plaintiffs would be without standing to challenge the target zoning re-

[*373*]

strictions. The specific-project standing defect affected low and moderate income challengers who alleged that they could not live in the target municipality, a public interest housing-promotion association, taxpayers in neighboring city whose taxes were allegedly higher because such city bore the burden of providing low and moderate income housing, and a home builders' association.

INDEX

References are to Pages

ACTIONS
    See also Judicial Review; Standing to Sue; Torts, this index
Declaratory judgment, 342
Federal Civil Rights Act, 357
Injunctive relief, 342
Judgments, satisfaction of, 361
    Execution, 361
    Garnishment, 361
    Mandamus, 342, 361, 368
Municipal immunity, see Torts, this index
Notice requirements, 345–348
    Claim, notice of, 346
    Defect, notice of, 346
    Injury, 346
Quo warranto, 342
Standing to sue,
    Generally, 362–374
    "Adverse effect" of government action, 363–365
    Federal court, requirements in, 370
    Taxpayer suits, 365–369
        Against municipalities, 367
        Municipal taxpayers compared with state and federal taxpayers, 370
        On behalf of municipalities, 365–367
        "Watchdog" suits, 368–369
Statutes of limitations, 345
Taxpayer suits, 365–369
    Against municipalities, 367
    On behalf of municipalities, 365–367
    "Watchdog" suits, 368–369

ANNEXATION
    See also Interlocal Relations, this index
    Generally, 54, 66
Avoidance of, by incorporation, 52–53

INDEX
References are to Pages

ANNEXATION—Continued
Constitutional challenges to, 78
Corridor annexation, 75
Defensive incorporation, 52–53
Disannexation, 73
"Environmental impact statements", 56
Extraterritorial powers, 65
Inflexibilities of, 66
Judicial review, 67, 70
Municipal approval, 67
Procedures,
    Arbitration, 67, 71
    Consent required, 67, 68–69
    Government approval, 67, 69–70
    Home-rule power, 67–68
    Legislative standards, 70
    New Mexico, 71
    North Carolina, 68
    Statutory, 69
    Texas, 68
    Unilateral power, 67
Requirements,
    Contiguous territory, 75
Special districts, of, 52
State legislative act, by, 67
Urban-problem solutions, for,
    Dilution of, 66–67
Voluntary, 77–78

APPROPRIATIONS
See Borrowing; Expenditure Controls; Taxation, this index

ASSESSMENTS
See Special Assessments, this index

AUTHORITY TO ACT
Consolidation, 82, 83
Delegated authority, governments of, 1
Delegation of implementation authority,
    Generally, 113
Eminent domain,
    Authority not inherent, 238
    Constitutional, 238
    Property held by another government entity, 243, 252

[*376*]

AUTHORITY TO ACT—Continued
Statutory, 238
Employees,
Creation of positions, 89
Expenditures, 338–341
Federal antitrust laws, 42, 207–208
Franchises, 265–267
Illustration, 10–13
Initiative, 115–116
Interlocal agreements, 82
Land use, 156
Limitations on,
Charters, 37–38
Constitutional, 1
Federal constitutional provisions, 40–45
Commerce clause, 139, 223
Confiscation, taxation amounting to, 277, 284–286
Contract clause, 24, 243
Fourteenth amendment, 98–100, 119–125, 129, 199–205, 223
Free speech, 129
Interstate commerce, 129, 277–283
Right of privacy, 36, 129
Preemption by State, 46
Campaign contribution disclosure laws, 93
State constitutional provisions,
Generally, 48–49, 138–139
Borrowing for investments, 26, 324
Compensation of public officers, employees and contractors, 28
Debt ceilings, 28, 324
Illegal claims, payment of prohibited, 28
Lending credit to private enterprises, prohibition, 28, 323
Public purpose, requirement of, 323
Revenues, 272
Uniformity of taxation, 274, 290, 296
Local government units,
Arbitration, 103–105
Executive, 112
Governmental authority,
Compared with proprietary authority, 104–105
Popular initiative, 109, 115–116

AUTHORITY TO ACT—Continued
Municipal property,
    Acquisition, 231–234
    Change of use, 260–263
    Federal constitutional use limitations, 259–260
    Gift, pledge and mortgage, 268–269
    Sale, disposition by, 269
    Use, 235–238
    Vacation of streets, 267
Police power, 126
    Estoppel, 153
    Licenses, permits and fees, 146
    Regulation vs. prohibition, 144
    Sanctions, criminal and civil, 150
Population requirements, 7–8
Public contracts, 212
    Apparent authority, doctrine of, 227
    Contractors charged with knowledge of limitations, 226
    Emergency, effect of, 214, 220
    Limitations to assure citizen vigilance, generally, 226
    Public purpose limitation, 231
    Ratification, 227
    Statutory and constitutional authority, 212–213
Recall, 115–116
Referenda, 115–116
Removal of officers for cause, 89
Revenues, 272
    Borrowing, 315–318
    Licenses, permits and fees, 274–277
    Taxation, 275
        Income taxation, 280
Sources of authority,
        Generally, 2, 14–24
    Charters, 15–16
    Constitutional home rule, 16–17
    Dillon's Rule, 14
    Federal licenses, 44
    Implied powers, 21–23
    Indispensable powers, 23
    Legislative home rule, 17
    Local-option legislation, 20
    Special or one-city legislation, 17–18
    Statutory grants, 17–18

INDEX
References are to Pages

AUTHORITY TO ACT—Continued
Special assessments, 288–289
    Reassessments, 300–301
Special metropolitan district, 83
Zoning, 126, 156
    Enabling legislation, 172, 173, 180, 188

BANKRUPTCY
See Borrowing, this index

BIDDING
See Public Contracts, this index

BONDS
See Borrowing, this index

BORROWING
    Generally, 315–337
Bankruptcy, 323
Bonds, 318–323
    Authority to issue, 318
    Default, 323–324
    General obligation vs. revenue bonds, 318
    Industrial revenue bonds, 329–333
        Challenges to, 331–332
        Impact on other municipal borrowing, 330
        Non-taxable interest, withdrawal of, 331
        Purpose of, 330
    Investor protection, 322
    Marketability, 320
    Referenda, 320, 325
Debt limitations,
        Generally, 324, 329, 334
    Applicability, 328
    Avoidance of, 325–329
    Debt ceiling restrictions, 317, 324
    Tort judgments, 360–361
Interest, exclusion from federal taxation, 336–338
Long-term leases, 325–327
Political restraint, 333–335
Warrants, 316–318
    Assignability and negotiability, 317–318
    Authority, 316–317
    Debt limitations, 317–318

BORROWING—Continued
Defined, 316–317
Interest, 317–318
Short-term, 316–317

BUILDING CODES
See Land Use, this index

CHARTER POWERS
Optional charter laws, 15–18

CITIES
See Government Units

CIVIL RIGHTS
Federal Civil Rights Act, 42 U.S.C.A. § 1943, pp. 41, 196, 241, 357

CIVIL SERVICE
See Employees, this index

CONDEMNATION
See Eminent Domain, this index

CONFLICTS OF INTEREST
See also Officers; Preemption Doctrine; Public Contracts; State-Local Relations, this index
Electoral candidates, 4
Public contracts, 213–215
Public officers, 4

CONSTITUTIONAL LIMITATIONS—FEDERAL
See Authority to Act; Federal-State-Local Relations, this index

CONSTITUTIONAL LIMITATIONS—STATE
See Authority to Act; State-Local Relations, this index

CONTRACTS
See Public Contracts, this index

COURT REVIEW
See Judicial Review

DEBT
See Borrowing, this index

DILLON'S RULE
Construction of statutes delegating authority, 14

EDUCATION
See also Federal-State-Local Relations; State-Local Relations; Taxation, this index
Fiscal support, 313–315
Pupils,
Children of illegal aliens, 314–315
Residency, 314–315
School segregation, 78–80

ELECTIONS
Generally, 88, 115–116, 119–125
Fifteenth Amendment, 119–125
First Amendment,
Establishment clause, 118–119
Fourteenth Amendment, 119–125
Residency requirements, 95–97
Candidates, 96
College students, 96
Continuing, 96, 97
Officers and employees, 96, 97
Prior, 96
Voters, 96
Voting Rights Act, 125

EMINENT DOMAIN
Authority not inherent, 238
Constitutional limitations, 238
Damages,
Consequential damages, 254
Offsetting benefits, 255–256
Severance damages, 254–255
Excess condemnation defined, 245–247
Extraterritorial power, 64–66
Inverse condemnation, 194–199, 240–241
Just compensation, 248–254
See also Damages, this topic
Comment on extent of, 257–258
"Highest and best use," 250

EMINENT DOMAIN—Continued
    Income-producing property, 249–250
    Leaseholds, 250
    Measure, 249–250
    Mineral deposits, 251
    Specialty property, 250
    Standards for determination of, 249–250
    Transferable development rights, 252–253
    Zoning status and possible rezoning, 251
Necessity, 243–244
Property held by another government entity, 243, 252–253
Property interests subject to,
       Generally, 239–243
    Abutter's rights, 239–240
    Contractual rights, 238, 242
    Property already devoted to a public use, 243
    Restrictive covenants, 241–242
Public use,
    Defined, 244–245
    Private benefits in, 244
Public vs. private use, 244–245
Quick condemnation, 247–248
Special assessments, 257
Statutory limitations, 238
"Taking",
    Defined, 194–199
    Distinguished from police power exercise, 194–199, 240–242
    Inverse condemnation, 194–199, 240–242
    Public health and safety, private condemnors, 246
Taking of municipal property by higher government authority, 271

EMPLOYEES
       See also Labor Relations; Officers, this index
    Generally, 86
Appointed officials, 88
Career service, 88, 89
Challenged employment practices, 97–102
Civil service appointees, 88, 89
Classified service, 87, 89
Compensation, state constitutional limitation on, 28
Conflicts of interest, 90, 92–93

EMPLOYEES—Continued
Creation of positions, 90
Discriminatory employment practices, 97–102
Distinguished from officers, 89–90
Dual office holding, 91–92
Due process, 97–102
Equal protection, 98–100
Loyalty oath, 91
Merit system, 88
Officers, 89–90
Open meeting-sunshine 90–91
Personal financial disclosure, 93–95
Public employee unions, 103–107
    Arbitration with government units, 104–105
    Collective bargaining and merit system, 103
    Prohibited, 103–104
    Strikes, 105–107
Residency requirements, 95–97
Restrictions on nepotism, outside work and political activity,
    95, 97
Statewide classification, effect of, 88

EQUITABLE RELIEF
    See also Judicial Review; Public Contracts, this index
Contracts improperly bid,
    Estoppel, 211, 222
    Unjust enrichment, 211, 221–222
Measure of relief, 228–230
Ultra vires, 230
Unjust enrichment of municipality, 228–230
Where both parties claim, 230

EXPENDITURE CONTROLS
Authority to spend, requirement of, 338
Contracting controls, see Public Contracts, this index
Expenditure method restrictions, 339–340
    Certification, requirement of, 339–340
    Intra-budgetary diversions of funds, prohibition of, 339
    Purposes of, 339
    Spending increases, limits on expenditure controls,
        Officer liability, 341
Public purpose restrictions, 330, 338
State constitutional limitations, 338–339

INDEX
References are to Pages

FEDERAL AID
See Federal-State-Local Relations, this index

FEDERAL–STATE–LOCAL RELATIONS
Annexation, constitutional challenges to, 78
Boundary alteration, constitutional implications, 74
Campaign contribution disclosure laws, 93–95
Competence, 39
Constitutional limitations, 55
Elections,
    Fourteenth Amendment, 119–125
Employees,
    Due process, 97–102
    Fifth Amendment rights, 91
    First Amendment rights, 91, 102
Federal antitrust laws, 42, 207–208
Federal constitutional limitations,
    Commerce clause, 42, 44, 139, 223
    First Amendment 91, 102, 129, 139–140, 259
    Fourteenth Amendment,
        Equal protection, 78–80, 98–100, 119–125, 129, 223, 259
        Exclusionary zoning, 199–205
    Right of privacy, 93–95, 129
    Spending and tax powers, 42
Federal involvement in local matters, 43
Federal preemption, 45
Federal sources of local power, 44
Federal supremacy, see Supremacy, this index
Interest earned on local obligations, exclusion from federal taxation, 336–338
Intergovernmental transfers of revenues, 303–305
Land use, 156
Limitation on federal power over the states,
    Federal constitutional provisions,
        Generally, 40–45
        Eleventh, Tenth and Twenty-first Amendments, 40
    Federal statutory provisions, 41
    Federal taxation, 42
    State sovereignty, 41
        Integral state governmental functions, 41
Limitations on state power over municipalities,
    Federal constitutional provisions,

FEDERAL–STATE–LOCAL RELATIONS—Continued
   Generally, 24–26
Referendum,
   Fourteenth Amendment, 119–125
Voting Rights Act, 125

FINANCING LOCAL GOVERNMENT
See Borrowing; Expenditure Controls; Revenues; Special
   Assessments; Taxation, this index

FORMS OF LOCAL GOVERNMENT
See Government Units, this index

FOURTEENTH AMENDMENT
See Federal-State-Local Relations, this index

GOVERNMENT EMPLOYMENT
See Employees; Officers, this index

GOVERNMENT OFFICERS
See Officers, this index

GOVERNMENT TORTS
See Torts, this index

GOVERNMENT UNITS
   Generally, 51–55
Benefit districts, 10, 81
Decentralized local government, 63
Defensive incorporation, 52–53
Extraterritorial exercise of power, 64
Federation, 84
Improvement districts, 81
Incorporated areas,
   Reasons for, 52–53
Incorporation,
   Alaska, 77
   Contiguous territory, 75
   Defensive, 75
   Hawaii, 77
   Home-rule power, 59
   Resistance to, 75–77
Legal classification, 7–8
Metropolitan district, 83

GOVERNMENT UNITS—Continued
Municipal administrative department vs. special districts,
    62–63
Organization of cities,
    Procedures and requirements, 55–62
Organization of special districts, 62
Proliferation of, 7
Separation of powers defined, 107–113
Special authorities, 10
Special districts, 9–10
    Decentralizing local government, 63
Unincorporated areas,
    Reasons for, 51–53

HOME RULE
    Generally, 15–16, 17, 25, 26, 32–38, 59
Annexation power, 66–71
Classified service, 88
Counties, 34
Extent of powers, 33–34
Forms of,
    Constitutional home rule, 15, 33
    Constitutional source of power, 15–16
    Legislative home rule, 16
Incorporation under, 59
Municipal restructuring by state, 54–55
Population requirements, 7
Problems, 34, 35–38
Source of power,
    Constitutional provisions, 15–16
    Statutory grants, 17
State or local affairs, classification, 35–38
    Acquisition of goods and services, 37
    Civil service, 37
    Land use, 37
    Police power, 37
Taxing powers, 274–275, 287

INTERLOCAL RELATIONS
Annexation,
    Defensive incorporation, 53
    Special districts, 52
City-city consolidation, 54
City-county consolidation, 54

INTERLOCAL RELATIONS—Continued
City-county relations, 85
Conflicts, power exercise, 47
Consolidation, 82
Cooperation,
    Council of governments, 83
Council of governments, 53, 83
Cross-boundary cooperation, 82
Decentralized local government, 63
Extraterritorial powers, 64
Federation, 53, 83
Incorporation, 55–62
Regional planning, 156–157
Special districts, interlocking governance, 62
Unincorporated areas, strong county government, 51

JUDICIAL RELIEF
See Actions; Equitable Relief; Judicial Review; Standing to
    Sue, this index

JUDICIAL REVIEW
        See also, Actions; Equitable Relief; Municipal Property
            Interests; Standing to Sue, this index
Annexation, 66
    Constitutional challenges to, 78
    Corridor annexation, 75
    Substantive review, 70
Anticompetitive activity, 42, 207–208
Arbitration, 104–105
Borrowing, debt limitations, 325–329
Citizen delegations, 113
Competence, 39
Contracts, see Public contracts, this topic
Delegation of legislative authority, 19–21, 113–119
Delegation of municipal powers,
    Adequacy of standards, 114–119
    Initiative, 115–116
    Recall, 115–116
    Referenda, 115–116, 119–125
        Constitutional limitations, 119–125
Detachment, 73
    Fifteenth Amendment, 78, 119–125
Dillon's Rule, 14
Disclosure laws, 93–95

INDEX

References are to Pages

JUDICIAL REVIEW—Continued
Discriminatory employment practices, 97–102
Dissolution, 72
Elections, 119–125
Emergency legislative sessions, 110
Eminent domain,
  Excess condemnation, 246–247
  Just compensation, 248–254
  Property interests subject to restrictive covenants, 242–243
  Public use, necessity of, 244–245
  Public vs. private use, 244–245
  "Taking," private condemnors, public health and safety, 246
Extraterritorial power, 64
Home-rule powers, extent of, 35–37
Implied authority, 21–23
Incorporation, 55–62
Land use,
  Master plans, 158, 165
  Official maps, 164
  Subdivision control, 167–169
  Takings, 194–199
Municipal activities, governmental-proprietary distinctions, 6
Municipal property,
  Change or expansion of use, 234
  Dedication, 234–235, 236
  Expansion vs. change of use, 235–238
  Sale of, 269
Municipal restructuring,
  Adjustment of assets and liabilities, 74
  Contiguous territory, 75
One-person-one-vote, 119–125
Overlapping state and local laws, 3–5, 45–47
  Public disclosure, 46
Police power exercises, 65–66
  Nuisances, 148
  Presumption of reasonableness, 132, 143
  Regulation vs. prohibition, 144
  Relation of means to object, requirement of, 135
  Unreasonableness, 134–135
Preemption, 45

INDEX
References are to Pages

JUDICIAL REVIEW—Continued
Public contracts,
    Against public policy, 209, 215–219
    Bidding requirements, generally, 219–225
    Defectively entered into, 209
    Estoppel, 209
    Illegal, 209
    Limitations to assure citizen vigilance, 226
    Measure of relief, 228–230
    Ratification, 209, 227
    Ultra vires, 209, 213
    Void for conflict of interest, 213–215
    Where no ratification, 227
Public employee unions, 103–106
Questions of authority, 18–24
    General considerations, 2–3
    Interpretation and implication, 18–23
Referendum, 119–125
Residency requirements, 95–97
    Candidates, 96
    Continuing, 96, 97
    Officers and employees, 96, 97
    Prior, 96
    Voters, 96
Revenues: licenses, permits and fees, 276–280
Right to vote, 119–125
School district reapportionment, 78
Special vs. general legislation, 26–27, 30–32
State or local matters, 41, 46–47
      Generally, 35–38
    Acquisition of goods and services, 37
    Civil relationships, 38
    Civil service, 37
    Felonies, 38
    Land use, 37
    Standard of care, 38
Taxation, assessments, 307
Zoning,
    Administrative implementation, 157–160
    Exclusionary zoning, 199–205
    Floating zones, 175–176
    Legislative decisions, 157
    Non-conforming uses, 186

JUDICIAL REVIEW—Continued
Presumption of validity, 172
Requirement of reasonableness, 172
Standing to sue, 155–159, 194

LABOR RELATIONS
See also Employees, this index
Generally, 86
Discriminatory employment practices, 97–102
Public employee unions, 103–106
Strikes, 106–107
Prohibition enforcement, 107

LAND USE
See also Eminent Domain; Zoning, this index
Generally, 79
Aesthetic construction, restrictions based on, 190
Building codes, 193–194
Comprehensive plans, 161
Floor space requirements, 189
General welfare powers, 189, 190
Housing codes, 191–192
Income-producing property, regulation of, 192–193
Judicial review, generally, 79
Local control of 27, 37
Master plans, 162
Nuisances, regulation of, 189
Official maps,
Compensation, when required, 163–165
Definition, 163
Function of, 163–165
Planning,
Entities, 156
Role of, 160–161
Subdivision controls, 166
Developments subject to, 169
Private developers,
Conditions and standards, generally, 166–167
Land dedication requirements, 166–167
Performance bonds, 167
Plat approval, 166–167
Purpose of, 166
Zoning maps, 163

LICENSES, PERMITS AND FEES
See Authority to Act; Police Power; Revenues; Taxation, this index

LOCAL GOVERNMENT TORTS
See Torts, this index

MANDAMUS
See Actions, this index

MUNICIPAL PLANNING
See Land Use; Zoning, this index

MUNICIPAL POWERS
Administrative,
    Compared with legislative, 106–107, 112
Arbitration, 104–105
Delegation by state, 53
Delegation of, 113
    Adequacy of standards, 114–115, 117
    Administrative, 114
    Discretionary authority to private citizens, 117
    Initiative, recall and referendum, 115–116
        Constitutional limitations, 119–125
Enactments,
    Administrative,
        Executive session, 110
    Legislative, 109–110
Executive, 112
Governmental authority, compared with proprietary authority, 109–110
Hearings, investigatory, 110
Initiative, 115–116
Legislative enactments, 109–110
    Procedures, 109
        Emergency sessions, 110
Mayoral veto, 112
Open meeting requirements, 110
Ordinances,
    Equal dignity rule, 109
Ordinances and resolutions, 108–112
Popular initiative, 115–116
Recall, 115–116
Referendum, 115–116

MUNICIPAL POWERS—Continued
Resolutions, 108–112
Separation of powers, 107–108, 112–113

MUNICIPAL PROPERTY INTERESTS
Acquisition,
    Adverse possession, 233–234
    Dedication, 232
        Easement, 235
        Implied, 234–235
        Limitations, constitutional, 232
        Statutory, 236
    Easement, 235–238
    Prescription and user, 235
    Transfer with conditions, 237
Change or expansion of use, 234
Disposition,
    Franchises, 265–267
    Gift, pledge and mortgage, 268–269
    Leases, 264–265
    Sale, 269
    Vacation of streets, 267
Eminent domain, see Eminent Domain, this index
"In trust" property, 260
Limitations,
    Constitutional constraints, 259–260
    Municipal purposes, 232
    Public use, 231–232
Loss,
    Abandonment, 263–264
    Adverse possession, 270
    Change of use, 262
    Estoppel to claim title, 270–271
    Reversion, 271
Trusts,
    Cy pres doctrine, 260
Use of property,
    Nuisances, 258
    Privately imposed conditions, 236–237, 260–262
    Purprestures, 258–259

MUNICIPAL RESTRUCTURING
    Generally, 53, 77

INDEX

References are to Pages

MUNICIPAL RESTRUCTURING—Continued
Adjustment of assets and liabilities, judicial action, by, 74
Annexation, 66–71
Charter, 61
Consolidation,
    Generally, 69, 83–84, 85
  City-city, 52, 83
  City-county, 53, 85
  Federation, 84
Constitutional considerations, 78–82, 119–125
    Elections, 119–125
    Improvement district, 81–82
Council of governments, 83
Decentralization, 54
Detachment, 73
Disconnection, 54
Dissolution, 72–73
Division, 73
Extraterritorial exercise of power, 64–66
Federation, 84
Judicial restructuring, 78–79
    Deference to existing boundaries, 79
    Multidistrict remedies, 79
Metropolitan districts, 53, 83, 85
Political realities, 74
Requirements, contiguous territory, 75
"Secession," 54, 72
Separate incorporation, 75
State powers, 54–55
Unincorporated status, return to, 54
Voting Rights Act, 125

NUISANCES
See Land Use; Municipal Property Interests; Police Power,
    this index

OFFICERS
    Generally, 86
Appointed, 88
Compensation, state constitutional limitations on, 28
Conflicts of interest,
    Campaign contribution disclosure, 93–95
    Personal financial disclosure, 93–95
    Remedies, 92–93

OFFICERS—Continued
Council of governments, 83
Distinguished from employment position, 90
Dual officeholding, 91–92
    De facto assumption of office, 92
    Prohibitions against incompatible offices, 92
Duration of office, 89
Elected, 88
Excepted from merit system, 88
Liability for unlawful expenditures, 341
Powers, 89
Removal for cause, 89
Residency requirements, 95–97
Restrictions on nepotism, outside work and political activity,
    95, 97
Special districts, 62

PLANNED UNIT DEVELOPMENT (PUD)
See Zoning, this index

PLANNING
See Land Use; Zoning, this index

POLICE POWER
    Generally, 126
Challenges to,
        Generally, 127–128
    Improper exercise, 127–128
    Lack of reasonable relation to objective sought, 128
    Preemption, 127
Definition of, 126
Enforcement,
        Generally, 149–152
    Discriminatory, 153–154
Estoppel, 154–155
Federal constitutional limitations,
    Confiscation of property, 141
    Due process, 140, 141–142
    Equal protection, 142
    Freedom of association, press, religion and speech,
        139–140
    Right to travel, 140
    Vague or overbroad laws, 140
Investigation for violations, 149–150

POLICE POWER—Continued
Land use planning and control, 155–205
    See Land Use, this index
Licenses, permits and fees, 146–148, 274–280
Nuisances, regulation of, 148–149
    Definitions, 148
    Enforcement, 148–149
Objects of,
        Generally, 131–135
    Health and safety, 132–133
    Public morality, 133
    Public welfare, 133–135
Ordinances, 108–112
Public employee unions,
    Strikes, 106–107
Regulation vs. prohibition, 144–148
Regulations,
    Illustrations, 43, 128, 132–135, 136–138, 145
Sanctions, criminal and civil, 150–153
State constitutional limitations, generally, 138–139
Zoning power, relation to, 126–127

POPULATION
Classification of municipalities by, 7–8

POWERS
See Authority to Act; Police Power, this index

PREEMPTION DOCTRINE
Competence, 40
Federal, 43, 45, 145
Local, 47–48
State: overlapping and conflicting state and local laws, 45–47
    Elections, 21
    Complementary, 46
    Income taxation, 280–281
    Occupation of the field, 46
    Police power, 127
    Public disclosure laws, 4–5, 36, 46
    Referendum, 119–125
    Taxation, 36

INDEX
References are to Pages

PUBLIC ACTIONS
See Actions, this index

PUBLIC CONTRACTS
Against public policy,
       Generally, 215–219
    Governmental vs. proprietary function, 217–218, 219
    Unreasonable duration, 216–219
Agency,
       Generally, 226–227
    Apparent authority, doctrine of, 227
    Contractors charged with knowledge of limitations of,
       226
    Ratification, 227
Arbitration, 104–105
Bidding requirements,
    Advertisement, 219, 222–223
    Amendments to properly awarded contracts, 220–221
    Attempted ratification of unbid contracts, 222
    Constitutional considerations, 223
       Commerce clause, 223
       Foreign trade, 223
       Fourteenth Amendment, 223
       Right to travel, 223
    Emergency, 220
    Equitable relief,
       Estoppel, 222
       Unjust enrichment, 221–222
    Lowest responsible bidder, 224–225
    Mistake in bid, 225
    Not applicable, 220
    Procedures, 222–225
    Specifications, 222–223
    Unlawful evasion, 221
Conflict of interest, 213–215
    By charter, 214
    By statute, 214
    Common law, 214
    Emergencies, 214–215
    Employee influence, 214
    Equitable relief, 214
    Void or voidable, 214
Equitable relief, see Equitable Relief, this index

PUBLIC CONTRACTS—Continued
Governing principles: implied contracts, quasi-contractual relief, restitution, etc., 206–207
Limitations,
    Citizen vigilance, 226
    Contractors, 226
    Emergency, 226
    Public purpose, 231
Quasi-contractual relief, and restitution, generally, 208–212, 228–231
Ultra vires, 212–213

PUBLIC EMPLOYEES
See Employees; Officers, this index

QUO WARRANTO
See Actions, this index

REMEDIES
See Actions; Equitable Relief, this index

REVENUES
Borrowing, see Borrowing, this index
Fiscal crisis, reasons for, 272
Intergovernmental transfers,
      Generally, 303–305
    Federal transfers to local governments, 303, 304–305
      Grants, 303, 304
      Revenue sharing, 304–305
    State transfers to local governments, 303
Licenses, permits and fees, 146–148, 274
    Judicial review of, 276–280
Municipal bankruptcy, 323–324
Special assessments, 288–302
    See Special Assessments, this index
Taxation,
    See Taxation, this index

REVIEW
See Actions; Judicial Relief, this index

SOVEREIGNTY
State, see Preemption Doctrine; Supremacy, this index

SPECIAL ASSESSMENTS
Challenges to,
Generally, 293
Absence of local improvement, 294
Absence of special benefit to the property assessed, 295
Assessment in excess of benefit, 296
Failure to comply with procedures, 294–295
Insufficient performance by contractor, 300
Lack of authority, 294
Necessity, 294
Uniformity of "taxation," 296
Eminent domain,
Offsetting benefits from taking under, 256
Liability for, 299–301
Procedures for, generally, 291–293
Process of,
Construction, 292
Contracting, 292
Cost estimate and determination, 290, 301
Determination of amounts assessed, 292
Hearings, 291
Levying of assessments, 293
Notice of assessments, 293
Objections to assessments, 293
Opposition, 291
Ordinance, enactment by, 291
Petition, 290
Plans, maps, and specifications, 292
Resolution, 290–291
Reassessments, 300–301
Special benefit rule, 296–298
Theory of, 288

SPECIAL DISTRICTS
Generally, 62
Annexation of, 52
Compared with incorporated city, 52
Compared with municipal administrative department, 62–63
Consolidation, 85–86
Criticism of, 10
Decentralized local government, unsuitability for, 63
Flexibility, lack of, 52
Functions, 9

SPECIAL DISTRICTS—Continued
Improvement districts, 79
Interlocking governance, 62
Judicial review, 119–125
Political control, 62
Powers of, 52
Procedures and requirements, 62
    Boundary ascertainments, 62
    Referendum, 62
Reasons for, 52, 62
Types and nature of, 9–10

STANDING TO SUE
See Actions, this index

STATE–LOCAL RELATIONS
Anticompetitive activity, 42, 207–208
    Remedies, 42, 207–208
Competence, 40
Constitutional limitations, 26–38
    Debt ceilings, 28
    Expenditure limits, 338
    Lending of credit, prohibition of, 28
    Public purposes, requirement of, 28
Home rule, 32–38
Intergovernmental transfers of revenues, 303–305
Land use, control over, 155–160
Limitations on state power over municipal activities, 26
    Land use, 37
    State constitutional provisions,
        Generally, 26–38
      Delegation of local powers to state commission, pro-
        hibition of, 29
      Home rule, 32–38
      Municipal or corporate functions, interference with
        prohibited, 29
      Special legislation, prohibition, 30
      Taxation, subjects reserved to localities, 29
Overlapping state and local laws,
    Conflict of interest, 4–5
    Public disclosure, 4–5
Preemption by state,
    Elections, 20–21
    Income taxation, 280

INDEX
References are to Pages

STATE–LOCAL RELATIONS—Continued
Public disclosure, 46
Special legislation, 46
State authorization of extra-territorial powers, 64
State constitutional limitations,
    Education, 314–315
    Equal protection, 314–315
    Exclusionary zoning, 199–205
State constitutional protection for individuals, 48, 78
State sovereignty, 24–26
Taxation, competition for, 287–288

STATE SOVEREIGNTY
See Preemption Doctrine; Supremacy, this index

SUPREMACY
Federal constitutional supremacy,
        Generally, 44
    Air traffic and noise, 45
    Air transportation, 44
    Local regulation of commerce, 44, 139
    Nuclear power plant construction, 43, 145
    Police power, 45, 139

TAXATION
Business and occupation privilege taxes, see Licenses, per-
    mits and fees, this topic
Earnings or wage taxation, 280
Federal constitutional limitations,
    Confiscation, taxation amounting to, 277, 283–286
    Interstate commerce, 277–280, 281–282, 283
Gross receipts taxation, 282–287
    First Amendment implications, 284
Income taxation, 280
    Graduated or flat percentage, 280
    Non-resident liability, 281
Licenses, permits and fees, 145–148, 274
Miscellaneous sources of tax revenues, 287
Multistate Tax Compact Commission, 282
Preemption by state, 35–36
Property taxation,
        Generally, 305–315
    Assessed valuation, 306–308
        Challenges to, administrative, 307

INDEX
References are to Pages

TAXATION—Continued
      Judicial review, 307
   Efficiency of, 308–312
   Enterprise zone, 180, 311
   Exemptions, 308, 310–311
   Federal constitutional limitations,
      Equal protection, 313
      Establishment and free exercise, 313
      Export-import clause, 312
      Interstate commerce, 312–313
   Limits of, 306, 308
   Reform of, 311–312
   State constitutional limitations, 306
      Equal protection, 314–315
      Thorough and efficient public education, 314–315
Sales taxation, 282, 286
Tax increment financing, 319
Taxation replacement strategies, 288
Taxpayer revolt, 273, 308

TAXPAYER SUITS
See Actions, this index

TORTS
Customary theories of recovery, 343–345
Damages, 359
   Punitive damages, 353
      Common law, 359–360
      42 U.S.C.A. § 1983, 357
Debt limits and tort judgments, 359
Exemptions from liability, 353–354
Federal civil rights legislation, 357
Immunity of political subdivisions vs. immunity of the state, 354
Indemnity and contribution, 361–362
Inverse condemnation, 194–199, 343–344
Judgments, satisfaction of, 361
   Execution, 361
   Garnishments, 361
   Mandamus, 361
Municipal immunity, 348–359
   Abrogation of, 349–355
   Effects of abrogation, 352–355
      Judicial, 352–354

INDEX

References are to Pages

TORTS—Continued
Legislative, 354
Exceptions to, 350
Federal Civil Rights Act, 357
Municipal liability insurance, 351, 354
Notice requirements, 345–348
Claim, notice of, 347
Defect, notice of, 345
Injury, notice of, 346
Public officer immunity, 356, 358
Statutes of limitations, 345
Ultra vires, recovery, 345

VARIANCES
See Zoning, this index

VOTING
See Elections; Employees; Federal-State-Local Relations;
Municipal Restructuring; Officers, this index

ZONING
Generally, 156–205
Accessory uses, 181–182
Challenges to land use restrictions, 194–199
Cluster or density zoning, 177–180
Comprehensive plans, 161
Conditional zoning, 175–176
Contract zoning, 176–177
Cumulative zoning, 187–188
Delegation of municipal powers, 113–118
Density zoning, 177–180
Development pressures, response, 169–170
Enforcement, 188–189
Enterprise zones, 180, 311
Euclidean zoning, 174
Exceptional uses, 180–189
Accessory uses, 181, 182
Exemptions,
Municipal property, 180–181
Non-conforming uses, 186–187
Special exceptions, 183
Variances, 184–187
Exclusionary zoning, 199–205
Challenge to, 201

ZONING—Continued
Judicial review, 160–161, 201–205
Motivation for, 200–201
Regional considerations, 199
Standing to sue, 370–374
See Actions; Standing to Sue, this index
Timed-growth plans, 204–205
Trailer parks, 199, 203
Exemptions, 180–181
Extraterritorial zoning authority, 161
Floating zones, 175–176
Flood plain ordinances, 165
General standards, 172–173
Cluster or density zoning, 177–180
Euclidean zoning, 172, 174
Floating zones, 175–176
PUDs, planned unit developments, 178–179
Inverse condemnation, 196, 240–241
Taking issue, 194–199, 240–241
Transferable development rights, 197, 241, 252–253
Judicial review,
Exclusionary zoning, 199–205
Floating zones, 175–176
Non-conforming uses, 186–187
Requirement of reasonableness, 172–173, 190
Role of court, 158
Standing to sue, 158–159
Landmark and historic preservation, 198, 241–242
Master plans, 162, 165
New towns, 179
Non-conforming uses, 186–188
Official maps,
Definition, 163
Function of, 163–165
Plan implementation, 163–170
Powers, source of, 155–157
PUDs, planned unit developments, 178–179
Purposes and objectives, generally, 170–173
Regional planning, 156
Review procedures, 158–159
Rezoning, 173–174
Special exceptions, 182–183
Spot zoning, 173–174

[*403*]

ZONING—Continued
Strip zoning, 173–174
Subdivision controls, 166–169
Supreme Court role, 194
Transferrable development rights, 197, 241, 252–253
Variances, 184–186
Zoning, planning, process and participants, 156–162
Zoning maps, 163

†